Rick Stein's

Taste of the Sea

Rick Stein's

Taste of the Sea

Photographs by Graham Kirk

BAY BOOKS

First published in 1997 by BBC Books. North American Edition published 1998 by Bay Books & Tapes, Inc., by arrangement with BBC Books, an imprint of BBC Worldwide Publishing.

This book is published to accompany the television series entitled *Rick Stein's Taste of the Sea*, which was first broadcast in 1995. The series is a production of BBC Television by Denham Productions and directed by David Pritchard.

Bay Books may be purchased for education, business, or sales promotional use at attractive quantity discounts. For information, address: Bay Books & Tapes, Inc., 555 De Haro Street, No. 220, San Francisco, CA 94107.

Publisher: James Connolly
Art Director: Jeffrey O'Rourke
Design: David Albertson Design, San Francisco
Production: Ken Rackow
American Editor: Sharon Silva
Proofreader: Sabrina Rood-Sinker

U.K. Edition:
Design: Barbara Mercer
Photographs: Graham Kirk
Photograph on page 2: Guy Newman
Home Economist: Louise Pickford
Styling: Helen Payne

Recipe for *Crab Newburg* on page 177 taken from *Cross Creek,* © the estate of the late Marjorie Kinnan Rawlings courtesy of Scribner, A Division of Simon and Schuster Inc.

Extract from *The Chef Has Imagination, or It's Too Hard To Do It Easy* on page 51 reprinted by permission of Curtis Brown Ltd. Copyright © 1953 by Ogden Nash, renewed

Library of Congress Cataloging-in-Publication Data

Stein, Rick.
    Taste of the sea / Rick Stein: photographs by Graham Kirk.
        p.   cm.
    Reprint. Previously published: London: BBC Books, 1995.
    "Companion to the Public Television series."
    Includes index.
    ISBN 0-912333-56-1 (pbk.)
    1. Cookery (Seafood) 2. Cookery (Fish) I. Taste of the Sea
(Television program). II. Title
    TX747.S67   1997   97-36266
    641.6'92–dc21   CIP

ISBN 0-912333-56-1

Printed in China

10 9 8 7 6 5 4 3 2 1

Distributed to the trade by Publishers Group West

Contents

ACKNOWLEDGEMENTS

Special thanks to Paul Ripley, David Pope and the other chefs at The Seafood Restaurant for all the time spent recipe testing. Particular thanks to Jane Rees, who typed most of the manuscript. Thanks to Heather Holden-Brown, Anna Ottewill and Frank Phillips at BBC Books for all their expertise, and their considerable patience with my failure to meet deadlines; to Graham Kirk and Louise Pickford for their sensitive interpretation of my dishes in the photography and to Barbara Mercer for her attractive and clear page design.

Lastly, thanks to the director of the television series, David Pritchard, the source of most of the ideas for the series, and consequently the book, for many hours spent talking about fish, fishermen and seafood in the London Inn, Padstow - and the source of some irritation to my wife, Jill, who cannot see why men have to have a couple of beers before they can talk about anything!

1 Why Should We Eat More Fish?

Imagine it is early spring and you have just arrived in Padstow. You have passed through the narrow lanes and slate walls of Cornwall, seeing only the odd tree, bent over to one side by the Atlantic gales, and the village churches across the open fields. You've taken more time to get there than you planned having stopped at St. Issey and caught sight of the estuary for the first time.

Then finally, here you are; the sky is a pale blue, the sand spreads all the way across the estuary with the Camel River to one side. Can you really still be in England?

Away from the quay, with its view across the estuary to the sand dunes at Rock, past the lobster pots with the smell of filmy seaweed still clinging to them, you walk into a seafood restaurant for *Sea Bass with Beurre Blanc, Moules Marinières, Helford Oysters* or some *Razor-Shell Clams with Garlic Butter*. You will be longing for some fresh ozone-scented seafood on such an optimistic sort of day before you've even sat down.

This book is about that sort of exhilarating experience. It encompasses not only recipes but my enthusiasm for fish cookery. I make no claims for a comprehensive coverage of all species of fish, only the ones that I love and the recipes that I think bring out the best in them: just a taste of the sea.

Since I started my own restaurant in Padstow, Cornwall, in 1975 I have witnessed, with amazement, how seafood has grown in popularity. At first I sold grilled plaice and lemon sole, sea bass, mackerel, lobster, crabs, crayfish and the occasional scallop—and that was about it. I would never have dreamed of selling fish like cod or haddock because that was what fish and chip shops sold. Now there is literally not a fish that swims in our waters that I can't sell. To give

you an example, not long ago I went out on a trawler and found a species of fish called dragonets in the nets, a fish I didn't know about. They're a bit like monkfish in texture and taste, but very small and a beautiful yellow and blue color. I brought some back, skinned them, filleted them, deep-fried them, put them on the menu with some chili sauce and we sold them all that night. So a species, totally unknown to the people that were eating it, including a Michelin Guide inspector, was enormously popular. If I'd put the dragonets on the menu 20 years ago I'd have thrown them away. I can sell any fish now—gurnard, weever fish, conger eel, trigger fish—and I put this down to the fact that people are at last beginning to appreciate how bountiful the mackerel-crowded seas around us are.

Coupled with an interest in eating seafood has been a growing understanding about the important part played by fish and shellfish in our diet. A book called *The Eskimo Diet* notes a correlation between the declining consumption of oily fish, like herring, in Europe and North America and the increase in diseases due to eating too much saturated fat. Fish is what you might call protein without tears; it's completely lean and easily digestible with none of the side effects of fatty meat. Indeed, it seems clear that oily fish might reduce high levels of cholesterol caused by eating too much meat and dairy products. Even nonoily fish, such as tuna, trout, salmon, mullet, sea bass, squid and even mussels and oysters, contain the cholesterol-reducing fish oil known as omega 3.

I must say I'm optimistic about the future of fish cookery and our continuing interest in fish, but we still have a long way to go. There are still an awful lot of people who are indifferent to seafood. I find it interesting to try to analyze why this is. I still think one of the main problems is one of perception. Fish and shellfish are still regarded as being, in some way, not quite a full meal. I noted a comment in Jane Grigson's excellent *Fish Cookery,* written in 1973, which is still, I'm afraid, all too relevant today.

> The writer remarked that "fish could not be served as a main course when men were present as they needed steak or some other red meat."

The incorrect belief that fish is not as nourishing as meat persists.

Fish bones are another reason mentioned to me for why people don't like fish. Speaking as someone who's spent a whole morning in the Radcliffe Infirmary in Oxford having a kipper bone removed from his throat, I should have given up fish long ago. But I haven't, and anyway, there are plenty of fish that don't have any small, throat-stabbing bones in them: flat fish, monkfish and all of the shark family, to name but a few.

The smell of fish is a problem to some. I do a number of demonstrations in local schools every year and children usually complain about the smell. This could be where poor fishmongers or perhaps poor turnover of fish is to blame. I'm always at pains to tell people that fresh fish doesn't smell fishy. But if you look round one or two fishmongers and even large stores at the quality of fish they have on sale, I'd be tempted to agree with those people who dislike the smell. Poor, sunken-eyed, flabby fish all sold at astoundingly high prices are fortunately not representative but definitely not acceptable.

I think the main reason for our reluctance to eat more fish is a lack of handed-down information. I was brought up in Oxfordshire, about as far from the sea as you can get in the British Isles, and I recall the fish that we had to eat in those days being dull. The transport of fish then was far less efficient than it is now. Fish was what everyone ate on Fridays; it was something that no one really looked forward to. I imagine most people have had similar experiences, unless they were brought up on the coast. I was brought up on a farm. I knew how to pluck chickens, remove guts from various animals. I saw pigs being slaughtered and all the bits made into something: headcheese, chitterlings, hams. We had rabbits, partridges and pheasants and ate them regularly; my mother is a natural cook. Apart from the odd salmon, fish was not a great part of my experience except when we went to Cornwall every summer for our long holidays. It was almost like going to another country; the fish, the lobsters, the crayfish, the enormous crabs were so exotic.

Through lack of handed-down information, many of us suffer from ignorance as far as fish preparation is concerned, so that when we're faced with a whole fish we don't know what to do with it. And because we don't know what to do with it, we lack imagination about the possibilities it offers.

One of the fishermen who catches sea bass for us describes his favorite way of cooking fish as being to fry them with mushrooms and tomatoes, rather as though he were frying bacon and kidneys. I wouldn't be surprised if the majority of people in this country considered that to be appetizing. But there is so much more he could do to cook those bass so as to pass on the excitement and quality of a beautiful fish. Think of roasting the whole fish and serving it with some *beurre blanc,* or grilling it and serving it with some basil, lemon juice and virgin olive oil with maybe a bit of rough sea salt sprinkled over it.

But I do have every reason to feel optimistic. One day, while we were filming the television series that this book accompanies, we went into a café just opposite the fish market in Newlyn and, having been excited by all the beautifully fresh fish in the market, we asked if we could have some simply cooked cod for breakfast. "We don't serve fish here, it's a fisherman's café," came the astonished reply.

We left feeling a little despondent—but you can either respond by thinking, "This is an example of how indifferent we all are to fish in these islands," and be generally depressed and demoralized about it, or, you could think, "Okay, this is how it is now, but it isn't going to last for much longer." And the more I think about it, the more I realize the truth in the latter viewpoint.

We are going through a revolution in our eating habits in this country and within the next 25 years I am confident that you will be able to find shops selling fish anywhere in the British Isles where there is a fishing community, as well as plenty of seafood restaurants. We tend to think there's something wrong with us as a nation because we don't appreciate and make use of our natural resources, like fish. I think over the past hundred years or so people forgot how to enjoy eating. We moved away from fish in our diets partly as a result of the Industrial Revolution when much of the population moved from the countryside and coast to the cities, leaving behind a whole tradition of living off the land and sea. Of course, some people still eat well off the land to this day, but most of us have lost sight of our natural culinary heritage.

I want to reverse the unhappy situation on this island where three-quarters of the fish caught are exported. I want to show you the unrivaled advantages of a diet containing fish. I have already stressed the invaluable health benefits but really hope to persuade you to eat more fish through the dishes themselves. By sampling just one of the recipes in this book, I think you will be bowled over not only by the marvelous flavor and texture of fish but also by the simple pleasure, ease and satisfaction there is in cooking with fish. Believe me, a whole new experience awaits you!

A Note About My Style of Cooking

The success of British cooking depends on the very best ingredients being treated in the very simplest way, and when that happens I think there is nothing to beat it in the whole world. The problem with British food is that it really doesn't lend itself to commercial cooking, and its downfall has been that the most indifferent raw materials when cooked simply, taste boring. If you have to use indifferent ingredients, then you need to have a more inventive cuisine to go with it. Nobody could claim that farmed carp has much taste to it, but put it into a Thai or Chinese context with ginger, garlic, chili, soy sauce and lime, and something very acceptable is produced. In British cooking we always rely on the quality of the ingredients, and if it isn't there, the cooking is not worth consideration. When indifferent ingredients are badly cooked, you have something truly awful, and that is what a lot of British cooking ends up being.

But the basic idea is what influences my cooking: keep the cooking simple and keep the ingredients good. I spend far more time in my restaurant on checking the quality of the fish, shellfish and vegetables than I do on inventing new dishes or endlessly refining a stock or a sauce. Much as I enjoy elaborate French food, I enjoy, far more, dishes like plain grilled lobster with herb butter, turbot with hollandaise sauce, salmon with mayonnaise, plain boiled crab and mayonnaise, skate with black butter and plain grilled Dover sole. If they're accompanied by a dish of freshly dug new potatoes and followed by a bowl of Cornish strawberries, I'm even happier.

My recipes reflect my enthusiasm. Most of them are easy to make and most of them are not overendowed with ingredients. But they all require the very best raw materials, and if you haven't got the very best raw materials, you'll wonder what all the fuss is about.

Notes on the Recipes

Any unusual cooking implements like mortars and pestles, conical sieves or fish scalers are described in Chapter 2.

Ingredients are listed in the order in which they are used in the methods.

BUTTER

Most of my cooking is done with unsalted butter these days. This is because salted butter tends to increase the amount of salt in a recipe and because I prefer the flavor. Nevertheless, sometimes it doesn't really matter which you use, in which case the recipe will say butter rather than unsalted butter. Salted butter is still significantly cheaper than unsalted because it keeps much better.

THAI FISH SAUCE

I use the Southeast Asian anchovy sauce called Thai fish sauce or *nam pla* in a large number of my recipes. It has a clean salty taste, and I like to use it in place of salt because it enhances flavors without actually being noticeable itself. I use a brand called Squid, which we have found to have the cleanest taste. Viet Huong Three Crabs brand and Flying Lion brand are two good alternatives available in the United States.

Thai fish sauce has a much better flavor when it has been recently manufactured. You can tell how old it is simply by checking its color. It is always dark brown in color but the fresher it is, the lighter the brown.

If you can't get hold of fish sauce, just use salt. Alternatively, you can use anchovy extract.

CELERY HERB

This herb, a member of the parsley family, has the same flavor as celery leaves but is much stronger. So strong, in fact, that a little goes a long way, but it is a valuable flavoring herb in stocks and robust sauces.

OLIVE OIL

In the recipes, I specify olive oil for general cooking when the flavor and expense of a fine olive oil would be wasted. I specify extra-virgin olive oil when the aromatic flavors of a good oil are all-important.

By olive oil I mean general purpose blended olive oil; by extra-virgin olive oil I mean oil produced by the first cold pressing of the fruit. I use about five different oils for different purposes. I tend to go for a good extra-virgin Italian oil for using warm in my fish dishes and a French extra-virgin for dressings for salads. The Italian tends to be stronger and more vigorous in flavor, the French softer and more subtle.

CHILIES

I've used Dutch chilies throughout this book because the heat factor is consistent. If you are not able to get hold of these, bite the very end of the tip off the chili you use to taste for strength before using.

WINE ACCOMPANIMENTS

I have often suggested wines to accompany the dishes. On the whole, I've recommended white wine accompaniments but occasionally a light red wine instead that will go wonderfully well with that particular dish.

WEIGHING HERBS

I have been experiencing some difficulty in trying to describe a measure for herbs in my recipes. The expression "a small bunch of parsley" smacks a little of "how long is a piece of string?" So I have specified the amount of herbs in a recipe by the tablespoonful. This means that you will have to guess roughly the amount of herbs to buy to produce a tablespoon. This might be a bit frustrating for you, but at least it does ensure that exactly the right amount of herbs are put into the recipe. As a guideline 1 ounce of parsley sprigs generally produces 1/2 cup of chopped parsley.

It is a good idea to invest in a salad spinner for washing and drying your herbs as well as your salad greens. Cilantro and parsley both tend to be dusty and therefore gritty. They particularly benefit from being washed and dried.

A Note About the Chapters in the Book

One of the hardest parts of organizing a cookery book is trying to fit the dishes into logical chapters. The last time I wrote a fish cookery book, the chapters were based on the courses of a meal, but this didn't work particularly well because so many fish dishes can be served as either a starter or a main course. I thought about making the recipes follow the seasons. But this is particularly difficult with fish because seasonal catches vary dramatically, plus I have always found cookery books based on the seasons to be particularly irritating to follow. I thought about an alphabetical list of fish, but that seemed so uninspiring. Finally I thought that perhaps, by being illogical, I might get a more logical order! So I have grouped the fish in ways that seem to fit together. Oily fish seem to be a group to me, as do flat fish and fish I associate with the Mediterranean—the sort I would cook on a barbecue. In one group I have considered appearance, in another their cooking qualities; illogical, but it seems to work.

2 Choosing, Preparing and Cooking Your Fish

How to Choose Fresh Fish

I know, because people often tell me, that choosing fresh fish is not as easy as it should be. I have always told people to trust their instincts—if the fish looks shiny and attractive, it will probably taste good. But it is a bit like asking somebody who doesn't know much about wine to comment on the quality of a new vintage. It is very difficult unless you have spent years and years tasting

all kinds of wine and have built up a fund of knowledge of colors, tastes and smells. So let me run through a few general points you need to look out for when buying fish.

A food writer visited my kitchen not long ago and paid me, what I consider to be, a very high compliment. She said, "It's extraordinary but your kitchen doesn't smell of fish." Fresh fish doesn't smell fishy. It has a smell in the same sort of category as green fields in spring or indeed dried sheets, taken off the washing line in a country garden on a breezy day. The appearance of the fish should be bright and shiny, it should be firm to the touch and, perhaps most important, if you lift up the gill cover, the gills underneath should be a lustrous pink or red. There should be no sign of brown in them and they should not look washed out. The eyes of the fish should be clear and bright and not dull or red and the scales should be tight.

An extra bit of advice to add about choosing fresh fish is that it's much easier to make judgments about one thing by comparing it with another. I would suggest you look for the nicest looking fish on the slab and, when you have found it, use it as a yardstick to judge the others. You can then ask yourself, "Why are the other fish less fresh looking?" The fish that looks better than the others is the fish to buy. So don't be too dogmatic about choosing fish. On p. 221 I've listed all the fish used in the recipes and given some alternatives if the specified fish is not available or is not in the best condition. You'll get much better results, for example, by using haddock instead of cod in a recipe if the cod doesn't look too good. Also, see the listing of fish by local names on p. 219.

If you see something on the slab that looks fresh but is unknown to you, go ahead and buy it, although I don't expect you to be quite as foolhardy as I was when I once bought jellyfish. I had had jellyfish in a Chinese restaurant where it was served as a salad with a julienne of chicken, cucumber with cilantro, and soy sauce. So enthusiastic was I about this dish that I was determined to try and make it myself. I asked one of the net fishermen to bring me some in. They started off about the size of footballs but when I boiled them, they reduced in size by about 90 percent. Then I thinly sliced what was left. When I ate them, though, it was a bit like eating a bunch of stinging nettles, the whole of my mouth came up in a wild rash. But I would still suggest you try anything that you see in a fishmonger's shop because they're not going to sell you jellyfish that sting your mouth!

I know that, sometimes, fish can be startling in their uncouth appearance, and I'm no less affected by the look of unfamiliar fish than anyone else. I have been taking winter holidays in Goa on the west coast of India for the last four or five years. I go to the same hotel, where the food is excellent and where I've struck up a very productive relationship with the manager, who used to be a chef. He has taken me round the local fish market a couple of times, and I must say the first time I went round it I was overwhelmed by the sight of so many strange fish. I have to admit that the smell was pretty overwhelming, too—not of stale fish but, on the one hand, of a dried fish that has a particularly pungent odor, and, on the other, the smell of tropically heated fish guts. Everyone has the same mixed feelings when going to markets in India: fascination and excitement about how exotic it all is, but also a dread of some of the smells and sights. Having been to the market a couple of times, I began to see patterns emerging in comparison with our own fish and thanks to Rui, my guide, I soon began to feel perfectly at home there. What became clear to me was, that although the fish looked strange to me, it could be classified in the same sort of way as our own fish and, indeed, adapted to the same sort of dishes that appear in this book. I don't think there is anywhere in the world that I could now go and not feel at ease in buying fish and cooking it in ways that I know.

Where to Buy Fish

It is always best to buy whole fish at the fishmonger's where it can be filleted or skinned by an expert, and where you can get a good look at the quality of the fish before you buy. It is much easier to tell the freshness of fish from a whole fish than a ready filleted one. A whole fish is also fresher because once it has been filleted, it tends to oxidize and will never taste as fresh again.

Anyone with a serious interest in fish will always find a dedicated fishmonger to supply them. I know that fishmongers have been closing in their dozens over the last few years, but I don't myself think that this is so much to do with a waning interest in fish as the fact that people are now buying fish from other sources, notably supermarkets, which have had a radical effect on the way we all shop. Supermarkets have been responsible for the demise of many small shops but no one can deny the extraordinary improvement in the supply of good-quality and wide-ranging food that they provide. I think that a dedicated fishmonger will survive. You only have to compare the enormous variety of fish and shellfish in the shop of a good fishmonger with what is offered at most supermarkets to see what I mean. Both types of outlet can exist side by side, on one hand, the convenient prepacked supermarket product, on the other, the skillfully prepared, carefully chosen fish and shellfish of the fishmonger.

Apart from actually buying fish and shellfish you can always go and catch your own. It always seems to me extraordinary how little shellfish is gathered from the beaches that exist around our coastline. I'm an avid picker of shellfish from the beach, and what could be more satisfying than going and collecting your food, coming home and cooking it, appealing, I guess, to some deep-rooted hunter-gatherer instinct?

The Preparing and Cooking of Fish

I wrote, in my last book, that I find cleaning and filleting fish is a very relaxing pastime. It's a job where my hands and brain are working in complete coordination because I've done it so often before. The feeling that I'm doing something right when I'm doing this job is one of the great pluses about being a cook; there's something about working with my hands that makes me happy, optimistic and calm. I watched a Filipino fishmonger fillet a yellowfin tuna in a Sydney fish market once. I videoed it as well because it was so beautiful. He was like a surgeon, parting the flesh from the bone with such apparent ease that it looked like the simplest job in the world. I love to watch the filleting of large cod at the fish market in Plymouth, or the swishing off of sides of salmon in a salmon smokery with one sweep of a long-bladed, serrated knife, or watching fishermen at sea gutting flat fish. A single cut and a flick and all the guts are removed. All these things are so fascinating. At the restaurant, we never achieve the speed or perfection that these people do because they are doing one job all the time, whereas we have to do hundreds. Nevertheless, the preparation of fish in our kitchen is one of the most important parts of our jobs, and all the chefs have to attain a high level of skill to avoid wastage.

Storing Fish

Domestic refrigerators are not ideally suited for storing fish. They are usually set at about 42°F and fish should be stored at about 32°F with plenty of ice to provide a moist atmosphere.

Despite this, I have found that it is possible to keep fish quite successfully in a domestic refrigerator if it's only for a short time and if you follow this procedure. Put the fish in a shallow dish and wrap both the dish and fish in plastic wrap. Then, dot cubes of ice around the top of the plastic wrap and put the dish in the coldest part of the refrigerator.

Whole fish keep better than filleted fish, which is why, at the restaurant, we always buy fish on the bone. Once a fish has been filleted, the cut surface tends to oxidize and turn an unappetizing yellow color. You can slow down this process by wrapping the fish as I've suggested, but the oxidizing and discoloring will still take place, albeit at a much slower pace.

It is not worth keeping fish for more than a couple of days. If you're going to keep it any longer, you would probably do better to freeze it. Some fish freezes better than others; the firmer the flesh, the better it freezes. So Dover sole, turbot and monkfish freeze very well and bass, lemon sole and flounder freeze less well. If you are certain that the fish is very fresh and no more than a day or so old when you get it, then I can see nothing wrong with freezing it, as long as you use what you have frozen within a week or two. Ungutted fish freeze best of all, as long as they're perfectly fresh when you get them.

The problem with buying frozen fish is that you don't know how long it's been frozen, and over a period even fish stored at the lowest temperatures will deteriorate. This is particularly the case with oily fish like mackerel or herring. Something seems to happen to the oil in them. It turns slightly rancid even after a short period of freezing.

When defrosting fish, give it plenty of time to thaw. The best method is to put it in the refrigerator straight from the freezer.

Whelks

Tellin Clams

Swimming / Velvet Crab

Razor Clams

Spider Crab

Norway Lobster

Brown Crab (Cock)

Cockles

Scallops

Spiny Lobster

Cherrystone Clams

Raw Mediterranean
Prawns

Mussels

Native Oysters

Rock Oysters

Octopus

Cuttlefish

Shark

Squid

Shrimp

Native Lobster

Winkles

Sea Urchin

Native Lobster

Green Crab / Shore Crab

Cleaning and Gutting Fish

If you buy fish ungutted, it is essential to remove the guts as soon as possible. Otherwise they will start to taint the flesh around the stomach. It is not a bad idea to remove the scales at the same time, even if you're not going to eat the fish for a while. They're much easier to get off while the fish is still moist. If you let the skin dry at all, the scales are difficult to remove.

ROUND FISH

Trimming

Snip off the fins with kitchen scissors. This is particularly important with spiky fish like bass. There is not a chef in my kitchen who has not caught his knuckle on the spines of a bass!

Scaling

This is best done on several sheets of newspaper so you can catch as many of the scales as possible. They tend to fly everywhere. You can then wrap up the newspaper, throw it away and have a relatively easy job cleaning up afterward. There is nothing worse than trying to clean a work surface with dried-out scales stuck to it.

Remove the scales by scraping the fish from tail to head using a blunt, thick-bladed knife, a special scaler or even a scallop shell. A scaler does the job best, if you can afford it. The one we use in the kitchen used to have a little plastic box on the back to collect the scales but, like a lot of smart implements in our kitchen, it disappeared a long time ago.

Gutting

Having removed the scales, slit the belly from the anal fin (two-thirds of the way down the fish from the head) to the head and pull most of the guts out with your hands, then cut away any pieces of entrails left. If you like you can also remove the gills at this time by cutting them away from the two places where they join the fish at the back of the head and under the mouth. Give the cavity a good wash. In salmon and steelhead you will need to remove the clotted blood on either side of the backbone. Do this by scraping at it with the point of a knife.

Gutting Round Fish for Stuffing

If you intend to fill a whole round fish with a large amount of stuffing, you can either fill the gut cavity and sew the flaps up with string, which you cut away just before serving, or you can remove the guts through the gill cavity to form a natural container.

To stuff the fish through the gill cavity, cut away the gills, then, reaching through the back of the head, pull out the insides with your fingers. Make a small opening in front of the anal fin and wash the cavity through from the gills.

Boning Round Fish for Serving Whole

You can remove most of the internal bones from a round fish so that when it is stuffed it can be eaten without the bones getting in the way. Gut the fish as normal, but slit it right along the belly, from head to tail, cutting through to the backbone and exposing the backbone along the whole length with your filleting knife. Snip the backbone with a pair of scissors where it joins the tail and behind the head, then pull out the backbone. We have a pair of thin-nosed pliers in the kitchen that we find ideal for removing bones. With the pliers, you can remove the bones around the gut cavity as well as from the backbone by pulling them out one by one.

FLAT FISH

Trimming

When cleaning flat fish snip off the side fins with a pair of scissors.

Scaling

Not many flat fish need scaling. Dover sole and petrale sole are the only ones with serious scales. See p. 20 for instructions on scaling.

Gutting

If you need to gut flat fish, make a small incision below the head where the guts cavity is. You can locate this by pressing on the white side of the fish where there will be an area that is much softer than the other side of this fish.

Pull the guts out with your little finger. If you want to remove the roe at this stage, make a larger incision on the same side and pull it out too.

Filleting Fish

I would expect you to get your fishmonger to fillet your fish. It's a bit of a specialist task really, and not many people are any more adept at removing fillets from a fish than boning a large side of beef. However, from time to time you are bound to get hold of the odd catch of whole fish or feel like doing it yourself and the following instructions are designed to help you as much as possible.

FILLETING ROUND FISH

Small Fish: Mackerel, Herring or Trout

Lay the fish on a chopping board with its back toward you. Cut across the fillet of the fish through to the backbone, behind the head. Turn the knife toward the tail and cut the fillet away from the backbone right down to the tail in one clean sweep using the flat of the knife against the backbone as a guide. Turn the fish over and repeat on the other side.

A simple way to fillet small fish like mackerel or herring without using a filleting knife is to cut off the head and make an incision from the gut cavity right down to the tail. Put the fish on a chopping board, belly-side down, and press the back firmly with the flat of your hand down into the chopping board, gradually flattening it out onto the board. Turn the fish over and pull out the backbone. Then remove any small bones left in the fillet with a pair of tweezers or pliers.

Larger Round Fish

Lay the fish on a chopping board and cut off the head behind the gills. Don't cut straight through but rather follow the line of the gills in a V-shape to make sure that you don't lose any of the fillet. Now lay the fish with its back toward you and cut down the length of the back keeping the knife above the back bones and the blade horizontal against them. As you cut, lift the flap of fillet up with your fingers to make it easier to see where you are cutting. Lift off the top fillet, turn over and repeat on the other side. This sounds easy, doesn't it? I'm afraid it's not really. To start with your knife won't seem to go where you want it to and you'll find yourself cutting into the fillet. Practice makes perfect. The only really difficult part of filleting round fish is the cutting round the rib bones. The rib bones, which surround the intestines, are different on all fish. In some species like hake, it is far better to cut around the rib bones; on others like salmon it is usually better to cut through them, then remove the bones from the fillet afterward. As I said earlier, filleting is tremendously satisfying when you've learned how to do it—if you've got plenty of fish and plenty of time, give it a try.

FILLETING MONKFISH

Cut the tail into two large fillets by running your knife against the spine. Monkfish has a membrane under the skin that should be partly removed; otherwise the

John Dory

Halibut

Salmon

Mackerel

Sprats

Cod

Red Bream

Brill

Tuna (Tail)

Red Mullet

Dover Sole

Gurnard

Pollack

Grey Mullet

fillet will shrink and twist unattractively in cooking. The membrane is best removed by pulling as much as you can off with your fingers and cutting some off. I don't think it is a good idea to try and completely remove the membrane because you will lose a lot of fillet by cutting it off; as long as a fair amount is removed, the rest will not be a problem. (See p. 25 for information on skinning monkfish.)

FILLETING FLAT FISH

This is much easier than filleting round fish because the bone structure lends itself to straightforward cutting. Slice through the fish from the head to the tail down to the backbone. Now slide the filleting knife under one fillet away to the side of the fish until the fillet is free. The angle of the knife is almost flat, using the long back bones as a guide. Do the same with the remaining three fillets.

FILLETING JOHN DORY

Because John Dory is actually a round fish rather than a flat fish, it has to be filleted in a slightly different way, even though it is flat! Lay the fish on a chopping board with its head facing you and insert the point of a knife into the right-hand side of the fish next to the tail and above the bony fins that run all around the body. Work right round the fish, cutting away a little flap all the way around one side. Now, gradually work your way right across one side of the fish with your filleting knife flat against the central bones. Lift the fillet off. Do the same on the other side.

Skinning Fillets of Fish

Place a fillet on the chopping board, skin-side down. Grasp the tail end with one hand and with the other work your filleting knife up the fillet against the skin, working away from your body in a series of short jerky cuts.

SKINNING DOVER SOLE

Lay the fish dark-side up and cut the skin across the tail. Work a finger under the cut and loosen the skin down both sides of the fish. Sprinkle the tail end with salt to make it easy to hold. Grasp the flap of skin with a tea towel and pull the skin away from the fish right over the head, holding the tail with your other hand. Repeat on the other side.

If the sole is particularly fresh, skinning it is tricky because it won't come away very easily. If pulling the skin away seems to be tearing the flesh, it is a good idea to cut the skin through at the head and start at the other end.

SKINNING EELS AND DOGFISH

To skin eels and dogfish, you will need some strong string, pliers and somewhere to hang the fish. Cut the fins and tail off the fish, then cut through the skin behind the neck and continue this cut right round the back of the head, so that the skin is parted all the way round. With the point of a thin-bladed knife, ease about 1/2 inch of skin away from the flesh all the way round. Tie a piece of string around this cut, with a long enough loose end to attach to some anchorage point like a hook on the wall or even a door handle. Attach the fish, grip the flap of skin with the pliers and pull the skin toward the tail. Some of the flesh will start to come away with the skin, but keep moving the pliers around different parts of the skin and pulling and you will find that the skin soon starts to pull away cleanly. Firmly and steadily pull the skin off the body.

SKINNING MONKFISH

Grasp the thick end of the tail in one hand and the skin in the other and pull away the skin. You will find that it comes away easily. (See p. 24 for information on filleting monkfish.)

Storing Crabs and Lobsters

Cooked crabs and lobsters keep very well in the refrigerator for up to four days. Live crabs and lobsters will stay alive for three or four days as long as they were lively when you bought them. You should keep them in the bottom of your refrigerator covered with a damp cloth. They should be checked regularly to make sure they're still alive, because once they have died their flesh deteriorates very quickly. If they have died, they should be boiled immediately.

Cooking Crabs and Lobsters

CRABS

Crabs should be killed before boiling. Take a small knife or screwdriver, turn the crab over and pierce it through the mouth straight up to strike the underside of the back shell, right between the eyes. Now pierce it again right in the middle of the undershell beneath the flap that folds over the shell. This flap is small in a male crab and large in a female.

Crabs should be boiled in plenty of water salted at the rate of 2/3 cup salt to 5 quarts water. This is roughly the salinity of seawater (in which the shellfish are actually cooked at my restaurant). Cooking times for crab are as follows (timing begins when the water has come back to a boil after the crab has been added).

Crabs up to 1¼ pounds	15 minutes
Crabs up to 2 pounds	20 minutes
Crabs up to 3½ pounds	25 minutes
Any larger crab	30 minutes

LOBSTERS

Killing lobsters presents a real problem in that it is impossible to kill them by piercing them in the same way as crabs. This is because they don't have a central nervous system but rather a series of nerves or ganglia throughout their body. Neither does the lobster have a brain. There is therefore no vital spot in a lobster to allow you to kill it humanely. It is pretty unlikely, however, that the lobster feels pain in the way that we or most other animals do, but we can't be totally sure about this. There was some talk a few years ago about manufacturing a small saline tank attached to the main electricity supply in which a lobster could be painlessly electrocuted, but nothing came of it. The British humane society has suggested that putting live lobsters in the deep freeze for two hours before cooking them will kill them painlessly. It is likely that if they do feel pain, putting them in cold salted water and bringing that water very slowly to a boil will probably kill them as painlessly as any other way, since heating the water will gradually drive out all the oxygen and they will drown.

The two methods used at the restaurant, while not painless, are mercifully quick. We either drop them into a great deal of very rapidly boiling salted water, salted at the same rate as for crabs—2/3 cup salt to 5 quarts water—so that the time taken for the water to come back to a boil once the lobster has gone in is minimized. The other way is to take a very large kitchen knife and cleave them in two. To cut the lobster in half, place it on a chopping board and drive a large knife through the middle of the main body section, lengthwise, cutting down toward and between, the eyes. Turn the knife round, place it in the original cut and bring the knife right down through the tail to split it in half. Pull off the claws, cut off the rubber band binding them and crack each claw open. Do the same with the other sections of the claws with a short, sharp chop from the thickest part of your knife

Whitebait

Conger Eel

Whole Monkfish

Sea Trout

Sardines

Sea Bass

Skate Wing

Haddock

Herring

Whiting

Hake

Lemon Sole

Turbot

Plaice

Pilchards

blade. Lobsters should be boiled for the following times. Again, as with crabs, timing begins when the water has come back to a boil after the lobster has been added.

Lobsters up to 1$\frac{1}{2}$ pounds	15 minutes
Lobsters up to 2$\frac{1}{2}$ pounds	20 minutes
Anything larger	Boil for an extra 5 minutes per pound

CRAYFISH OR SPINY LOBSTER

These are killed and cooked in the same way as lobsters. Instructions for removing the meat from crabs, lobsters and crayfish are given in the individual recipes.

Preparing Squid, Cuttlefish and Octopus

SQUID

Gently pull apart the head and body, the intestines will come away with the head, which is joined directly to the tentacles. Reach into the body with your fingers and pull out the rest of the insides, which will be the plasticlike quill and normally some soft white roe. Pull the purple skin off the body—it comes away very easily. Remove the two fins and pull the skin off them, too. Wash the body, cut the tentacles from the head in front of the eyes. Squeeze out the beaklike mouth from the center of the tentacles and throw it away. You may like to keep the ink sac, which is with the rest of the insides. It is easily identifiable being pearly white in color with a slight blue tinge. The only other part of the insides worth keeping are two pieces of muscle running down either side, which can be taken off and used with the body and tentacles. Discard everything else. You are now left with the body section, the fins, the tentacles, perhaps the ink sac and two pieces of muscle from the insides.

CUTTLEFISH

Cut off the tentacles in front of the eyes and remove the beaklike mouth from the center of the tentacles. Cut the head section from the body and discard it. Cut open the body section from top to bottom along the dark colored back. Remove the cuttle bone and the entrails. Skin the body and, with large cuttlefish, the tentacles. Cook in the same way as squid.

OCTOPUS

Cut off the tentacles in front of the eyes and, as with the squid and cuttlefish, press the mouth and beak out from the center of the tentacles. Cut the head section from the body sac at the round openings in the body. Discard the head. Turn the body inside out and pull away the insides. Discard. Pull off the small bonelike strips sticking to the sides of the body and discard also. Bring a pan of water to a boil and simmer the body and tentacles very gently for up to 1 hour, depending on the size of the octopus.

Oysters, Mussels and Other Mollusks

OPENING OYSTERS

Wrap one hand in a tea towel and place the oyster in it, put your hand on a work surface, push the point of an oyster knife or small, thick-bladed knife into the hinge of the oyster and, using firm but not excessive pressure, work the knife backward and forward into the shell, breaking the hinge. As the hinge breaks, twist the point of the knife to lever the shell up, then slide the knife under the top shell to sever the ligament that joins the oyster to the shell. The ligament is slightly off to the right of center of the oyster. Lift off the top shell, keeping the bottom shell upright at all times to avoid losing any of the juice. Pick out any little pieces of shell that might have broken off.

PREPARING MUSSELS FOR COOKING

Mussels should be washed in plenty of cold water. There is no need to steep them in buckets of cold water with or without oatmeal. Not only is this totally ineffective but more likely to kill them than anything else. None of the water in the bucket will get inside the mussels; they will remain tightly closed. Mussels only open their shells when they sense that they're in well-aerated water, seawater or brackish water. The same advice goes for all bivalves like clams or cockles: a good wash is all they need. Having washed the mussels, scrape off any barnacles that are sticking to them and any seaweed and pull out the beards. These are the threads called the byssus by which the mussel attaches itself to rocks. Raw mussels are excellent to eat as long as you accompany them with the *Shallot Vinegar* on p. 53. Without it the mussel leaves a bitter metallic aftertaste. To open a raw mussel, take a small, thin-bladed knife and force it between the two shells, then run the blade right round to separate them. Carefully scrape the live meat from one shell into the other and pull out any remaining beard.

PREPARING COCKLES AND CLAMS

As with mussels, cockles and clams need to be washed in plenty of cold water by swirling them round and round in it. The cockles or clams that you buy will already be free from mud and grit but another wash does no harm at all. The easiest way to open cockles and clams is to steam them open in a covered pan to which you have added a little bit of water or wine. However, both can be opened raw by inserting the blade of a small knife between the shells and twisting them open. With both cockles and clams, unlike oysters, the knife should be inserted on the opposite side to the hinge not into the hinge itself.

PREPARING SCALLOPS

Like mussels, scallops too should be washed in plenty of cold water. Place the scallop on a chopping board, flat shell uppermost, and slide the blade of a filleting knife between the two shells. Keep the blade of the knife flat against the top shell and find the ligament that joins the shell to the muscle meat of the scallop and cut right through it. The top shell will come off. Pull out all the material in the scallop shell except the bright orange coral and the muscle.

Cooking Fish

Fish cooks very fast and overcooks even faster so you really do have to be very attentive to get it right, particularly where you're dealing with very small pieces of fish. Whichever method of cooking fish you use, the one main point you need to remember is timing. These days recipes for fish in cookery books tend to be aware of this, but when you look at some older recipes, which talk about boiling fish for 11/2 hours or steaming scallops for 20 minutes, you wonder if there was anything left at the end that was worth eating. At the restaurant we use a temperature probe to gauge the internal temperature of the dish exactly, but you can also use the following methods. Take a small knife and part the fillet in the center. If it is cooked, the fish will have changed from a translucent color to solid white. Alternatively, take a metal skewer, push into the center and leave for 5 seconds. Remove and touch the tip on either your top lip or elbow. If it feels pleasantly warm the center will be about 113°F, if it feels hot, about 149°F. If it feels very hot it will be overcooked and you'll burn your lip as well! If you are cooking whole fish, you can also check the gills. If they are cooked they will have turned a gray brown with no traces of pink in them.

BAKING

These days, the words baking and roasting are pretty interchangeable because what we actually do with roast beef is to bake it in a baking oven. Roasting means cooking in front of an open fire. However, I do see a distinction between roasting in a baking oven and baking in the same oven, in that I take baking to mean cooking a fish in a reasonably high-sided dish with flavoring ingredients around it. The flavoring ingredients to some extent permeate the flesh of the fish and the high sides prevent both the fish and other ingredients from burning. The temperature for baking fish is lower than that for roasting, about 350°F.

COOKING IN A BAIN-MARIE

Fish terrines, like the *Shrimp Terrine with Zucchini Salad* on p. 194, are cooked in a moderate oven (325°F). The terrine is placed in a pan of boiling water and the pan and terrine placed in the oven. Cooked this way, the terrine cooks slowly in a very moist atmosphere.

BRAISING

Fillets, steaks or whole fish are placed on a bed of vegetables. Stock and white wine are added to come about halfway up the fish, herbs are sprinkled over and a loose-fitting lid or buttered parchment is placed on top. The dish can either be cooked gently on the top of the stove or else in a moderate oven. When the fish is just cooked, it is removed. The juice and vegetables are reduced down to make a thick sauce, which is then poured over the fish.

BOILING

The only fish dishes that are cooked by boiling are stews, where the idea is to force oil or butter to amalgamate with the liquid by rapid boiling. Most other cooking methods where fish is immersed in a liquid are described as poaching (see p. 33).

FRYING
Shallow frying

This is the process of cooking small fillets or even whole fish in oil or fat in a shallow pan. You can coat the surface of the fish with flour or other starchy materials like semolina, matzo meal, rolled oats or bread crumbs. You don't have to coat the surface of the fillets at all. If you are looking for a slightly oily finish, try frying them with some good olive oil and at a low temperature.

A couple of important tips about shallow frying: first, don't crowd the pan. The object is to cause the surface of the fillets of fish to caramelize by cooking at a high temperature. If you crowd the pan you will lower the temperature and caramelization will not occur. (Caramelization is when the sugars present in all foods are burnt by contact with a fierce heat. The burning, if arrested at the right time, is full of flavor; if you take it too far it becomes like carbon.) The other important tip is not to let the oil burn so that it carbonizes the surface of the fillets before the fish has had time to cook or caramelize.

With regard to the second point, pure butter is a bad cooking medium because there are lots of solids in butter that burn at a much lower temperature than that needed to caramelize the fish. Burnt butter will give you black and greasy results. Either use clarified butter or vegetable oil with a little knob of butter for flavor. (For notes on how to clarify butter see the recipe for *Hollandaise Sauce* on p. 40.) If you are going to cook a large steak of fish or a whole fish, you would be better off caramelizing the fish by starting it on the top of the stove, then finishing it off in a moderate oven. In this way you will avoid the risk of burning it.

A lot of people complain that one of the main reasons they don't like frying fish is the smell. If you have an oven that is well vented to the outdoors, you can avoid excessive cooking smells when frying fish by completing the operation in the oven.

Several of the baked dishes in the book call for coloring the fish by shallow frying first, for example

Haddock Boulangère (see p. 124). This shallow frying not only enhances the flavor through caramelization but also gives the fish a pleasing color that you would not otherwise get owing to the short cooking time of the fish in the oven.

Deep-frying

Deep-frying is one of the most successful ways of cooking fish because, provided you use a good solid batter like the *Yeast and Beer Batter* on p. 52, all the flavor and moisture of the fish is sealed inside. There are a few points to watch out for when deep-frying. Don't be stingy with the oil. Don't let it become too dirty before throwing it away. You will only ruin the food if the oil is bitter and black. If you only deep-fry things occasionally, it is a very good idea to let the oil cool down in the fryer and then pass it through a sieve into a container that you can seal. Oil picks up moisture from the air all the time and spoils quickly. If you keep it sealed it will last a lot longer.

Another important part of deep-frying fish successfully is getting the temperature of the oil right. Temperature-controlled fryers are available relatively cheaply, as are thermometers, but if you can't afford to buy one, the best way of testing the correct temperature of the oil is to drop a small piece of bread into the oil when you think its shimmering surface is hot enough. If the bread browns within 30 seconds, the oil is hot enough. If it blackens in the same time it is too hot. Fish should be cooked between 350°F and 380°F. Big pieces of fish in batter, like cod, should be cooked at the lower temperature, allowing the heat of the oil to penetrate right to the center of the fish before there is any chance of the outer coating burning. Conversely, small pieces of fish or small fish like whitebait should be cooked at the higher temperature to allow the pieces to crisp very quickly.

Stir-frying

The Chinese way of cooking is ideally suited to fish. By cutting food into small pieces, vegetables and fish need not be cooked so thoroughly.

Many people find undercooked fish a problem because they are put off by the chewiness, unless the fish is thinly sliced and presented as obviously raw, like the sashimi on p. 165. But when the fish is cut into small pieces and stir-fried, nobody notices. What they do notice is the tremendous amount of flavor in the fish. As with shallow frying, don't overload the wok. If you've ever seen the size of burner that Chinese and other Southeast Asians cook over, you will see how little one should put in a wok using our puny Western burners. I will always remember a visit I made to a restaurant on Sukhamvite Road in Bangkok a few years ago. The wok stoves they use there are like small volcanoes. Everything takes about 20 seconds to cook. The chefs are on show outside the restaurant. You go into a supermarket, choose your fish and vegetables, take them over to a chef and he cooks them in about a minute. The restaurant seats something crazy like 1200 people. It is one of the best dining experiences I've ever had.

BROILING

One of the faults in my last seafood cookery book was that I was a bit overfond of cooking fish in this way. This is because we use an overhead broiler in our restaurant a great deal. It cooks fish perfectly every time and yet it is a method of cooking that you can walk away and leave for a minute or two without anything going wildly wrong—very important this when you've got maybe six different dishes all cooked in different ways on the go at one time. The problem is (as has been pointed out to me since writing the book) that the sort of broilers we use at home are not as powerful, so I've tended to be a little less liberal in my use of such a method of cooking in this book.

However, if you do have a good broiler it is an excellent way of cooking fish, particularly fillets and whole fish, which should always be slashed right down to the bone so that the intense heat of the broiler cooks the fish quickly before any of its juices have leached out and dried away. On the subject of juices leaching out, one of the most influential books on cooking I have read recently, called *On Food and Cooking* by

Harold McGee, dismisses many cherished ideas about the science of cookery but none more so than the whole business of sealing meat or fish by searing. He proves conclusively that when you apply intense heat to a piece of protein you do not create a barrier that locks in the juices, you simply enhance its flavor by caramelizing the outside but the juices continue to run through. The reason that it appears that the juices have been locked in is that the intense heat dries them up so quickly that you can't see them coming out but, as soon as you take that piece of meat or fish away from the source of heat and leave it to rest, out they continue to run. So when we are broiling a fillet of fish in the restaurant, we always leave the cooking of it to the last minute. Only when a customer has finished his first course and has actually ordered a piece of broiled turbot for his second, do we start to cook the turbot. In this way the most flavor is delivered to the customer and doesn't leach out onto the broiler pan.

BARBECUING OR CHARBROILING

Barbecuing or charbroiling is one of my favorite ways of cooking fish. It is so popular at the moment, though, that we are in danger of being criticized for having too many grilled items on the menu at one time. But, not only do I love cooking fish this way, my customers enjoy eating it. So enamored am I of charcoal cookery that for five years in the restaurant we had just that, a broiler heated by charcoal. We bought charcoal by the ton and stoked up the fire every night because I love that little edge of flavor that you get from the gases that emanate from charcoal. That smell from hot balmy evenings in Greece, once experienced, is never forgotten. However, in the end we had to give it up because we couldn't keep the grill hot enough right through a busy lunch or dinner that could last as long as four hours. Although the grill was about a square yard in size, even building up one side with fresh charcoal as the other side died down didn't give us enough heat. Now we have an excellent gas charcoal grill. To get over the lack of charcoal flavor, we throw dried herbs and charcoal dust over the lava coals.

I'm sure most people are familiar with barbecue cookery. There's nothing much I can add except to say don't be stingy with the charcoal. I remember when I was in Australia lighting my first outdoor barbecue using wood, the girl that was with us said "You call that a fire?—this is a fire," and produced enough wood for Guy Fawkes night. Mine wouldn't have cooked a single shrimp. You must build up a really good fire, then let it die down. When barbecuing you cook on the residual heat to achieve the best results because the great enemy of good barbecue cooking is flame. What you really need is very hot ash because then, providing that the barbecue is very hot (and therefore the barbecue bars are very hot) and the fish, even fillets, are well oiled, they shouldn't stick. We have found that the best way to prevent a whole Dover sole from sticking is first to brush oil all over the sole and then sprinkle it liberally with sea salt and put it straight on oiled grill bars. A lot of cookery books suggest that you shouldn't season anything before you put it on a charcoal grill because you won't get a crisp charbroiled surface. This is total rubbish; it works perfectly and anything cooked on a grill should be preseasoned.

POACHING
Shallow poaching

Shallow poaching is the method used when fillets of fish, or perhaps whole flat fish, are laid in a shallow butter dish, perhaps on some chopped shallots or other finely chopped vegetables such as leek, fennel or celery. A little water and dry white wine is poured over the fish, it is covered with a butter paper and poached in the oven or gently on top of the stove until it has barely turned white. To finish the dish, the fillets are removed, the cooking liquid is reduced and a little butter or cream is added with whatever flavoring ingredients the dish calls for.

Poaching in a court bouillon or nage

Court bouillon is the term used for a flavored cooking liquor in which fish such as skate wings or salmon are poached. *Nage* is the word for a rather more strongly-flavored liquid used for poaching shellfish, in particular freshwater crayfish, which are notably lacking in flavor, at least when compared with their marine equivalent langoustine (lobsterette). I find that the flavor of a court bouillon or nage tends to improve after 24 hours or so of being left in the refrigerator with all the aromatic vegetables and herbs that went into making them. If the fish or shellfish to be poached is of the best quality I tend to favor either plain water with salt or the very simplest court bouillon maybe with a couple of slices of lemon, a bit of salt and some peppercorns. Generally, the lesser the flavor of the ingredient to be poached, the more flavor one should put into the court bouillon.

ROASTING

Thick fillets or steaks of fish or whole fish like bass can be successfully roasted in the oven at a high temperature, even as high as 450°F. The object in subjecting the fish to such a fierce heat is to crisp the skin on the outside while cooking the inside as quickly as possible. It works very well and in terms of the appeal of dishes on the menu, there is something rather special in an old English cookery sort of way about the idea of roasting fish. It has a sort of echo of Elizabethan banquets.

Menu writing is a tricky business. The object is and always must be first to tell the customer what he or she can expect to eat. This might seem fairly obvious but it is not so at all. Many menus promise one thing and deliver something totally different. The second and equally important object of menu writing is to stimulate the customer's appetite. Words like roasting, baking and grilling are stimulating; words like boiling and steaming are not so attractive. If you're going to use boiling or steaming in a menu, you need to be careful that you explain how the dish is assembled.

STEAMING

Steaming is a brilliant way of cooking fish. The heat never gets much above boiling point so that, as with poaching and boiling, the cooking is a comparatively leisurely affair compared with, say, roasting or deep-frying. In addition, because the fish is constantly bathed in moisture, it tends to come out moist and delicate.

In a busy kitchen it is a godsend, partly because of the need to get the cooking just right in fish cookery, which steaming allows, and partly because steaming is relatively slow, so you're given a little bit more time to do other things before you start to run the risk that the dish will spoil. If I am tasting a new species of fish for the first time, I always steam it first because that is the best way of getting the true flavor of fish without being diverted by any additional flavors added through the cooking. The great experts of steam cookery are the Chinese—a visit to a Chinese kitchen is like entering a steam bath. The recipe for *Steamed Scallops with Ginger, Soy, Sesame and Green Onions* on p. 212 is one of my favorites and taken straight from a Chinese restaurant.

STEAMING IN A PRESSURE COOKER

Cooking in a pressure cooker is faster because when the pressure is increased in a closed, sealed vessel, the boiling temperature of water is also increased and therefore, the water being hotter than boiling point, the food is cooked much more rapidly. As a matter of fact, if you're steaming or boiling food, it cooks faster at sea level than it does at the top of a mountain, simply because at the top of a mountain water boils at a lower temperature. Since fish cooks so quickly anyway, there is not a lot of point in using a pressure cooker. Its great advantage is in drastically reducing the cooking times of long-simmering dishes like stews of tough cuts of meat. The only serious application for seafood would be for the tenderizing of octopus (see p. 204).

MICROWAVE COOKERY

I'm not an expert on microwave cookery because I don't use them in the restaurant. This is not because I have anything against microwave ovens, it is simply that they're actually too slow when it comes to commercial cookery. This seems a bit paradoxical but the advantage of a microwave is more in the speed of reheating food rather than cooking it. In terms of cookery, good broilers, stoves and steamers can do the job better and for larger quantities than microwave ovens.

But for reheating food, a microwave is invaluable and some of the dishes in this book, like the *Hot Shellfish with Garlic and Lemon Juice* on p. 205, require previously cooked food to be reheated. In this case a microwave is the best piece of equipment. You can also cook fish in a microwave and, as long as you are aware that cooking continues after the microwave has stopped and you make the necessary adjustments for this, you can get very good results. A microwave is also invaluable when it comes to defrosting shrimp that you've forgotten to do earlier.

Special Equipment for Cooking Fish

The longer I remain a cook the less enthusiastic I am about gadgets. There was a time when whenever some new electrical whizzer or hand-operated shredder came on the market I was keen to buy it but, probably owing to the relentless grinding down of any equipment other than the most basic knives, spoons and spatulas by chefs in too much of a hurry, I now tend to think that most jobs are better done by hand. A skilled chef can do more or less all the work done by a machine in about the same time. There are notable exceptions, in particular the food processor. Thank goodness the days of making fish mousselines with a mincer and drum sieve have gone!

There are, however, some pieces of equipment you may not have in your kitchen that are particularly useful in fish cookery.

First is a **fish filleting knife**. Even if you buy all your fish filleted from the fishmonger there will still be occasions when you want to, say, remove some skin or slide a thin-bladed knife between the two shells of a scallop. I think it is an essential part of any kitchen.

Next, I would suggest that anybody who is serious about fish cookery purchase a **fish poacher**. They look rather decorative in a kitchen, apart from anything else, and most people are bound to poach salmon from time to time. They also double up as a steamer if you raise the perforated plate on stands such as two egg cups, and bring a couple of inches or so of water in the bottom to a boil. If you don't want to go to the expense of a fish poacher, a fish up to 3 pounds will normally fit into a large oval casserole dish if you bend it. Or, you could remove the head and tail and fit it into your largest pan.

If you are going to cook a lot of whole fish, a **fish scaler** is also a wise investment, as is a **wok**, which is a pretty standard general-purpose pan used not just for Chinese cookery these days.

I would earnestly suggest that you buy a **conical sieve** and a **ladle** for passing soups and stocks through, and a length of **cheesecloth** through which you can pass sauces.

Perhaps the most valued piece of equipment I have in my kitchen at home is a **mortar and pestle**. If you want to grind or purée large quantities of anything, then a food processor or blender is fine, but there are many times when you only want to make up a little fresh spice or a spoonful or two of *salsa verde*, grind a few peppercorns for *steak au poivre* or make up some *aïoli*. On these occasions, a blender or food processor is too big. You can buy small mini versions of food processors for doing small quantities, but I've had about four and each one has soon broken. I bought my mortar and pestle in a Thai food shop in London and it's made out of granite. You could drop it from a great height and it wouldn't split, it never breaks down and it's dead easy to clean.

There are also a few other small items that would be worth buying. If you don't have a **steamer**, there's a very simple petal-shaped perforated one that you can get at any hardware store. It expands to fit any pan.

A **second pepper grinder for white peppercorns** is also a good idea. I use white peppercorns or *mignonette* pepper (meaning dainty) a great deal in fish cookery.

If you haven't got **a large chef's knife** with a, say, 10-inch blade, it's a good investment for cutting lobsters and crayfish in half.

A good pair of **kitchen scissors** for cutting off fins and a small pair of **long-nosed pliers** or **tweezers** for extracting bones from fillets of fish will make life infinitely easier, as will some **lobster picks** and some **periwinkle pickers**. Curiously I've never seen the latter on sale in England, but hat pins would probably do the trick.

A **mandoline** would also be a wise investment. A good one not only allows you to slice potatoes wafer thin, but it will also cut the thinnest of julienne vegetables.

A **pasta machine** is a wonderful invention and lastly a **cast-iron ribbed grill pan** for all the charbroiled dishes that I love. You can now buy a large double-sized grill pan to fit over two rings or burners so that you can do some serious charbroiling.

Basic Recipes

STOCKS AND OTHER BASIC PREPARATIONS

You can make good fish stock out of any fish bones except oily ones. At the restaurant two stocks are made, first class and second class. First class is made out of any of the cod family and all flat fish and the second-class stock is made from anything else. The first-class stock is used for all sauces and the second-class for fish soup. You can store stock in a covered container in the refrigerator for up to four days. You can keep it indefinitely if you reboil it every four days or so. Otherwise, store it in small quantities in the freezer.

Fish Stock

Although a precise recipe for fish stock is given here, the quantities are actually not very important. By simmering the fish bones in stock first, then removing the bones and simmering the vegetables in the resulting stock, more flavor can be extracted. I have not included salt in the recipe because normally the stock will be greatly reduced and so could become too salty. The seasoning should therefore be added after the stock has been reduced.

Place the fish bones in the water and bring to a boil. Simmer for 20 minutes, then pass through a sieve lined with cheesecloth.

Return the stock to the pan and add the vegetables. Bring to a boil and simmer again for 45 minutes. Strain again, then use or store (see above).

Makes 5 cups

3   pounds fish bones, including heads
7   cups water
•   A handful of fresh white button mushrooms, sliced
1   large onion, chopped
1   large leek, chopped
1   large carrot, chopped
1   celery stalk, including the leafy top, sliced

Shellfish Stock and Shellfish Reduction

A lot of shellfish removed from its shell is sold in the restaurant, so we use the shells for making a basic stock that is used to flavor sauces, soups, terrines and mouses.

You can make this stock by using whole unpeeled prawns or shrimp in their shells, preferably raw ones. The little green crabs that you find all round Great Britain and along the Atlantic coast of the United States also make excellent shellfish stock.

To make the shellfish stock, fry the carrot, onion and celery in the butter for 2–3 minutes. Add the shrimp and the cognac and fry for another couple of minutes. Add the remaining ingredients and simmer for 40 minutes. Pass the stock through a sieve lined with cheesecloth. To store see p. 36.

To make the shellfish reduction, transfer the unstrained stock to a blender and liquidize it. Then pass it first through a conical sieve, then through a fine-mesh sieve. Return the strained liquid to the heat, bring to a boil and reduce the volume down to about 2/3 cup. Store as for the shellfish stock.

1/2	cup chopped carrot
1/2	cup chopped onions
1/2	cup chopped celery
1	tablespoon unsalted butter
12	ounces whole prawns, small crabs or shrimp
1	tablespoon cognac
2	tablespoons white wine
1	teaspoon chopped fresh tarragon
1/2	cup roughly chopped tomato
5	cups *Fish Stock* (see p. 36)
•	A pinch of cayenne pepper

Makes 4 cups Shellfish Stock or 2/3 cup Shellfish Reduction

Chicken Stock

I read a sad but amusing article about Agas, the permanently hot heating and cooking range that no middle class country home in Britain seems to be able to live without, a symbol of comfort and reassurance. The subject was that of making stocks using the cooler of the two Aga hot plates.

The stock in the writer's house was made from the leftover bones from roast chicken out of a sense of thrift. But it was destined to go sour and be thrown away. The fate of the stock was actually inevitable but never admitted. I thought this a poignant statement on the way we live today. The chicken stocks that you need for fish cookery are not to be made from the remains of roasts. You need fresh chicken trimmings or drumettes (which you can now buy in supermarkets). You will find that if you prepare beautiful clear stock from fresh raw ingredients rather than old roast bones, you will end up with something you really want to look after. Making stock is easy, relatively cheap and only needs to be done periodically. I find it one of the most satisfying jobs in the kitchen. The quantities in this recipe are for the carcass, wing tips and other trimmings of one medium-sized chicken obtained after having removed the meat for use in another recipe. →

Put all the ingredients in a large pan and simmer very gently for a couple of hours. Make sure you do simmer everything gently, as boiling stock will force the fat from even the leanest chicken into an emulsion with the water, making it cloudy.

Pass the contents of the pan through a sieve lined with cheesecloth. Set aside and leave to go cold, then chill. Remove the film of fat from the surface. For storing see p. 36.

Makes about 7 cups

- Bones of one 3- to 3¹/₂-pound chicken or 1 pound chicken drumettes
- 2 tablespoons vegetable oil
- 1 large carrot, chopped
- 2 celery stalks, sliced
- 2 leeks, sliced
- 2 fresh or dried bay leaves
- 2 fresh thyme sprigs
- 2¹/₂ quarts water

Court Bouillon

This is a general purpose poaching liquid for skate, salmon and any occasion when you want to cook fish with plenty of flavor. After poaching the fish, you can use the bouillon and vegetables as part of the stock for fish soup. You can also strain it for use as an unreduced fish stock.

Place all the ingredients in a large pan and bring to a boil. Simmer for 30 minutes. To complete the infusion of flavors, leave to cool before using. For storing see p. 36.

Makes 5 cups

- 1¹/₄ cups dry hard cider
- 5 cups water
- 6 tablespoons white wine vinegar
- 2 fresh or dried bay leaves
- 12 peppercorns
- 1 onion, roughly chopped
- 2 carrots, roughly chopped
- 2 celery stalks, roughly chopped
- 1 teaspoon salt

A Court Bouillon for Poaching Smoked Fish

Place all the ingredients in a pan and bring to a boil. Simmer for 10 minutes before using to poach the fish.

Makes 4 cups

- 1¹/₄ cups milk
- 2¹/₂ cups water
- 1 medium onion, thinly sliced
- 2 fresh or dried bay leaves
- 6 peppercorns
- ¹/₂ lemon, sliced

Vegetable Stock

This is also a good general-purpose vegetable stock that you can use for poaching lobsters or langoustine (lobsterettes). You can then reduce the bouillon to a beautiful sauce with a little butter whisked in at the end. We do a poached lobster dish at the restaurant like this using a small lobster poached to order. We rapidly reduce the stock in a vast shallow copper pan, beat in some basil butter (butter pounded in a mortar with basil), a handful of peeled, seeded and chopped tomatoes and a few small vegetables (tiny carrots, fennel, green onions, beans and snow peas) and serve the lobster out of the shell.

Place all the ingredients except the wine in a large pan and bring to simmering point for 30 minutes, then add the wine. Bring to a boil for 30 seconds, then cool. Leave for at least 12 hours before straining. To store see p. 36.

Makes 1³/₄ pints

2	carrots, sliced
1	leek, white part only, sliced
¹/₂	medium onion, sliced
5	cups water
1	tablespoon salt
•	Zest and flesh of ¹/₂ lemon
2	garlic cloves
15	white peppercorns
5	star anise
1	small bunch fresh parsley
1	fresh or dried bay leaf
1	fresh fennel sprig
1	fresh thyme sprig
1¹/₄	cups white wine

SAUCES

Velouté

A good velouté should taste neither heavy nor floury, so the flour must be thoroughly cooked by long, slow simmering.

Place the stock and milk in a pan and bring to a boil. Melt the butter in a heavy-based pan and add the flour. Cook for about 2 minutes, stirring constantly, without letting it color too much. When it starts to smell nutty, remove from the heat and cool slightly.

Gradually add the hot stock, stirring all the time, until smooth. Return to the heat when almost all the stock

has been incorporated. Add the remaining stock. Turn the heat down immediately and simmer for 40 minutes.

Pass the sauce through a conical sieve into a bowl, cover with a butter parchment or plastic wrap to prevent a skin forming and allow to cool. Chill if not using immediately. To store, place the sauce in a covered container in the refrigerator. You can keep it indefinitely if you reboil it every three or four days. Flour-based sauces don't freeze well.

2¹/₂	cups reduced *Fish Stock* (see p. 36)
1¹/₄	cups milk
¹/₄	cup unsalted butter
¹/₄	cup all-purpose flour

Makes 1 pint

Hollandaise Sauce

I like my hollandaise sauce to be well flavored with plenty of lemon juice and cayenne, and well sea-soned. You will need a wire whisk, a stainless steel whisking bowl and a saucepan into which it will fit.

Clarify the butter by heating it gently in a pan until the solids fall to the bottom. Pour off the clear butter and reserve. Discard the butter solids.

Half fill a pan with water and bring to a boil. Reduce to a simmer and place a stainless steel bowl on top of the pan. Pour in the 2 tablespoons of water, add the egg yolks and whisk the mixture until it is voluminous and creamy.

Remove the bowl from the heat and whisk in the clarified butter a little at a time, building up an emulsion as if making mayonnaise. Add the lemon juice, the cayenne pepper and the salt.

Hollandaise is best used immediately but you can hold the sauce for anything up to 2 hours if you keep it in a warm place (about 140°F) with a lid on. If the sauce does split, it is actually very easy to reform it. Just take a new pan, warm it and add one tablespoon of hot water. Then whisk in the curdled sauce a little at a time.

1	cup unsalted butter
2	tablespoons water
2	egg yolks
•	Juice of 1 lemon
•	A good pinch of cayenne pepper
1/2	teaspoon salt

Serves 4

Pastis and Fennel Hot Butter Sauce

This sauce is very good with grilled fillets of fish; it's especially good with hake.

Put all the ingredients except the hollandaise sauce and 1 teaspoon of the pastis in a small pan then boil rapidly to reduce to about 2 tablespoons. Strain and stir the strained liquor into the hollandaise and add the remaining teaspoon of pastis.

1	tablespoon chopped fennel
1/2	cup *Fish Stock* (see p. 36)
2	tablespoons pastis, Ricard or Pernod
1	quantity *Hollandaise Sauce* (see above)

Serves 4

Maltaise Sauce

This sauce is good with grilled fillets of red mullet.

Mix the juice and zest of the oranges with the hollandaise sauce and serve.

- Juice of 2 blood oranges
- Grated zest of 1 orange
1 quantity *Hollandaise Sauce* (see p. 40)

Serves 4

Mussel Sauce

You can serve this with thick, poached fillets of cod, halibut, turbot or bass. Alternatively, you can place the poached fish in a gratin dish, cover with the sauce and glaze under a hot broiler. Either will be perfect if accompanied with new potatoes and spring greens thinly sliced and cooked gently in a little butter.

You can also make the sauce using oysters. Open the oysters gently by poaching them in their own liquor with a little white wine, some shallots and a little parsley. Then proceed as for the mussels.

Place the mussels, white wine, shallot and parsley in a pan and cover tightly. Place over high heat, shaking the pan occasionally. Remove the pan from the heat as soon as all the mussels have opened.

As soon as they are cool enough to handle, remove the mussels from their shells and pull out any beards. Stir all but the last tablespoonful of the cooking liquor (the dregs will contain some grit) into the hollandaise sauce. Add the mussel meats to the hollandaise.

1 pound small mussels
- A splash of white wine
1 small shallot, finely chopped
1 teaspoon finely chopped fresh parsley
1 quantity *Hollandaise Sauce* (see p. 40)

Serves 4

Seafood Sauce

Pass this sauce at the table or use as a glaze for fish, as with Mussel Sauce *(see above).*

Make the shellfish reduction. Mix the reduction into the hollandaise sauce.

1 quantity *Shellfish Reduction* (see p. 37)
1 quantity *Hollandaise Sauce* (see p. 40)

Makes 4 cups

Beurre Blanc

There is nothing complicated about beurre blanc, neither is it particularly unstable. If it does separate, it is much easier to reconstitute than an egg-based sauce like hollandaise. All you do is add a bit more water and boil it vigorously to emulsify the butter and water. You may lose some lightness in having to do this, but at least the embarrassment of producing a separated and greasy sauce will have been avoided.

Use with poached and grilled fillets of fish like turbot, bass, lemon sole, cod.

Put the shallots, vinegar, wine and water in a small pan, bring to a boil and simmer until nearly all the liquid has evaporated. Add the cream and reduce a little more, then remove the pan from the heat and whisk in the butter a little at a time until it has all amalgamated.

You can also make the sauce by reducing down and adding the cream as before, then adding a couple of tablespoons of water. You then bring the sauce to a rapid boil and whisk the butter in while boiling. This method will produce a perfectly acceptable sauce but it will be a little less light than if you choose the first method. This second method is also the way to reconstitute a sauce that has got too hot and separated. At the restaurant we replace the water with well-reduced fish stock, which gives the sauce a roundness, but it still tastes good made with water.

2	ounces shallots or onions, finely chopped
2	tablespoons white wine vinegar
4	tablespoons dry white wine
6	tablespoons water or fish stock
2	tablespoons heavy cream
³/₄	cup unsalted butter, cut into pieces

Serves 4

Beurre Rouge

This is excellent with any grilled fillets of fish from the cod family, like cod, hake or haddock.

Place all the ingredients, except the butter, in a pan and simmer until the onions are soft. Beat in the butter as for *Beurre Blanc* (see above).

8	ounces red onions
²/₃	cup red wine
6	tablespoons *Fish Stock* (see p. 36) or *Chicken Stock* (see p. 37)
6	tablespoons red wine vinegar
¹/₄	teaspoon sugar
•	A pinch of salt
¹/₂	cup unsalted butter

Serves 4

Olive Oil Mayonnaise

This is one of two recipes I have for mayonnaise. This one is of the utmost simplicity and uses best extra-virgin olive oil, while the second uses peanut or sunflower oil and is strongly flavored with mustard. You will find that using extra-virgin olive oil for this mayonnaise produces a waxy, slightly green finish that tastes bitter. Too strong you may think but, like most sauces, mayonnaise should be a bit strong on its own. When combined with the rest of the dish, like poached salmon, everything falls delightfully into place.

Make sure all the ingredients are at room temperature before beginning. Put the egg yolks, vinegar and salt into a mixing bowl, then place the bowl on a tea towel (to stop it slipping). Using a wire whisk, beat the oil into the egg mixture a little at a time until you have incorporated it all. Once you have carefully added about the same volume of oil as the original mixture of egg yolks and vinegar, you can add the oil more quickly.

2	egg yolks
2	teaspoons white wine vinegar
1/2	teaspoon salt
1¼	cups extra-virgin olive oil

Serves 4

Mustard Mayonnaise

This sauce goes particularly well with crab.

Make sure all the ingredients are at room temperature before beginning. Put the mustard, egg yolks, vinegar, salt and pepper into a mixing bowl, then place the bowl on a tea towel (to stop it slipping). Using a wire whisk, beat the oil into the egg mixture a little at a time until you have incorporated it all. Once you have carefully added about the same volume of oil as the original mixture of egg yolks and vinegar, you can add the oil more quickly.

1	tablespoon English mustard
2	egg yolks
1	tablespoon white wine vinegar
1/4	teaspoon salt
•	Few turns of the white pepper mill
1¼	cups peanut or sunflower oil

Serves 4

The science of all cold and hot butter sauces is as follows. Oil or hot butter likes to stay in one large puddle. Beating separates it into millions of tiny droplets that reform into one large puddle as soon as you stop. But if you add oil to egg yolk and whisk, the egg yolk will tend to coat each droplet of oil and prevent it from joining the rest. A little egg yolk will go a very long way with oil, provided you add a little oil at a time and beat well.

Fennel Mayonnaise

Mix all the ingredients together.

Serves 4

3	tablespoons Pernod
1	teaspoon chopped fresh chives
1	tablespoon chopped fresh fennel
1	quantity *Olive Oil Mayonnaise* (see p. 43)

Tartare Sauce

Mix all the ingredients together and use with deep-fried, breaded fish.

Serves 4

1	quantity *Mustard Mayonnaise* (see p. 43)
1	teaspoon green olives, finely chopped
1	teaspoon gherkins, finely chopped
1	teaspoon capers, finely chopped
1	teaspoon chopped fresh chives
1	teaspoon chopped fresh parsley

Aïoli

Peel and crush the garlic and mix with the mayonnaise.

If you don't have a garlic crusher, mash a peeled clove of garlic with the large flat blade of a knife. Place the garlic on a firm, nonslip surface (a wooden chopping board is best), position the widest part of the knife on the garlic then hit it with the palm of your hand. Chop the flattened clove, then sprinkle it with salt and mash with the knife to a purée.

8 garlic cloves
1 quantity *Olive Oil Mayonnaise* (see p. 43)

Serves 4

Sauce Verte

Blanch the spinach and arugula leaves in boiling water for 1 minute. Refresh under cold running water and squeeze dry. Blend together in a food processor with the fresh herbs and mayonnaise. Best served with poached salmon.

1 cup spinach leaves
1 cup arugula leaves
1 cup mixed fresh parsley, chervil, chives and tarragon leaves, roughly chopped
1 quantity *Olive Oil Mayonnaise* (see p. 43)

Serves 4

Rouille

To make this fiery accompaniment to fish soup and bouillabaisse quickly, mix mayonnaise with garlic and mashed seeded and chopped red chilies. Alternatively, use this version, which includes harissa, *an aromatic sauce from Africa.*

Put all the ingredients, except the olive oil, in a food processor and blend. Then, gradually pour in the oil until it is incorporated into the egg yolks.

Serves 4

1	slice dry bread soaked in fish stock
3	garlic cloves
1	egg yolk
2	tablespoons *Harissa* (see below)
1/4	teaspoon salt
1	cup olive oil

Harissa

Harissa *is a chili, red pepper, saffron and coriander sauce that comes from North Africa. It is available in small cans from good specialty-food shops, but our own recipe has evolved over time and it is a lot more aromatic than the store-bought variety.*

Place all the ingredients in a food processor or blender and blend until well incorporated.

Makes enough for the rouille recipe above.

1	teaspoon tomato paste
1	teaspoon ground coriander
•	A pinch of saffron strands
1	red bell pepper, seeded, roasted and skinned
2	red chilies
1/4	teaspoon salt
1/4	teaspoon cayenne pepper

Charmoula

This is another hot aromatic paste from North Africa. Use it to marinate fillets and whole fish prior to grilling on a barbecue.

Place all the ingredients in a blender or food processor and blend until well incorporated.

Makes about 3/4 cup

2	tablespoons roughly chopped fresh cilantro
3	garlic cloves, peeled and chopped
1 1/2	teaspoons ground cumin
1/2	red chili, seeded and chopped
1/2	teaspoon saffron strands
4	tablespoons extra-virgin olive oil
•	Juice of 1 lemon
1 1/2	teaspoons paprika
2	teaspoons salt

Salsa Verde

This sauce, used with the Grilled Sea Bass with Straw Potatoes and Salsa Verde on p. 116, is one of the most versatile sauces for fish. Its piquant herb flavor brings out the best in most fish, particularly the blander cod family. A thick fillet of poached cod with salsa verde is pure bliss. Also try it with skate wings or even a pile of boiled whelks (conchs) or long-simmered octopus.

Blend together all the ingredients in a food processor or in a mortar with a pestle to form a thick paste. (I use a mortar and pestle but I don't pound the ingredients too much, as I like the sauce to have a coarse texture.)

Makes 1 cup

- 3 tablespoons roughly chopped fresh parsley
- 1 tablespoon roughly chopped fresh mint
- 3 tablespoons capers
- 6 anchovy fillets
- 1 garlic clove, chopped
- 1 teaspoon Dijon mustard
- · Juice of 1/2 lemon
- 1/2 cup extra-virgin olive oil
- 1/2 teaspoon salt

FLAVORED BUTTERS

These are perfect sliced into rounds and placed on grilled fish. They are also ideal for flavoring sauces and for stuffing fish fillets.

All can be easily made by simply putting the flavoring ingredients and the butter (which should be soft) into a food processor and blending until smooth. The butter can then be turned out onto a sheet of plastic wrap or parchment paper, rolled into a sausage shape and chilled.

Montpellier Butter

Blanch the spinach and arugula leaves in boiling water for 1 minute, refresh in cold water, then squeeze dry. Place in a food processor with the herbs, shallot, gherkins, capers, garlic, anchovies, egg yolk, hard-boiled egg yolks and softened butter. Season with salt and pepper then blend until smooth before adding the olive oil in a steady stream. Continue to blend until all the ingredients are thoroughly mixed, then turn out onto plastic wrap, roll into a sausage shape and refrigerate until firm.

Serves 4

- 1 cup spinach leaves
- 1 cup arugula leaves
- 1 cup fresh mixed parsley, chervil, chives and tarragon
- 1 shallot, cut up
- 3 small gherkins
- 1 teaspoon capers
- 2 garlic cloves
- 6 anchovies
- 1 egg yolk
- 2 hard-boiled egg yolks
- 1/2 cup butter, softened
- 1/2 teaspoon salt
- · Freshly ground black pepper
- 6 tablespoons olive oil

Anchovy Butter

Blend together all the ingredients, then place on a piece of plastic wrap, roll into a sausage shape and refrigerate until firm.

{ **Serves 8**

6 anchovy fillets
1 tablespoon roughly chopped fresh parsley
• Juice of ¼ lemon
³⁄₄ cup unsalted butter, softened

Mustard Butter

This butter is good with grilled oily fish like herrings, mackerel and sardines.

Blend together all the ingredients, then place on a piece of plastic wrap, roll into a sausage shape and refrigerate until firm.

{ **Serves 4**

1 tablespoon Dijon mustard
½ cup unsalted butter, softened
• Salt and freshly ground black pepper

Garlic Butter

Blend together all the ingredients, then place on a piece of plastic wrap, roll into a sausage shape and refrigerate until firm.

{ **Serves 8**

1 cup unsalted butter, softened
4 large garlic cloves
1 cup fresh parsley leaves
1 teaspoon brandy
1 teaspoon lemon juice
• A good pinch of salt

Pink Peppercorn Butter

Perfect served with grilled small sand dabs.

Blend together all the ingredients, then place on a piece of plastic wrap, roll into a sausage shape and refrigerate until firm.

{ **Serves 4**

2 teaspoons chopped pink peppercorns
6 tablespoons unsalted butter, softened
• Freshly ground black pepper
½ teaspoon salt
1 teaspoon brandy

Garlic and Roasted Hazelnut Butter

Turn on your broiler. Roast the hazelnuts under the broiler, turning them to ensure even coloring. When the skins are dark brown, tip them onto one-half of a tea towel, fold over the other half and roll off the skins. Open out the tea towel and roll the nuts to one side, leaving the skins behind.

Mix all the ingredients in a food processor, place on a piece of plastic wrap, roll into a sausage shape and refrigerate until firm.

$2/3$ cup hazelnuts
1 quantity *Garlic Butter* (see p. 49)

Serves 8

Cilantro and Hazelnut Butter

This is excellent as a stuffing for mussels.

Blend together all the ingredients, then place on a piece of plastic wrap, roll into a sausage and refrigerate until firm.

$2/3$ cup roasted hazelnuts (see *Garlic and Roasted Hazelnut Butter*, p. 50)
1 cup unsalted butter, softened
1 cup fresh cilantro leaves
$1/2$ cup fresh parsley leaves
1 shallot, cut up
• Juice of $1/2$ lemon
• Freshly ground black pepper

Serves 4

Shrimp Butter

Mix together all the ingredients in a blender or food processor. Pass the butter through a sieve, pushing it with the back of a ladle or wooden spoon. Place on a piece of plastic wrap, roll into a sausage shape and refrigerate until firm.

3 ounces shrimp in the shell
$1/2$ cup unsalted butter, softened
1 teaspoon lemon juice
• A pinch of cayenne pepper

Serves 4

Noisette Butter

Once you're familiar with the taste of Noisette Butter (and you need to make it as per these instructions at least once), all you need do is heat the butter to taste and throw it straight over the fish. →

Melt the butter in a small pan. Pour cold water into a bowl that is large enough to take the base of the butter pan. Keep it ready nearby.

Heat the butter until it turns a golden brown and starts to smell nutty. Remove from the heat and immerse the base of the pan in the cold water to prevent any further cooking.

½ cup butter

DRESSINGS FOR SALADS AND CONDIMENTS

A dressing is not a compot,
A dressing is not a custard;
It consists of pepper and salt,
Vinegar, oil, and mustard
　　　　—Ogden Nash

There could, to my mind, be no more urgent a call to chefs to keep it simple than in the matter of dressings. Ogden Nash's title to the above verse is The Chef has Imagination or It's Too Hard to Do it Easy. *No dressing tastes better in a salad than one made with good olive oil, good vinegar and, for me, just a little salt.*

Lemon Olive Oil

You can buy a brand of extra-virgin olive oil with natural essence of lemons, which is superb for salads. I use it in many of my recipes as a dressing for salad greens. With a little of this and only a faint sprinkling of salt and perhaps a little Preserved Lemon *(see p. 52), you can make a perfect and very simple dressing. You can also make your own, as follows, but use the best olive oil you can find.*

Carefully pare the zest from the lemon with a potato peeler. Slice the zest into thin strips, then add to the olive oil. Leave to infuse for 12 hours.

1　lemon
2½　cups extra-virgin olive oil

Olive Oil Dressing

If I use vinegar in a dressing, I use the tiniest amount, and I only make the dressing just before tossing the salad. Once the two are combined, the vinegar begins to knock out the fragrance of the olive oil. This is why in Italy they bring oil and vinegar to your table in separate containers. If you make the dressing there and then, you get perfection; if you make it some time before, the flavor of the oil fades. Only use the best olive oil you can find.

Combine the ingredients and toss into the salad just before serving.

6　tablespoons extra-virgin olive oil
½　tablespoon white wine vinegar
½　teaspoon salt

Mustard Dressing

This dressing is a much more rugged affair than Olive Oil Dressing and goes very well with bitter leaves like Belgian endive, dandelions and radicchio. It can also be made some time in advance of being used. Add some chopped chives for an extra dimension to the flavor.

Combine all the ingredients by shaking in a screw-top jar. Serve as required.

6	tablespoons peanut or sunflower oil
1	tablespoon white wine vinegar
1/2	teaspoon salt
1/2	small shallot, finely chopped
1/2	small garlic clove, finely chopped
1	teaspoon English mustard

Preserved Lemons

This is a way of keeping lemons that makes them more of a condiment than a citrus fruit. Preserved lemons are much used in Moroccan cuisine.

Cut the lemons almost in quarters, leaving them joined at one end. Sprinkle a little salt into the center of each, then arrange them, tightly packed, in a plastic or glass container. Bring the water and the rest of the salt to a boil in a large pan. Boil until the salt has dissolved, then remove from the heat and leave to cool. Pour the brine over the lemons, weigh them down with some sort of nonmetallic weight and leave for 3–4 weeks. Use as required. They will keep indefinitely. Finely chop the flesh and skins and add to salads or dressings.

10	lemons
5	cups water
1 1/4	cups salt

BATTERS FOR DEEP-FRYING

Yeast and Beer Batter

I don't think there is a nicer batter than Yeast and Beer Batter. It is a perfect combination of lightness, crispness and flavor and in my opinion the only batter for fish and chips. In addition to producing carbon dioxide that makes the batter light, yeast also matures the dough and gives the batter a flavor of hops and bread. The only drawback is that it needs to be made some time in advance.

Dissolve the yeast with a little of the beer. When they have been mixed to a paste, gradually add the rest of the beer, stirring continuously. →

Makes enough for 4 servings

1	package (2 1/2 teaspoons) active dry yeast
1 1/4	cups beer, or Guinness for a deep brown batter
1 2/3	cups all-purpose flour
1	teaspoon salt

Sift the flour and salt into a bowl and make a well in the center. Pour in the beer and dissolved yeast and whisk into a batter. Leave covered for 1 hour before using at room temperature.

Tempura Batter

This is a very light, thin batter that barely coats the food. The secret of making good tempura batter is to leave mixing it to the very last minute and to have the batter ingredients really cold.

Chill the water and egg, then whisk together the ingredients just before dipping the food. The batter should be only just amalgamated.

Makes enough for 4 servings

$7/8$	cup water
1	egg
$3/4$	cup all-purpose flour
$1/2$	cup cornstarch
$1/2$	teaspoon salt

MISCELLANEOUS RECIPES

Kachumber (Tomato and Cilantro) Salad

This is a great Indian salad that goes well with spicy fish dishes like the Mackerel Recheado *(p. 91),* Tandoori Monkfish with Tomato and Cilantro Salad *(p. 137) or the* Grilled Sea Bass with Straw Potatoes and Salsa Verde *(p. 116).*

Mix together all the ingredients.

3	tomatoes, halved and thinly sliced
1	medium onion, halved and thinly sliced
2	tablespoons fresh cilantro, roughly chopped
$1/4$	teaspoon ground cumin
$1/8$	teaspoon cayenne
1	tablespoon white wine vinegar
$1/2$	teaspoon salt

Shallot Vinegar

This is perfect with oysters and essential with raw mussels.

Mix together all the ingredients.

6	tablespoons red wine
6	tablespoons red wine vinegar
1	shallot, finely chopped

Salt Cod

Put a fillet of cod in a plastic bowl or ice cream container and completely cover with a thick layer of salt. Refrigerate for 24 hours.

After a day, most of the salt will have turned to brine with the water it has drawn out of the cod. The fish will be sufficiently preserved now to keep for up to a week.

To prepare the salt cod for cooking, simply soak it in plenty of cold water for an hour or two if only lightly salted, or up to 24 hours if it is very dried out.

Brandade

Poach the cod in a little water for about 10 minutes, then drain and remove skin and bones.

Bring the olive oil and cream to a boil in a pan. Put the cod fillet and the garlic in a blender or food processor and turn on. Gradually pour in the hot oil and cream to build up a thick emulsion.

Serves 4

Serve with plenty of French bread.

4	ounces *Salt Cod*, soaked (see p. 54)
½	cup olive oil
½	cup heavy cream
4	garlic cloves

Quatre Épices

Mix together all the spices and store in a screw-top jar out of the way of direct sunlight.

¾	teaspoon freshly ground black pepper
1	teaspoon ground nutmeg
¾	teaspoon ground ginger
¼	teaspoon ground allspice

Egg Pasta Dough

Mix together all the ingredients and knead until smooth. Roll the pasta to the thickness you want, then leave to rest for 10–15 minutes before cutting.

Serves 4

¾	cup all-purpose flour
•	A large pinch of salt
¼	teaspoon olive oil
1	egg
2	egg yolks

4

Soups, Stews, Pies

I judge the quality of a fish restaurant by its soup and, to my mind, nothing indicates the talent of a cook better than his ability to make a fish soup. When I started my restaurant 20 years ago, I didn't actually know much about cooking (not a great handicap to running a restaurant in those days!), but over the next ten years or so, I attended a large number of courses at the

local technical college that taught me a great deal about cooking; the rest I learned through cooking, making mistakes, reading books and going to lots of restaurants. At the college, it was my extreme good fortune to be taught by a chef who had spent many years cooking for a famous fish restaurant in London, Madame Prunier. He was an inspiring teacher who was probably more influential in turning me into a proper chef than anyone else.

One day, the whole class was given exactly the same ingredients and told to make a fish soup. At the end of it, we all tried each other's. None of them was the same. Mine wasn't bad, but the best was cooked by a young Chinese woman and, extraordinarily, it tasted Asian. It had a depth that none of the other soups had. She knew about concentrating flavors. The basis of fish soup is a concentrated flavor; it must be deep and powerful. More fish and vegetables than you might think are necessary to achieve that vital fullness of flavor.

Fish soups, shellfish bisques and fish stews are among the most well-loved of seafood dishes, so nothing makes me happier than when a delighted customer remarks on the heady aroma of warm fish, peppers, tomatoes, garlic and saffron that seems to permeate the restaurant because this is the scent of our popular fish soup and bouillabaisse. Of all the dishes that we cook at the restaurant, this soup is the one

that must never be allowed to grow tired, even though it is cooked every day, year in and year out. The recipes in this chapter include a *Bouillabaisse* (see p. 60), which uses lots of whole fish and is simple to make. It has been designed to be eaten with great gusto by people who don't mind a few bones. There are also recipes for *Cotriade* (see p. 65–6) and *Bourride* (see p. 64), where the fish is filleted.

To me both approaches to fish stew are equally valid. Sometimes I prefer the easy preparation and the simple cooking to produce stews that would be little different to those cooked by the fishermen who first invented the dish, and other times, I like to take the essence of the dish and enhance it to make a sophisticated dish. I think everyone has the same approach to fish: sometimes you want bone-free fillets with reduced, aromatic sauces and other times you want to pile into a great plate of *Fruits de Mer* (see pp. 197–201) using your fingers and throwing shells all over the place.

There is also in this chapter a fish pie (see p. 72), a seafood thermidor (see p. 76) which is just a rather upmarket fish pie, and a fish pasty (see p. 77) dish that we sell in our delicatessen. I have also included some mixed seafood dishes like risotto (see pp. 68–9), seafood salad (see p. 68) and a tremendous dish of mixed seafood deep-fried in tempura batter (see p. 73).

Fish Soup with Croutons

This French soup is Mediterranean in origin, but you can find the same sort of soupe de poissons *in virtually any French coastal restaurant. I love fish soup. I think it is one of those dishes, like roast beef and Yorkshire pudding,* aïoli Provençal *or Chinese crispy duck, that is so deeply satisfying that it has a special place in everyone's heart. Produce indifferent roast beef or fish soup at your peril, for you will not be forgiven.*

The best fish for this soup are conger eel, skate, cod and shark, but virtually any other fish is suitable except the oily ones, like mackerel and herring. You can also use shrimp and other shellfish scraps, like lobster, crab, lobsterette or mussels.

Fillet all the fish (see instructions in Chapter 2) and use the heads and bones to make a fish stock with the 2½ quarts of water.

Heat the olive oil in a large pan and add the onion, celery, leek, fennel and garlic. Cook gently for about 20 minutes without coloring until the vegetables are very soft. Add the orange zest, tomatoes, bell pepper, bay leaf, thyme, saffron, prawns and fish fillets. Cook briskly, stirring, then add the stock and orange juice. Bring to a boil and simmer for 40 minutes.

Purée the soup in a blender or food processor, then pass it through a conical sieve, pushing it through with the back of a ladle to extract all the juices. Return to the heat and season with salt, pepper and cayenne. The soup should be a little on the salty side, with a subtle but noticeable hint of cayenne.

To make the croutons, thinly slice the baguette, then fry in olive oil. When cool enough to handle, rub the croutons with garlic. Serve the soup, Parmesan and *rouille* separately. The idea is that each person spreads some rouille onto the croutons, floats them in the soup and sprinkles them with Parmesan.

2½	quarts water
⅔	cup olive oil
1½	cups roughly chopped onion
1½	cups roughly chopped celery
1½	cups roughly chopped leeks
1½	cups roughly chopped fennel
5	garlic cloves, sliced
·	Juice of 1 orange plus 2-inch piece zest
1	can (14 ounces) of tomatoes
1	red bell pepper, sliced
1	fresh or dried bay leaf
1	fresh thyme sprig
¼	teaspoon saffron strands
4	pounds fish
8	ounces prawns or shrimp in the shell
·	Salt and freshly ground black pepper
·	A large pinch of cayenne pepper

For the Croutons

1	baguette
·	Olive oil
2	garlic cloves
½	cup freshly grated Parmesan cheese
2	tablespoons *Rouille* (see p. 45)

Serves 6-8

Crab Bisque

The little green crabs you find on the beach are almost as good as lobsters for making bisque. Bisques are soups made with both the shells and meat of shellfish. If you can't get hold of green crabs, you can use any other cooked shellfish, including larger crabs, prawns, lobsterettes, shrimp and, of course, lobsters, either on their own or together.

Bring a large pan of well-salted water to a boil, drop in the crabs, then bring back to a boil and cook for 2 minutes. Strain and let the crabs cool a little, then chop with a large knife.

Melt the butter in a heavy-based pan and add the chopped onion, carrot, celery and the bay leaf. Cook without browning. Stir once or twice then add the crab. Stir, then add the cognac. Allow to boil off, then add the tomatoes, tomato paste, wine, tarragon and stock. Bring to a boil and simmer for 30 minutes.

Remove the tough claw shells from the soup before processing in a blender or food processor in two or three batches. Process in short bursts until the shell is broken into small pieces about the size of your fingernail. Avoid producing puréed shell; the aim is to extract all possible flavor from any meat left sticking to the shell, particularly in the body section, rather than to extract flavor from the shell itself. Strain the soup through a conical sieve, pushing it through with the back of a ladle to extract all the juices. Then, pass the soup through a fine sieve before returning to the heat. Bring to a boil, add the cream, then season with cayenne pepper, lemon juice, salt and black pepper. Reduce the volume by simmering if you think the flavor needs concentrating.

Serves 4

2	pounds green crabs or other shellfish
1/4	cup butter
1/2	cup chopped onion
1/2	cup chopped carrot
1/2	cup chopped celery
1	fresh or dried bay leaf
2	tablespoons cognac
4	tomatoes
1	teaspoon tomato paste
6	tablespoons dry white wine
1	good-sized fresh tarragon sprig
7	cups *Fish Stock* (see p. 36)
1/4	cup heavy cream
•	A pinch of cayenne pepper
•	Juice of 1/4 lemon
•	Salt and freshly ground black pepper

Mussel, Leek and Saffron Soup

This is one of three or four recipes I have included from my first fish cookery book, English Seafood Cookery, *published by Penguin, and which are what I would call classic dishes. This soup is quite special; mussels with leeks and saffron seem to combine so well.*

Wash the mussels thoroughly, scraping off any barnacles, pulling out the beards and discarding any that are open and don't close when given a good tap. Place in a large pan and add a dash of wine. Cover tightly and cook over high heat for about 5 minutes, shaking the pan frequently, until the mussels have opened. →

Strain the liquor through a colander into a bowl, shaking the colander well to drain off all the juices lodged in the shells. Pull any remaining beards from the mussels and remove the meat from all but 12 of the shells.

Chop the 1 pound leeks and the onion. Melt the butter in a pan and add the vegetables. Cook on low heat in the butter for about 3 minutes.

Stir in the flour until smooth. Gradually add the mussel liquor, remaining wine and fish stock to the pan, stirring thoroughly until smooth. Bring to the simmering point, then add a good pinch of saffron and continue to cook for 25 minutes.

Serves 4

Blanch the matchstick leeks in a little salted water. Remove the mussel meats from all but 12 of the shells and set aside. Process the soup in a blender or food processor and then strain through a sieve into a clean pan. Stir in the cream and reheat. Just before serving, add the mussel meats, the 12 mussels in their shells and the matchstick leeks.

3	pounds mussels
4	tablespoons white wine
1	pound leeks, plus 2-inch piece leek, cut into matchsticks to serve
1	small onion
6	tablespoons unsalted butter
2	tablespoons all-purpose flour
•	Scant 2 cups *Fish Stock* (see p. 36)
•	A good pinch of saffron
1/4	cup heavy cream

Panache of John Dory, Turbot and Goatfish with Young Summer Vegetables

I ate this recently at an excellent fish restaurant in Brittany. It is a typically French combination— extremely fresh seafood with plenty of crème fraîche and wine made into a rich fragrant sauce. Many English chefs, being much more eclectic in their search for ideas than the French, have tended to steer away from these simple but enormously popular creamy seafood dishes, but I love them. They are what holidays in Brittany are all about—those and the heavenly platters of Fruits de Mer *(see p. 197).*

Boil all the vegetables in well-salted water until just tender. Drain and refresh in cold water. This can be done some time before making the dish. You will need to construct some sort of steamer for this dish (see pp. 35 and 205 for some suggestions).

Cut the fillets of fish into 4 equal portions. Season with salt. Place the John Dory and turbot in the steamer and steam for about 6 minutes. Remove the fish from the steamer and keep warm. Put the vegetables in the steamer to warm through for a couple of minutes. While you are steaming the fish, take a frying pan, add the olive oil and season the goatfish with salt and →

Serves 4

1/4	cup shelled fresh fava beans
1/4	cup shelled English peas
1	small leek
2	ounces tender cabbage
4	very small new season's carrots
4	very small rutabagas
8	ounces John Dory fillet
8	ounces turbot fillet
1	tablespoon olive oil
8	ounces goatfish (red mullet) or sea bass fillet
•	Salt and pepper
6	tablespoons white vermouth
3/4	cup *Fish Stock* (see p. 36)
3/4	cup crème fraîche or heavy cream
•	Fresh parsley sprigs

pepper. Fry for 4 minutes, skin-side down. Remove and keep warm with the other fish. Add the vermouth to the frying pan and boil off for 1 minute. Then add the fish stock and the crème fraîche and reduce to a sauce that will coat the back of a spoon. Lay the fish on 4 warm plates all together on one side of the plate and a pile of vegetables on the other. Pour the sauce over the fish, decorate with the sprigs of parsley and serve.

Clam Chowder with Cod

A simple, and perfect, creamy soup. Any clams will do and if you can't get fresh clams in their shells, frozen clam meats are acceptable. When we can get them, we use razor clams, so called because they look like old straight razors. They have a beautiful sweet flavor.

You can make salt pork by simply sprinkling 1 tablespoon salt over a 2-ounce slice of pork loin 30 minutes before using. Because you need the starch to thicken the liquid, don't wash the potatoes after they are cut.

Wash and scrub the clams, then place them in a large pan with a splash of water. Cover tightly and cook over high heat. As soon as the clams open, take the pan off the heat and drain them in a colander, saving the cooking liquor in a bowl. When cool enough to handle, remove the clams from their shells and cut the meat into 1/2-inch pieces.

Melt the butter in a pan, then fry the diced pork until it starts to brown. Add the onions and fry until softened.

Place the potatoes in a large pan with the milk, cream and bay leaf. Bring to a boil, then reduce to a slow simmer until just cooked but still firm. Add the pork, onions and clam cooking liquor and simmer for a further 5 minutes, then add the cod fillet. Simmer until the cod is cooked, then add the clams. Warm through, then season with salt (if necessary) and white pepper.

Pour the chowder into a serving tureen, then garnish with the chopped parsley and crushed water biscuits.

Serves 4

16 large or 32 small clams
2 tablespoons butter
2 ounces salt pork, cut into small dice
1 cup diced onions
8 ounces potatoes, diced but not washed
1 1/4 cups milk
1/2 cup heavy cream
1 fresh bay leaf, cut into fine shreds, or 1 dried bay leaf, crushed
• Cooking liquor from the clams
4 ounces cod fillet, skinned and cut into 1/2-inch pieces
• Salt and freshly ground white pepper
1 tablespoon chopped fresh parsley
2 water biscuits, chopped into little pieces

Bouillabaisse

Fish stews, like bouillabaisse, are wonderful for big parties where everyone can sit around a large, deep tureen filled with all kinds of fish, adding lots of rouille to their bowls and mopping up the rich aromatic bouillon juices with crusty bread.

Any of the following fish may be used in the Bouillabaisse: wrasse, shark, porgy, red snapper, monkfish, cod or hake, searobin, goatfish, bass, John Dory, sunfish, skate, conger eel, mullet. The more variety there is the better. Use either small fish or slices of bigger fish. For the shellfish, choose between: lobster, crayfish, lobsterette, shrimp or prawns in their shells.

To make the croutons, heat the oil in a frying pan and fry the slices of bread on both sides until golden. Rub each crouton with garlic, set aside and keep warm.

To make the bouillabaisse, heat the olive oil in a pan large enough to hold all the fish and the water. Add the onions, leeks, celery, fennel and garlic. Cook until soft. Season with black pepper, then add the orange zest, tomatoes, chili, saffron, thyme, bay leaves and water and bring to a boil. Simmer for 10 minutes.

Add the fish, putting the firmer-fleshed fish like conger eel, and skate in first. Add the softer fish 3 minutes later and the mussels 1 minute after that. While adding the fish, put in the herbs and the Pernod. Continue to boil only until the fish is just cooked (about 8 minutes).

Finally, add the shellfish and boil for a further 1 minute. Strain the soup through a colander and place all the fish, mussels, shellfish and vegetables in a large warm dish. The mussels and shellfish should be served in their shells. Set aside and keep warm.

Return the strained bouillon to the pan, add the extra-virgin olive oil and concentrate the flavor by rapid boiling. Check the seasoning and add cayenne pepper if you like it (I do).

Pour the bouillon over the fish and vegetables and scatter the croutons over the top. You can separate the fish from the soup as they often do in France, if you prefer, but I like to eat fish and soup together served with a dollop of *rouille*.

Serves 8–10

Serve with a dry, fresh, nutty rosé.

6	tablespoons olive oil, for frying
2	medium onions, roughly chopped
•	White of 2 large leeks, roughly chopped
4	celery stalks, thinly sliced
2	large bulbs fennel, thinly sliced
10	garlic cloves, chopped
2	pieces orange zest, each 2 inches long
2	pounds tomatoes, peeled and chopped, peels reserved
1/2	red chili, seeded and chopped
1	teaspoon powdered saffron
2	sprigs of thyme
4	fresh bay leaves
3½	quarts water
7	pounds fish (see above)
1½	pounds mussels, washed and scraped clean
1	teaspoon fennel tops, roughly chopped
1	teaspoon fresh oregano
1	teaspoon fresh thyme leaves
2	tablespoons Pernod or Ricard
1½	pounds shellfish, sliced (see above)
2	tablespoons extra-virgin olive oil
•	Cayenne pepper (optional)
•	Salt and freshly ground black pepper

For the Croutons

	Olive oil, for frying
12	thin slices French bread
2–3	garlic cloves
1/2	cup *Rouille* (see p. 45), to serve

Lobster, Turbot and Mussels with Star Anise Nage

A nage *is a court bouillon that is specifically for fish. The word comes from* nager, *which is French for "to swim."*

This dish also works well with mussels, oysters, crayfish or lobsterette. The only essential requirement is that the fish and shellfish should be slightly undercooked. Allow 12 hours for the nage to cool and for the flavors to develop before using. Star anise is available from Chinese and Indian food stores.

Cut the turbot into pieces about 1 inch wide and cut the lobster into 1/2-inch slices.

Peel the carrot, slice it thinly lengthwise, then cut these slices into long, thin straws. Top and tail the green beans and cut them in half lengthwise.

Add the cream to the *nage,* bring it to a boil, then boil rapidly to reduce the volume by half. While the *nage* is reducing, blanch the carrots, beans and snow peas in boiling salted water for 3 minutes, then refresh in cold water.

Wash the mussels, scrape them clean and pull out the beards. Place the mussels in a pan with a splash of the *nage,* then cover tightly and cook over a fierce heat until the mussels have opened. Add the resulting liquor to the *nage,* straining it through a sieve to remove any grit. When cool enough to handle, remove the meat from half the mussels, discarding their shells. Leave the rest intact.

Add the zucchini, spinach and fish to the reduced *nage* and simmer for 1 minute, then add the blanched vegetables, all the mussels and the lobster. Simmer for 1 minute. With a slotted spoon, lift the fish, shellfish and vegetables onto four warmed soup plates. Whisk the cold butter into the sauce, then add a small pinch of ground star anise. Pour the sauce over the fish and vegetables.

A Sauvignon Blanc or a Fumé Blanc is an ideal wine to accompany this soup.

6	ounces turbot fillet, skinned
4	ounces cooked lobster meat, from a 1 pound lobster
1	carrot
8	slender green beans
1/2	cup heavy cream
1	quantity vegetable stock (see p. 39)
4	snow peas
24	small mussels, washed and scraped clean
1	small zucchini, thinly sliced lengthwise
8	small spinach leaves
1/4	cup cold unsalted butter, cut into pieces
•	A pinch of ground star anise

Serves 4

(TOP LEFT) Lobster, Turbot and Mussels
with Star Anise Nage (*see page 61*),
(ABOVE) Fish Soup with Croutons
(*see page 56*), and (LEFT) Mussel, Leek
and Saffron Soup (*see page 57*)

Bourride of Goatfish, Petrale Sole and Salt Cod

I make bourride with salt cod because it makes the unsalted fish taste delightfully sweet. In all my recipes, I look for ways of extending the complexity of the tastes, so in this dish I have included a recipe for croutons spread with chili and sun-dried tomato—an idea I picked up from none other than Keith Floyd, a well-known British TV chef. I think it is an inspired combination.

You will need a large shallow serving dish that can contain about 4 cups of sauce.

To make the croutons, heat the oil in a pan and fry the bread until crisp. Remove from the pan and set aside. Mix together the chili and sun-dried tomato and bind with a little of the *aïoli.* Spread over the croutons and keep warm.

To make the *bourride,* heat the oil in a pan large enough to hold all the vegetables, stock and fish. Add the onion, leek, fennel, garlic and orange zest and fry gently without coloring for about 5 minutes, then add the tomatoes, bay leaf, thyme, fish stock and salt.

Bring to a boil and simmer for 30 minutes. Add all the fish, including the salt cod, and simmer very gently for 5 minutes. Remove the fish carefully and set aside in the warm serving dish. Strain the cooking liquor through a sieve into a clean pan, pressing down with a ladle to extract as much flavor as possible.

Put the *aïoli* in a large bowl and whisk in a good splash of the warm stock, then pour in the rest, whisking continuously (if you add all the stock at once, the *aïoli* won't amalgamate properly). Return the sauce to the pan and, continuing to whisk, heat to the temperature of an egg custard (hot enough to be uncomfortable to your little finger) to thicken it. Pour the *bourride* over the fish, sprinkle with the chopped parsley and arrange the croutons on top. Serve with boiled potatoes.

Serve with a bottle of aromatic white wine such as a Sauvignon Blanc or a French white.

Serves 4

2	tablespoons olive oil
1	medium onion, chopped
1	small leek, chopped
1/2	bulb fennel, chopped
4	garlic cloves, chopped
2	strips orange zest
2	tomatoes, sliced
1	fresh or dried bay leaf
1	fresh thyme sprig
5	cups *Fish Stock* (see p. 36)
1/2	teaspoon salt
8	ounces goatfish (red mullet) or sea bass fillet, with the skin left on
8	ounces petrale sole (brill) fillet, with the skin left on
8	ounces *Salt Cod* (see p. 54)
1	cup *Aïoli* (see p. 44)
•	Chopped fresh parsley to garnish

For the Croutons

2	tablespoons olive oil
4	slices French bread, about 1 inch thick, cut on the diagonal
1	red chili, seeded and finely chopped
4	sun-dried tomatoes in oil, chopped

Cotriade

Cotriade *is a fish stew from Brittany. It differs from other fish stews in that it uses oily fish, like mackerel, herring and smelt, along with the more unusual fish used in a stew. All fish stews are really very simple dishes that were originally concocted by fishermen using whatever fresh fish and vegetables were available. In the case of a* cotriade, *I believe it was quite common for the stew to be made on board ship. But although I had long known about* cotriade, *I had never been particularly interested in cooking what seemed to me to be a fish stew lacking any excitement until last year, when I went to Brittany.*

I stayed at the hotel of one of France's top chefs, Olivier Roellinger, and, in the second of his two restaurants (the first restaurant has won many stars and is much feted), I had a cotriade of such brilliance that I resolved to have a go myself. What really distinguished this dish was the astonishing pungency of the fennel in the bouillon. In the spring, the fennel is just appearing in the hedgerows everywhere in Brittany. Used in this dish with searobin, mackerel, monkfish and bass, it seemed all the more romantic because it evoked the scents and flavors of spring on the coast of France.

Being very close to Brittany, Cornwall has exactly the same fish, so I decided that it was just the sort of dish that I should be serving at the restaurant. In my recipe, I have also added slices of sorrel and anchovy butter, which is served separately so each guest can stir as much or little into the dish as they wish.

Because there is quite a lot of work involved I have written this recipe for eight people, making it suitable for a dinner party. But just one word of warning about using oily fish in stews: unless you are absolutely sure that the fish is extremely fresh, leave it out because the smell and flavor of the slightly-less-than-fresh oil in those oily fish will ruin the dish.

You can use almost any fish fillets in this recipe, but my suggestions are to use a few of the following: searobin, flounder, petrale sole, lemon sole, mackerel, herring, smelt, cod, hake, haddock, goatfish, mullet, red snapper, John Dory, turbot and whiting.

Use the smallest new potatoes you can find for this recipe.

You will need a large, shallow serving dish that can contain the fillets and about 3 cups of sauce.

To make the sorrel and anchovy butter, put all the ingredients in a food processor and blend until smooth. Place on plastic wrap and roll into a thick sausage shape. Chill until required.

To make the *cotriade,* put all the court bouillon ingredients except the crème fraîche and sprigs of fennel in a large pan, bring to a boil and simmer for 30 minutes. Strain through a sieve into a clean pan, pushing the liquid through with the back of a ladle to extract as much of the flavor as possible. Bring the strained bouillon to a boil and continue boiling to reduce the volume by about half. Add the crème fraîche and all but one of the sprigs of fennel and simmer for 5 minutes before straining again. Add the potatoes to the strained stock and boil until just tender.

Preheat the broiler. Brush the oily fish fillets with a little butter and season lightly with salt. Wash the mussels and scrape them clean, removing the beards with a →

sharp knife. Put a generous splash of the bouillon in a large pan; then add the mussels. Cover tightly and place over high heat until they steam open. Remove the mussels from the pan and keep warm. Strain the mussels' cooking liquor through a sieve into the bouillon.

Broil the oily fish under the broiler until just cooked. Poach the rest of the fish in the bouillon and try to keep the fillets in one piece. Cook them in batches until they are just firm. They will continue to cook after you have removed them from the heat. As each batch is cooked, set it aside and keep warm.

Serve in the large shallow dish. Unlike most fish stews it is important to try and keep the fillets intact and lay them out neatly. Add the mussels and pour over only enough bouillon and potatoes to cover half the fillets. Sprinkle with the chopped fennel and serve the rest of the bouillon separately. Serve the sorrel butter cut into thick slices on a plate.

Serves 8

2	pounds new potatoes, sliced in half
4	pounds fish fillets (see above)
1/2	cup unsalted butter
2	pounds mussels
•	Salt

For the Court Bouillon

2	carrots, chopped
1	leek, chopped
2	celery stalks, chopped
1	bulb fennel, chopped
1/2	onion, chopped
2 1/2	quarts water
•	Rind and flesh of 1/2 lemon
2	garlic cloves
1	fresh or dried bay leaf
2/3	cup dry white wine
2	tablespoons Ricard or Pernod
6	black peppercorns
1	tablespoon salt
1/2	cup crème fraîche
2	ounces fresh fennel sprigs, including stems and leafy fronds (about 2 cups)

For the Sorrel and Anchovy Butter

10	sorrel leaves
4	anchovy fillets
1/2	cup unsalted butter, softened

A Meurette of Flounder and Lemon Sole with Beaujolais

This Burgundian freshwater fish stew calls for plenty of fruity red wine to produce a robust, full-flavored dish.

First, make the croutons. Using a 1-inch round cutter, cut out 8 disks from the slices of bread and fry them in the peanut oil, adding a little knob of butter to the pan to give them a golden color.

To make the stock, melt the butter in a pan and add the chopped mixed vegetables (known as *mirepoix*) and fry them until they are just beginning to brown. Add the brandy and boil off the alcohol before adding 4 cups of the chicken stock, the Beaujolais, bay leaf and thyme. Bring to a boil and simmer for 30 minutes. →

Meanwhile brown the shallots with the sugar and butter in a shallow pan. Add the remaining chicken stock and simmer the shallots gently until they are tender, then turn up the heat and reduce the shallots and stock until you have a shiny brown glaze. Set aside and keep warm.

To make the garnish, cut the bacon into thin strips and fry gently in the butter. Add the mushrooms and continue to fry until soft. Season with salt and black pepper. Then set aside and keep warm.

Finely chop the garlic and parsley together, to make the *persillade.*

Strain the red wine stock into a shallow pan, bring to a boil and boil rapidly to reduce the volume by half. Add the fish fillets and cook gently until just tender. (This should take about 5 minutes.)

Remove the fillets from the pan and place neatly on a warmed serving dish. Break the *beurre manié* into small pieces and stir into the red wine sauce. Continue to stir until the sauce thickens. Add the *meurette,* the mushroom and bacon garnish and the *persillade.* Check the seasoning and add a little salt, if necessary. Spoon the sauce over the fish, top with the croutons and serve. Serve with plainly boiled new potatoes and green beans.

A bottle of good Beaujolais, such as Fleurie, or other light, fruity, aromatic red wine is excellent with the Meurette.

Serves 4

For the Croutons

2   slices white bread
2   tablespoons peanut oil
•   A knob of butter

For the Fish

12 ounces flounder (plaice) fillets, skin on
12 ounces lemon sole fillets, skin on
2   tablespoons unsalted butter mixed with 1½ tablespoons all-purpose flour *(beurre manié)*
•   Salt and freshly ground black pepper

For the Stock

2   tablespoons butter
8   ounces equal quantities carrot, celery, leek and onion, chopped and mixed together
1   tablespoon brandy
5   cups *Chicken Stock* (see p. 37)
½   bottle Beaujolais or other light, fruity red wine
1   fresh or dried bay leaf
1   fresh thyme sprig or ½ teaspoon dried thyme

For the Persillade

1   small clove garlic
1   small bunch fresh parsley

For the Meurette

24 shallots, peeled
¼   teaspoon sugar
1   tablespoon butter

For the Mushroom and Bacon Garnish

1   slice bacon, rind removed
1   tablespoon butter
8   ounces button mushrooms, cut into quarters

Thai Seafood Salad

This dish is designed for large numbers and it is always a great success. The aromatic flavors of lemongrass, lime, fresh chili and cilantro are just the sort of positive and attractive highlights that make a buffet dish like this memorable. I made it for about 50 last May Day. In Padstow, May 1st is known as Obby 'Oss Day, a pagan festival when the coming of summer is celebrated with dancing, singing, eating and just a little drinking!

Heat the oil in a large frying pan and fry the squid in batches until it has turned brown and is beginning to take on color. Use the same pan and oil to fry the monkfish. Again, do this in batches so that the fish fries and takes on some color rather than sweats. Repeat the process with the scallops, frying them for only about 1 minute. Set aside all the cooked seafood and leave to cool. Deglaze the frying pan with the water. Mix these pan juices with the fish sauce, lime juice and sesame oil in a small bowl. Set aside.

Cut the lobster, if using, in half lengthwise and remove the meat from the tail and claws. Pick out the meat from the head section. This is done in the same way as for the body section of a crab (see p. 177). Set the meat aside and discard the shells.

To make up the salad, gently turn over all the ingredients in a large salad bowl.

Serves 20

4	tablespoons olive oil
2	pounds squid, cleaned and cut into strips (see p. 28)
2	pounds monkfish fillet, sliced
20	scallops, cut in half
3/4	cup water
1/2	cup Thai fish sauce (*nam pla*)
•	Juice of 4 limes
2	tablespoons Asian sesame oil
1	lobster, 3 pounds, cooked (optional)
1	pound large shrimp, cooked and peeled
2	cucumbers, diced
3	stalks celery, diced
3	bunches green onions, sliced
4	stalks lemongrass, finely sliced
6	cloves garlic, peeled and finely chopped
3	ounces ginger, peeled and finely chopped
6	red chilies, seeded and finely chopped
1/2	cup fresh cilantro, roughly chopped
6	Kaffir lime leaves, very finely sliced (available in Asian markets; optional)
1	iceberg lettuce, thinly sliced

Seafood Risotto

Risotto is one of those dishes, like bouillabaisse, where stern warnings about correct ingredients and cooking abound. But like many a simple dish there is really very little to it. It reminds me of an essay by Elizabeth David called "An Omelette and a Glass of Wine," where the omelettes of Annette Poulard, proprietress of a restaurant on Mont Saint-Michel, were analyzed and secret ingredients like foie gras and cream and special methods were ascribed to her delightfully light dishes. Years after she had retired she replied to a letter asking what was in her omelettes by saying, "I break some good eggs into a bowl, I put a good piece of butter in the pan, I throw the eggs into it and I shake it constantly." There's nothing to it, and the same goes for risotto. →

This seafood risotto is very simple to make and makes a perfect starter. You can use any of the following risotto rices: Arborio, Carnaroli, Maratelli, Roma, or Nano Vialone.

Peel the shrimp, reserving the shells for the stock. Set the shrimp aside until needed. Wash the mussels, scrape them clean and pull out the beards. Open by placing in a pan with a splash of water, covering tightly, then setting over high heat until they have opened. Strain through a colander to remove any grit. Save the liquor for the stock. Remove the meats from all but 8 of the shells, discard the empty shells. Leaving a few whole mussels in the risotto makes it look very appetizing. Set the mussels aside until needed.

To make the stock, heat the oil in a large pan and add the garlic, carrot, celery, onion, leek and chili. Fry for 5 minutes without coloring. Add the reserved shrimp shells and cook for another couple of minutes, then add the tomato, saffron, fish stock and mussel liquor. Bring to a boil and simmer for 30 minutes, then push through a conical sieve with the back of a ladle to extract as much flavor as possible.

To make the risotto, melt the butter in a heavy-based pan (this will lessen the chance of the risotto burning on the bottom as it cooks), then add the shallots and garlic and cook until softened. Add the rice and stir for a couple of minutes until well coated with butter. Pour in the wine. Bring to a boil, then remove from the heat and let the rice absorb all the liquid. You can make the risotto to this stage some time before completing the dish. The final cooking time, about 20 minutes, is reduced to about 10 by doing this.

Return the pan to medium heat and add the shellfish stock to the rice in three stages, allowing the liquid to be absorbed each time before adding the next amount. Stir continuously until the stock is almost completely absorbed.

When the rice is just tender but still firm to the bite (al dente), add the Parmesan. (The small amount of stock left at this stage will be absorbed by the cheese.) While the risotto is cooking, brush the rest of the seafood with olive oil and broil for 3–4 minutes. To serve, carefully mix the seafood, including the mussels, into the risotto. Leave a few pieces on top to garnish.

1	pound shrimp in the shell
36	small mussels
4	ounces monkfish fillet, thinly sliced
2	ounces cleaned squid, thinly sliced (see p. 28)

For the Stock

2	tablespoons olive oil
1	garlic clove, chopped
1	medium carrot, chopped
1	celery stalk, chopped
1	small onion, chopped
1	small leek, chopped
1/4	red chili, chopped
1	tomato, chopped
1/8	teaspoon saffron strands
4	cups *Fish Stock* (see p. 36)
•	Cooking liquor from the mussels

For the Risotto

1/4	cup unsalted butter
2	shallots, chopped
1	garlic clove, chopped
1 3/4	cups risotto rice (see above)
1/2	cup dry white wine
1/4	cup freshly grated Parmesan cheese
1	tablespoon olive oil

Serves 4

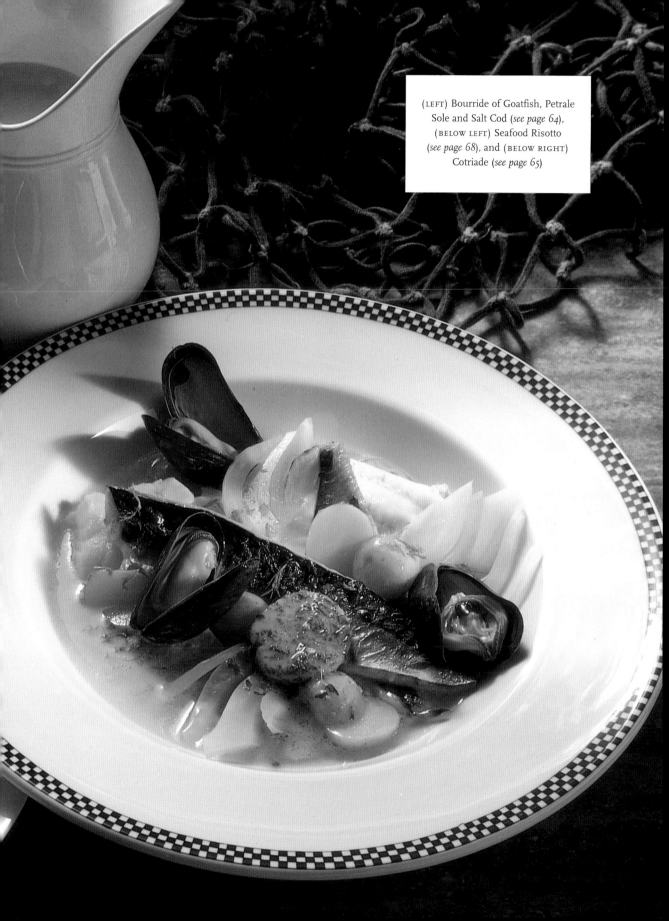

(LEFT) Bourride of Goatfish, Petrale
Sole and Salt Cod (*see page 64*),
(BELOW LEFT) Seafood Risotto
(*see page 68*), and (BELOW RIGHT)
Cotriade (*see page 65*)

Charles Fontaine's Fish Pie

Charles Fontaine is a French chef who loves English food. He runs the Quality Chop House in Farringdon Road, London. The restaurant has had quality English food like chops and fish pies on its menu for over a hundred years. While making the television series, we filmed him making a fish pie. My recipe is identical to the fish pie made by M. Fontaine but with two important differences: first he adds 2 pounds of mussels to the pie and second, he omits the boiled eggs.

To make the pie in Charles's way, wash the mussels thoroughly, scraping off any barnacles and discarding any that are open and don't close when given a good tap. Place in a large pan and add a dash of dry white wine. Cover tightly and cook over high heat for about 5 minutes, shaking the pan until the mussels open. Strain the liquor through a colander into a bowl and add the liquor when making the velouté sauce. Remove the mussel meats from the shells and remove the beards. Add the mussels with the rest of the fish to the fish pie.

Preheat the oven to 400°F.

Place the milk, water, onion and ½ lemon in a large pan. Bring to a boil, then simmer for 5 minutes. Add the fish and poach gently for 5 minutes. Remove the fish, then strain the liquid into a shallow pan and boil rapidly to reduce the volume by half.

Melt the butter in a heavy-based pan and stir in the flour. Cook for about 2 minutes, stirring continuously without letting it color too much. When it starts to smell nutty, remove from the heat and allow it to cool slightly. Gradually add the hot poaching liquid, stirring until smooth. Return to the heat and simmer over very low heat for about 40 minutes, stirring occasionally.

Meanwhile, remove the skin and bones from the fish. Break the fillets into good-sized chunks.

Boil the eggs for 10 minutes until they are hard-boiled. Cool slightly, then peel and quarter and place with the fish in a shallow ovenproof dish. Sprinkle with the parsley.

Remove the sauce from the heat, then add the grated cheese, stirring until smooth. Check and adjust the seasoning, then pour over the fish.

Boil the potatoes in lightly salted water until very soft. Drain, then mash until smooth, adding the butter and milk. Spread over the top of the sauce. Pull a fork across the top of the potato to make a wavy-line pattern.

Bake in the oven for 30 minutes and serve hot.

2½	cups milk
2½	cups water
½	onion, sliced
½	lemon
2	pounds white fish fillets, such as pollack or ling
¼	cup unsalted butter
¼	cup all-purpose flour
2	eggs
2	tablespoons fresh parsley leaves, roughly chopped
½	cup grated cheddar cheese
•	Salt and freshly ground white pepper

For the Mashed Potatoes

3	pounds white potatoes, peeled
2	tablespoons unsalted butter
½	cup milk

Serves 4

Tempura of Seafood with Roasted Red Chili and Onion Pickle

This recipe is best served as a first course because it makes heavy demands on the deep-fryer, and if you tried to cook it as a main course for any more than a couple of people, you would find you were cooking an awful lot of batches. However, it is extremely popular; deep-fried seafood always is. The batter recipe given here has the enviable quality of remaining crisp for a very long time.

To give the best possible visual impact, I have chosen seafood that can be cooked partly in the shell and partly out. Only the tail shells are removed from the shrimp and only one half of the shells from the mussels. This makes the finished dish look much more attractive than if you just served the mussel meats or shrimp tails in the batter.

Carefully remove the shells from the tails of the shrimp, taking care to avoid separating the tail from the head. Grip the sides of the tail with your thumb and forefinger and push the bottom edges together to crack the shell. Gently peel the tail shell back the other way. Try not to put any pressure on the shrimp where the tail goes into the body section.

To open the mussels, place them in a small pan with just a splash of water. Cover tightly and set over high heat until they open. Discard any mussels that don't open when cooked. Remove from the pan. Strain through a fine sieve to remove any grit. When cool enough to handle, carefully remove one shell from each mussel, leaving the meat in the other. Also remove any stringy beards still attached to the meat. Prepare the scallops by cutting each one in half and the sole by cutting the fillet into 8 small pieces.

To make the roasted red chili and onion pickle, heat the oil in a pan, then add the garlic and ginger and fry until the garlic is beginning to brown. Add the onion and reduce the heat, allowing it to cook gently for 5 minutes. Add the chilies, sugar, vinegar and oyster sauce and cook gently for 30 minutes. Add the lime leaves (if using), fish sauce and green onions and cook for a further 3 minutes. Leave to cool.

To deep-fry the fish, preheat the oil in the deep-fryer to 375°F. Drop the scallops and sole fillets into the batter, then remove and drop immediately into the hot oil.

Fry for 3 minutes. Remove and drain on paper towels. Next, cook the shrimp for 2 minutes and, finally, cook the mussels for 1 minute.

Assemble the seafood onto four warm plates with a dollop of the extremely hot aromatic and delightful chili pickle. Serve immediately.

Serve with a full-bodied Chardonnay or Semillon.

8	large shrimp or prawns, shells on
16	mussels, cleaned
4	scallops
4	ounces flounder fillet
•	Vegetable oil, for deep-frying
1	quantity *Tempura Batter* (see p. 53)

For the Pickle

2	tablespoons vegetable oil
3	garlic cloves, finely chopped
•	2-inch piece ginger, finely chopped
1	medium onion, finely chopped
2	red chilies, seeded and finely chopped
2	tablespoons sugar
4	tablespoons white wine vinegar
2	tablespoons oyster sauce
2	Kaffir lime leaves, very finely sliced (available in Asian markets; optional)
1	tablespoon Thai fish sauce (*nam pla*)
3	green onions, sliced into thin rounds

Serves 4

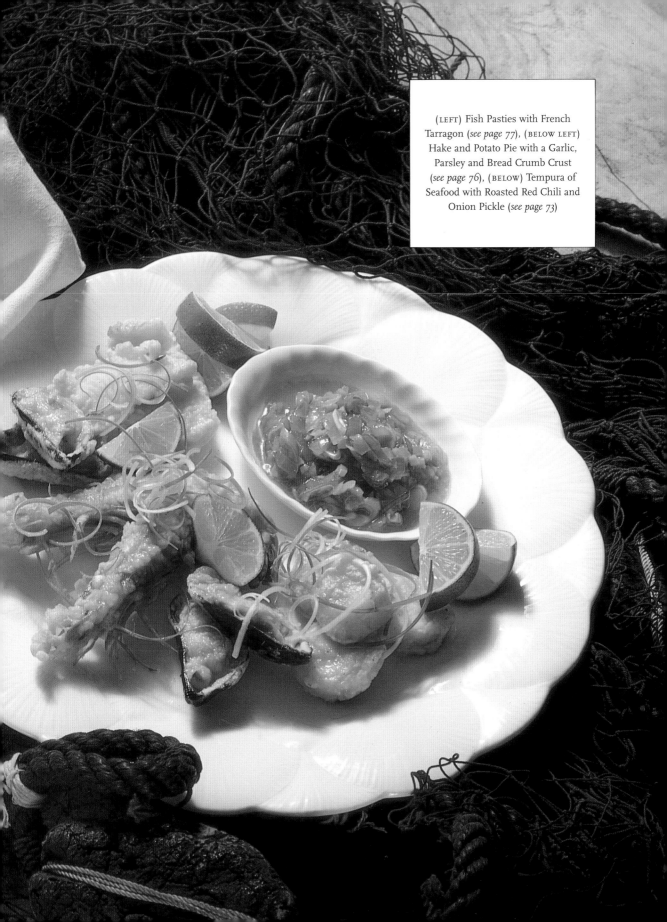

(LEFT) Fish Pasties with French Tarragon (*see page 77*), (BELOW LEFT) Hake and Potato Pie with a Garlic, Parsley and Bread Crumb Crust (*see page 76*), (BELOW) Tempura of Seafood with Roasted Red Chili and Onion Pickle (*see page 73*)

Seafood Thermidor

This is a star attraction at our deli.

Preheat the broiler. Melt the butter in a pan and fry the onion until softened. Pour in the white wine and boil to reduce a little, then add the stock and one-third of the mushrooms. Simmer for 10 minutes, then boil to reduce the stock by two-thirds.

In a separate pan, carefully heat the velouté, then add the reduced stock to it. Stir in the cream and leave to simmer on very low heat while you prepare the fish.

Cut the sole and monkfish into 1/2-inch pieces and slice each scallop into three. Put all the fish in a large, shallow gratin dish. Sprinkle the rest of the mushrooms on top. Melt the butter and brush over the mushrooms and fish. Season with salt and place under the broiler. Remove when the fish is white but still a little undercooked. Sprinkle over the shrimp.

Add the mustard to the sauce so it is slightly hot but not overpoweringly so. Pour the sauce over the fish and mushrooms.

Mix together the grated cheese, bread crumbs, cayenne pepper and a couple of twists of black pepper and sprinkle over. Place under the broiler until golden brown.

1	tablespoon butter
1	medium onion, finely chopped
6	tablespoons dry white wine
1 1/4	cups *Fish Stock* (see p. 36)
3	ounces fresh button mushrooms
2 1/2	cups *Velouté* (see p. 39)
1/2	cup heavy cream
6	ounces lemon sole fillet, skinned
6	ounces monkfish fillet, skinned
4	large scallops
·	Melted butter for brushing over fish
4	ounces large shrimp, cooked and peeled
1	tablespoon English mustard
3/4	cup grated Parmesan cheese
1/4	cup fine dried bread crumbs
·	A pinch of cayenne pepper
·	Salt and freshly ground black pepper

Serves 4

Hake and Potato Pie with a Garlic, Parsley and Bread Crumb Crust

I'm very fond of this simple French fish pie.

Preheat the oven to 400°F.

Parboil the potatoes for 2 minutes and drain. Grease an ovenproof dish with half the butter. Cut the hake into 1-inch slices and layer in the dish with the potato slices. Season and dot with the rest of the butter. Cover and bake for 15 minutes, basting with the butter twice.

Process the bread, garlic and parsley to crumbs. Season, then sprinkle over the pie and bake, uncovered, for 15 minutes or until crisp.

1	pound potatoes, cut into 1/4-inch slices
1/2	cup butter
1	pound hake fillet, skinned
2	slices white bread
2	garlic cloves
1/2	cup fresh parsley leaves
·	Salt and freshly ground black pepper

Serves 4

Fish Pasties with French Tarragon

Use the cheapest fish fillet you can find for this dish. Ling, pollock or cod (in that order of preference) are all fine. This is the recipe I use in our bakery and very good it is too!

Preheat the oven to 400°F.

Mix all the ingredients, except the pastry, in a bowl. Roll out the pastry about 1/4 inch thick. Using a pastry cutter, press out five disks each 7 1/2 inches in diameter. Divide the filling evenly among the disks. Moisten the edges of the pastry, fold in half, then pinch them together to seal. Crimp the edges, then place on a lightly greased baking sheet and bake for 35 minutes. Serve hot or cold.

Makes 5 pasties

1   large leek, about 5 ounces, cut into 1/2-inch dice
1   onion, about 5 ounces, cut into 1/2-inch dice
8   ounces potatoes, cut into 1/2-inch dice
•   Scant 1 pound fish fillet (see above), cut into 1-inch pieces
2   tablespoons white wine vinegar
2   tablespoons butter
1/4   cup grated aged cheddar cheese
1/2   teaspoon chopped fresh French tarragon
1/2   teaspoon freshly ground black pepper
1   teaspoon salt
2   pounds flaky pastry or shortcrust pastry dough, chilled (Either buy ready-made or use your favorite recipe.)

Fish Cakes

You can use any white fish or, indeed, any oily fish to make these fish cakes, but cheaper white fish like ling, pollock, whiting and cod are ideal for this dish. I have included a couple of teaspoons of anchovy essence in this recipe because it improves the flavor dramatically. You can also use nam pla (Thai fish sauce) if you want to, but if you don't want to use either, just add more salt to the recipe.

Break the cooked fish into small pieces, removing all the skin and bones. Mix the mashed potatoes with the eggs and melted butter, then fold in the anchovy essence, fish sauce or salt, pepper and parsley.

Mold the mixture into fish cakes using your hands and a spatula. Coat each cake with flour, then beaten egg, then bread crumbs. Shallow fry or deep-fry as you prefer.

Serve hot with a green vegetable or a salad.

Serves 4

1   pound cooked white fish (see above)
2   cups mashed potatoes
2   eggs
2   tablespoons butter, melted
2   teaspoons anchovy extract or Thai fish sauce (nam pla) or 1 teaspoon salt
10   turns of a black pepper mill
2   tablespoons chopped fresh parsley
1/3   cup seasoned all-purpose flour
2   eggs, beaten
2 1/2   cups fresh white bread crumbs

5 Oily Fish

Oily fish are rich in omega-3 fatty acids that have the benefit of reducing cholesterol levels. We should all eat more mackerel, herring, salmon, trout, whitebait, smelt (sprats) and sardines. Not only are they healthy and nutritious, but their oil creates a delightful flavor when the fish are perfectly fresh and served simply grilled, fried or barbecued. They all lend themselves to being preserved in salt, smoked or pickled, too.

HERRING

The maritime countries of northern Europe have made use of herring in as many diverse ways as the rural people of France have used the pig. Just think of the different ways that herring is served up: kippers, bloaters, buckling, red herrings, rollmops, Bismarck herrings, salt herrings, pickled herrings, matjes herrings.

Large ports have built up over the years, particularly in the Baltic, the east coast of England and Scotland, and Holland, from the earnings made from the fishing and processing of herrings. Yet, because they have always been so cheap, I tend to think we underrate them. I once asked a very good food-writer friend of mine, Linda Brown, why she thought that we underrate herrings and she came up with a novel and, I suspect, truthful answer, that people really don't like the lingering smell of oily fish in their houses after they've fried them. I remember doing some research on sardines (pilchards) in Cornwall in the last century and reading an account of someone visiting the cottages of the poor at that time. They described the appalling smell of sardine oil in every house, which was used to light lamps in those days.

If you don't like the smell of frying oily fish, but love the taste, here are some suggestions: get a stove that vents to the outside of the house, start frying the fish, then transfer them to the oven, or get yourself a little barbecue and cook them outside! We barbecue fish outside the kitchen door even in the middle of winter. All of the herring family—sardines, smelt and herrings—when cooked perfectly fresh are amongst the best things you could ever eat.

MACKEREL

The best way to eat mackerel is to cook it on the day it is caught. For this reason, I wouldn't suggest cooking the *Fillets of Mackerel with Dill and New Potatoes* on p. 92 with anything but the freshest mackerel. Apart from that exception, mackerel from the fishmonger will be fine for all the other recipes. Make sure that the mackerel have some traces of blue or green in their skin. If they look gray, they won't be particularly interesting to eat. When we were filming for the television series we took my youngest son out mackerel fishing. He complained, having never been in a boat on the open sea before, about the rocking until we gave him a fishing rod and he had his first bite. He was totally absorbed from then on. For this I feel most grateful to mackerel: first, for being such a delicious fish when fresh; and second, for being in such abundance in in-shore waters so that small boys can catch them.

On the whole I've tried to keep separate the writing of the cookery book and the making of the TV series (which includes about 40 recipes from this book). However, once in a while the experiences of making the cookery series are so interesting as to make me want to mention them in the book. This is very much the case with mackerel.

David Pritchard, the producer, wanted me to do some voiceovers. These are little introductory pieces to various episodes in the series. We were particularly tired as we'd been up since 5 a.m. at the market in Newlyn and had just finished three days of pretty hard filming, so I suppose we were all a bit half-baked.

David said, "I want a piece about mackerel. If you remember there's a scene where Charles (my youngest son) is seen pulling in his first mackerel and then we cut to those same mackerel on a chopping board by the cooker. I want you to say, in line with what we have already been saying, that mackerel are, shall we say, ubiquitous. Let's call them the Mini Metros of the sea."

So I started, "One of the great joys about mackerel is that they make themselves so easy to be caught, they're everywhere, they're a bit like the Mini Metros of the sea."

"Hang on a minute," said Julian, the cameraman, "they're not Mini Metros at all, they're Ford Escorts."

There was a pause of aggrieved silence from David.

"Okay," I said, "Ford Escorts."

"No, Julian," said David. "They're not Ford Escorts, they're Mini Metros. What I mean is that they crop up everywhere."

"Okay," I said. "Fine. Mini Metros."

"Well they're not Mini Metros to me," said Julian.

"Look," I said, "does it really matter? Can't we just call them the Skodas of the sea?"

"That's not the point," said Julian. "Mini Metros are squat little cars, mackerel are sleek and shiny, much more like Ford Escorts."

"I don't think that Ford Escorts are particularly sleek or shiny," said David. "A Mini Metro's a far better car to compare them with. You just don't understand, do you Julian?"

"Look," I said, "we're all getting a bit tired, can't we just call them Ford Escorts, just for a quiet life?"

"Anyway," said the sound engineer, Tom, "what the hell's wrong with Mini Metros? My wife's got one."

"Okay," said David, "let's forget the whole thing."

SALMON

Well-produced farmed salmon is perfectly acceptable but even more delightful is wild salmon and the fishermen who catch it. There's a salmon fisherman in Cornwall called Charlie Bettinson who catches fish on the higher reaches of the Camel or Tamar at places like Golitha Falls. The single-mindedness, obsession and skill that he puts into catching a 12-pound salmon out of a pool where you would never have believed anything was swimming is a joy to behold.

When I see how much time and care it takes to get wild salmon from the water, I am filled with a sense of value of the fish. It is a real prize; firm flesh and the taste of fresh nuts.

Fish farming is vital if we wish to continue eating fish at all in view of the inexorable over-fishing that is going on in the seas around us. Inevitably, the taste of farmed salmon is not as good as wild. Don't worry about using farmed fish in any of the recipes. I'd far sooner you cooked them with farmed fish than not at all.

SEA TROUT

The sea trout, also known as steelhead, is a brown trout that has exchanged its habitat of rivers for the open sea. Its flesh develops a pink color from a diet of crustaceans but is slightly less pronounced than the salmon. If better known and more widely available, I'm sure it would rank very highly among people's favorite fish because it is so sleek and goodlooking. It suffers even more than salmon from overcooking and tastes far better if eaten slightly underdone. Some fish are inedible when undercooked, John Dory in particular, and monkfish, but those fish with soft flesh like salmon, sea trout, whiting and hake really benefit from being slightly undercooked.

WHITEBAIT

There is no such fish as whitebait. They are the young of fish in the herring family, normally smelt, herrings or sardines. As you eat the whole fish, guts and all, it is important not to buy them too big or the bones,

intestines and scales become unpleasant. The largest they should be is 2–21/2 inches in length. Wash the whitebait after you have bought them in case there is any sand clinging to them; it's not very pleasant when mixed with the flour and deep-fried!

EELS

I think we ought to eat more eels but having been the recipient of a polystyrene cup of jellied eels in a London pub on more than one occasion, I can see why we don't. It wasn't until I started buying fresh eels and cooking them myself that I realized of what value they were. Of all the oily fish, I think eels have the finest flavor—a perfect contrast of delicacy and richness. The flesh is firm and any stock made from eel trimmings is flavorsome and gelatinous.

Hot Smoked Eel with Lentils, Sauerkraut and New Potatoes

Smoked eel is one of my favorite smoked fish. This great warm salad makes a good first course if you halve all the ingredients, but you can also serve it as a main course. I really love this sort of central European food—totally wizard!

Wash the potatoes well and then peel them. Slice them lengthwise and boil in well salted water. Drain and keep warm.

Slice the eel fillet into finger-size pieces (being hot smoked, it is already cooked). Boil the lentils in salted water with the sprig of thyme until soft, drain and set aside. Gently stew the sauerkraut in a separate pan, with the butter and white wine, for about 20 minutes.

Place the eel, potatoes, lentils and dressing in a pan and warm through, turning carefully. Finally, add the watercress before dividing among four warmed plates. Serve with a portion of sauerkraut on each plate.

1	pound waxy new potatoes
4	ounces smoked eel fillet
1/3	cup Puy lentils or other tiny green lentils
1	fresh thyme sprig
4	ounces sauerkraut
2	tablespoons unsalted butter
2	tablespoons white wine
6	tablespoons *Mustard Dressing* (see p. 51)
1	bunch watercress, stalks removed

Serves 4

Fillets of Eel with Teriyaki Marinade

You can use almost any fish to make this dish, but it does seem to go particularly well with eel which, being oily, responds to grilling or barbecuing well. This dish is designed to be cooked on some sort of charcoal grill or grilling pan but, like most of my grilled recipes, it can also be cooked under a broiler, not quite so exciting but still well worth doing. Teriyaki is Japanese and uses two unusual ingredients, sake and mirin. If you can't get hold of the rice wine sake, use dry sherry. Mirin is a syrupy sake and I have increased the amount of sake and sugar in the recipe to allow for its omission.

Boil all the marinade ingredients in a small pan for 5 minutes. Leave to cool. Brush the eel fillets liberally with the marinade.

Preheat the broiler or ready the charcoal grill and cook the fillets for 2–3 minutes on each side. Brush them with the marinade twice more on each side during cooking. Serve the eel accompanied with the remaining marinade passed as a sauce at the table.

1½	pounds skinned fillets of eel
	For the Teriyaki Marinade
2/3	cup soy sauce
2/3	cup sake or dry sherry
2	tablespoons sugar
1	garlic clove, finely chopped
1	teaspoon finely chopped fresh ginger

Serves 4

Herrings in Oatmeal with Salad Greens and Tomato

The essential ingredient for frying herrings in oatmeal is the fat in bacon. You can adapt this recipe for other oily fish, too.

Bone the herrings as on p. 21. Season and press with the oats until they are well covered. Heat the oil in a frying pan and fry the bacon until crisp. Remove from the pan and keep warm. Fry the herrings in the same pan oil, flesh side first, until golden brown. Set the pan aside without washing it.

Divide the salad greens among four warmed plates and sprinkle with the tomatoes and bacon. Place one herring on each plate, beside the salad. Pour the dressing into the pan and heat through briefly before pouring over the salads. Serve immediately.

4	herrings, about 8 ounces each
1¹/₃	cup rolled oats
2	tablespoons vegetable oil
4	slices bacon, cut into thin strips
2	ounces salad greens
2	tomatoes, seeded and chopped
4	tablespoons *Mustard Dressing* (see p. 51)
•	Salt and freshly ground black pepper

Serves 4

Herring Beignets with Olive Oil, Marjoram and Cracked Spices

I had always imagined that oily fish, like herring, deep-fried in batter would be too rich but I had some fritters like this in Corsica once and they were delightful.

To make the batter, whisk the flour, salt, olive oil and beer together until smooth. Leave for an hour. Just before deep frying, whisk the egg white to soft peaks and fold into the batter. Remove the seeds from the cardamom pods, crack the coriander and peppercorns with a rolling pin and place in a small bowl with the marjoram, sea salt and olive oil. Set your deep fryer to 360°F, or heat some vegetable oil in a large pan. Fillet the herrings (see p. 21), cut into finger-sized pieces, dip in the batter and fry for 2 minutes. Drain and arrange in four neat piles on four plates. Place the salad greens next to the beignets and pour the dressing beside the salad greens. Serve with lemon wedges.

4	small herrings
1	ounce salad greens (about 1 cup)
1	lemon, cut into 4 wedges

For the Batter

³/₄	cup all-purpose flour
¹/₂	teaspoon salt
2	tablespoons olive oil
²/₃	cup beer
1	egg white

For the Dressing

2	cardamom pods
12	coriander seeds
6	black peppercorns
¹/₂	teaspoon chopped fresh marjoram
•	A large pinch of sea salt
6	tablespoons virgin olive oil

Serves 4

Panfried Herring Milt on Toasted Brioche with Noisette Butter, Capers, Salad Greens and Chervil

I have always loved fried herring milt, which is the roe of the male herring just fried and served on toast. My wife, Jill, suggested upgrading the idea by using brioche instead of toast and adding some salad greens so that we could serve it as a first course at the restaurant. It has been a great success. But, if you don't want to make brioche, use toast instead.

Preheat the oven to 400°F. To make the brioche, put the yeast, water, sugar, milk and 1 tablespoon of the flour in a bowl, whisk together then cover with a wet tea towel. Leave in a warm place until the mixture starts to froth. Put the rest of the flour and the salt in a large mixing bowl and add the eggs and yeast mixture. Mix thoroughly to form a soft dough. Turn out onto a floured surface and knead for 5 minutes. Add the butter and knead again to incorporate it into the dough. Cover with a clean tea towel and leave to rise in a warm place for 3 hours. Punch down, shape into a loaf and place in a 7½-by-3½-inch (1 pound) bread pan. Bake for 35 minutes.

Mix the salad greens with the olive oil dressing in a bowl then divide among four warmed plates. Scatter over the chervil. Cut four ½-inch-thick slices of brioche, toast lightly and place beside the salad.

Dust the roes in the seasoned flour; then fry in 2 tablespoons of butter for about 2 minutes; then place on top of the brioche.

Pour away the butter used to fry the roes and melt the remaining butter in the pan until it foams and starts to smell nutty. Pour over the herring roes, sprinkle with the lemon juice, scatter with a little salt and parsley and finish with a few capers. Serve immediately.

Serves 4

For the Brioche

1	package (2½ teaspoons) active dry yeast
3	tablespoons warm water
2	tablespoons sugar
3	tablespoons tepid milk
3¼	cups bread flour
1	tablespoon salt
4	eggs
½	cup unsalted butter

For the Salad

2	ounces salad greens (almost 2 cups)
2	tablespoons *Olive Oil Dressing* (see p. 51)
•	A small bunch chervil, with the larger stems removed

For the Herring Roe

12	ounces soft herring roe
3	tablespoons all-purpose flour, seasoned with salt and pepper
6	tablespoons unsalted butter, softened
•	Juice of ½ lemon
1	tablespoon chopped fresh parsley
1	tablespoon capers
•	Salt and freshly ground black pepper

(LEFT) Fillets of Mackeral with Dill and New Potatoes (*see page 92*), (BELOW LEFT) Panfried Herring Milt on Toasted Brioche with Noisette Butter, Capers, Salad Greens and Chervil (*see page 85*), and (BELOW) Grilled Herrings with Mustard and Onion Sauce and Fish Sausages (*see page 88*)

Grilled Herrings with Mustard and Onion Sauce and Fish Sausages

This dish of herrings and fish sausages makes a pleasingly robust supper dish. The fish sausages are made with fish forcemeat and flavored with lovage, a much underused herb mainly, I suspect, because it is so strong and has such a singular flavor. But a little lovage in a fish sausage is a delight. Unfortunately, unless you are a keen herb gardener, or have a friend that is, you will probably find it hard to get hold of, which is a shame really because it has long been used in English cookery. A suitable alternative to lovage is the tops of celery.

Ideally you should have some sort of sausage-making equipment to make these fish sausages, but a piping bag and 1/2-inch plain nozzle will do equally well. It is quite easy to buy sausage casings from your local butcher—4 ounces will be quite enough.

The best white fish fillets for the sausages are pollock, flounder or whiting.

Scale the herrings, then slash them diagonally three times on each side, cutting right down to the bone. Season well inside and out with salt and pepper and brush with a little melted butter.

Before starting to make the sausages, make sure that all the ingredients are cold.

Put the fish, bread crumbs, butter, egg, salt, white pepper and lemon juice into a food processor and blend until smooth. Add the lovage, parsley and onion tops and then quickly pour in the cream, taking no more than 10 seconds. Fill the sausage skins (see above) with the forcemeat and twist into 3½-inch-long sausages.

Gently simmer the onion, balsamic vinegar, salt and chicken stock in a pan for 30–40 minutes. If the liquid boils away, add a little water. The aim is to cook the onions until they are extremely soft and to boil off all, or almost all, the liquid. Add the butter as if making *Beurre Blanc* (see p. 42). Remove from the heat and stir in the mustard. Set aside and keep warm.

Preheat the broiler then broil the herrings for about 4 minutes on each side. Meanwhile, poach the sausages in lightly salted water for about 4 minutes. Drain, then serve immediately with the herrings and sauce, accompanied with mashed potatoes.

A good-quality hard cider would be an ideal accompaniment for this dish.

4	herrings, 8–10 ounces each
•	A little melted butter, for brushing
1	large onion, finely chopped
4	tablespoons balsamic vinegar
½	teaspoon salt
⅔	cup *Chicken Stock* (see p. 37)
½	cup unsalted butter
1	tablespoon Dijon mustard

For the Sausages

9	ounces white fish fillet, free of skin and bone
¾	cup fresh white bread crumbs
2	tablespoons butter
1	egg
½	teaspoon salt
•	A good pinch of white pepper
•	Juice of ½ lemon
½	teaspoon finely chopped fresh lovage
2	tablespoons chopped fresh parsley
3	tablespoons sliced green onion tops
½	cup heavy cream

Serves 4

Chilled Fillets of Mackerel with Cider and Aromatic Herbs

This recipe makes an excellent, cheap and simple first course. I think it is better than the similar dish, soused (pickled) mackerel. Unlike soused mackerel, which is cooked for far too long, the mackerel fillets are poached briefly in a sharp court bouillon then allowed to cool. It is at its best the day after it is made, so you need to plan in advance to make the most of this dish. For decoration, groove the whole carrot with an apple corer before slicing it for the court bouillon.

Bring all the ingredients, except the mackerel, to a boil in a pan, then simmer for 30 minutes.

Place the fish, skin-side up, in a shallow pan. Pour over the hot court bouillon and bring back to a boil. When it has bubbled once, remove it from the heat and leave to cool before chilling overnight. Remove the fillets from the court bouillon and serve on individual plates. Garnish with the sliced carrot and onions, and a few spoonfuls of sieved court bouillon.

Serves 4

2½	cups hard cider
1	carrot, thinly sliced
3	shallots, thinly sliced
½	teaspoon black peppercorns
1	fresh thyme sprig
1	bay leaf
1	fresh fennel sprig
1	fresh lovage sprig or celery tops (optional)
½	teaspoon pickling spices
1	teaspoon salt
4	large mackerel fillets or 8 small ones

Hot Mackerel Salad with Lettuce, Lemongrass and Cilantro

You really should try this recipe from Laos in Southeast Asia. The traditional way to eat the grilled fish and dressing is with a pile of whole lettuce leaves. The fillet is removed from the mackerel, laid on a lettuce leaf, and some of the dressing is poured over. Cilantro is sprinkled on top and the whole thing is wrapped up and eaten like a pancake.

Guests at the restaurant resisted eating it like this, so the whole fish is now served on the salad and the dressing is poured over the top. Eat it whichever way you like, but if you decide to use the "lettuce pancakes," peel off whole leaves rather than slicing them.

Slash the fish diagonally three times on each side, cutting right through to the bone. Brush with oil and season with salt and pepper. Broil the mackerel for 4 minutes on each side. Check to see if they are cooked by lifting up the gill covers. If there is no trace of pink left, then they are done.

Meanwhile, put the fish sauce, water, chili, lemongrass, lime and sugar in a small pan. Warm the dressing →

4	mackerel (small for a first course, large for a main course)
•	Vegetable oil, for brushing
•	Salt and freshly ground black pepper
	For the Dressing
2	tablespoons Thai fish sauce (*nam pla*)
⅔	cup water
1	green chili, seeded and finely chopped →

through (don't boil) over a moderate heat. Add the chopped cilantro just before taking the pan off the heat.

If serving the mackerel whole with the salad, divide the sliced lettuce among four plates and place the mackerel on top. Pour over the dressing and sprinkle with the cilantro leaves.

If serving lettuce pancakes, serve the fish, sauce, whole cilantro leaves and a pile of lettuce leaves separately.

Serves 4

- 1 lemongrass stalk, thinly sliced
- · Juice and finely sliced zest of 1 lime
- · 1/2 teaspoon sugar

For the Salad
- 1 tablespoon roughly chopped fresh cilantro and about 20 leaves
- 1/2 iceberg lettuce, thinly sliced, or 1 whole lettuce for "lettuce pancakes"

Mackerel Escabèche

This is a pleasant way of serving mackerel cold, as an hors d'oeuvre. The mackerel is fried in olive oil, then marinated with olive oil, wine vinegar, vegetables and herbs.

I made this dish one morning when Sandi Toksvig and John McCarthy arrived in Padstow by boat while making Island Race, a television series about their voyage around the coast of Britain. They had bought a string of mackerel in a shop on the quay. I knew I was going to be asked to cook some fish but I didn't know what. They asked me to do something quickly, so I filleted and fried the fish, sliced and cooked the vegetables and finished the dish all in, as they say in television, "real time." It took about 8 minutes.

Either ask your fishmonger to fillet the mackerel for you or see p. 21 for instructions on filleting it yourself.

Heat half the oil in a large frying pan, dust the mackerel fillets with the seasoned flour, shake off any excess, then fry the fillets on both sides until golden brown. Transfer to a shallow dish, which is just large enough to take the fillets side by side.

Pour the rest of the olive oil into the frying pan and fry the carrot, onion and garlic until they begin to color. Add the wine vinegar, water, herbs and seasoning. Simmer until the vegetables are cooked, then pour over the fish and leave to cool before serving.

Serves 4

- 2 mackerel, 8–10 ounces each
- 3/4 cup olive oil
- · Seasoned all-purpose flour for dusting
- 1/2 cup thinly sliced carrot
- 2/3 cup thinly sliced onion
- 2 garlic cloves, sliced
- 4 tablespoons wine vinegar
- 4 tablespoons water
- 1 bay leaf
- 1 teaspoon chopped fresh thyme
- · Salt and freshly ground black pepper

Mackerel Recheado

In this recipe from Goa in India, the head and bones are removed from a plump mackerel and the fish is stuffed with a "masala" made with ginger, tamarind and chili.

Traditionally the masala is made in a mortar, and if you have one, it is the easiest way to make this paste where dry and moist ingredients have to be ground together. If you don't have one, grind the dry ingredients in a spice mill or, in a pinch, a very clean coffee grinder, and then combine with the chilies, garlic, tamarind, ginger and vinegar in a blender. You can add a little water to the blender to assist in the blending required, but remember you need to end up with a paste not a liquid. The fish is panfried but the cooking is finished off in the oven. In Goa they serve the fish with freshly made naan bread, which is so wonderful that you begin to think you could live forever after all!

For the masala paste, grind together the cumin seeds, coriander seeds, peppercorns, cloves, turmeric, salt and sugar in a mortar, spice mill or very clean coffee grinder. If using a pestle and mortar, add the chilies, garlic, tamarind, ginger and wine vinegar and pound to a paste. Otherwise, combine the dry and wet ingredients in a blender using a little water to loosen the paste but not turn it to liquid.

Remove the backbone from the mackerel following the instructions on p. 21.

Preheat the oven to its highest setting. Apply a generous layer of masala paste to the insides of the fish. Reassemble the fish and tie each one in two places with string to secure. Dust the fish with the seasoned flour and shake off any excess. Heat the oil in a roasting pan and fry the fish on one side until deep brown. Turn the fish and cook in the oven for about 8 minutes. Serve the fish tied, snipping the string at the last moment. The *Kachumber Salad* (see p. 53) and naan bread make good accompaniments.

Serves 4

4	large mackerel, 10–12 ounces each
•	Seasoned all-purpose flour for dusting
•	Peanut or vegetable oil for frying

For the Masala Paste

½	teaspoon cumin seeds
2	teaspoons coriander seeds
1	teaspoon black peppercorns
½	teaspoon whole cloves
¼	teaspoon ground turmeric
½	teaspoon salt
½	teaspoon sugar
5	red chilies
3	garlic cloves
•	A walnut-sized piece of tamarind, seeded
•	2-inch piece fresh ginger
2	tablespoons red wine vinegar

Fillets of Mackerel with Dill and New Potatoes

This is one of my favorite dishes for early summer when I catch some mackerel, come back from sea, go straight into the kitchen and fillet them while they are still stiff. I don't even bother to wash them, just dust them with seasoned flour, fry them with a bit of oil and butter and sprinkle them with chopped fresh dill from my garden. I usually eat them with freshly dug new potatoes, boiled with dill, and served with lemon wedges. With a bottle of dry white wine to wash it all down, it's pure pleasure.

Either ask your fishmonger to fillet the mackerel for you or see p. 21 for instructions on filleting it yourself.

Boil the new potatoes in a pan of well-salted water with the dill stems.

Dust the fillets in the seasoned flour and shake off any excess. Heat the oil in a frying pan and add a knob of the butter. Fry the mackerel for 3 minutes on each side, then remove from the pan and keep warm. Pour away the fish-frying oil and butter. Add the rest of the butter to the pan and heat it until it smells nutty. Squeeze the juice of half the lemon into the pan, then pour over the fillets. Season the mackerel with salt, sprinkle over the dill and serve with the remaining half of the lemon cut into wedges.

- 4 mackerel, 6–8 ounces each
- 1 pound new potatoes
- 1 small bunch fresh dill, chopped, stems reserved
- 1/3 cup seasoned all-purpose flour
- 2 tablespoons vegetable oil
- 2 tablespoons unsalted butter
- 1 lemon
- • Salt

Serves 4

Salmon Marinated in Dill

The best cut of salmon for this dish known in Scandinavia as gravlax is the middle of the fish. Ask your fishmonger to cut the salmon in half lengthwise and remove the bones. Wash and scale it before beginning the marinating (see p. 20).

Place half the fish, skin-side down, in a shallow dish. Roughly chop the dill and mix it with the salt, sugar and crushed peppercorns. Cover the salmon with this dry cure and place the other piece of salmon on top, skin-side up. Cover the fish with aluminum foil or plastic wrap and place a plate, slightly bigger than the salmon, on top. Place a weight on top of the plate to press the fish down. Refrigerate for two days, turning the fish about every 12 hours and spooning over the liquid from the salmon. Remember to replace the weight each time.

Remove the salmon from the brine and slice it thinly, like smoked salmon. You can scrape off the dill coating if you like, but I think it looks rather nice to have a green line of dill on each slice. Serve with the *Horseradish and Mustard Sauce* (see opposite).

- 2½ pounds salmon
- 1 large bunch fresh dill
- ½ cup salt, preferably sea salt
- 6 tablespoons sugar
- 2 tablespoons white peppercorns, crushed

Serves 6

Salmon Steaks with Muscadet, Watercress and Dill Potatoes

In this recipe salmon steaks are fried briefly on both sides in clarified butter and then cooked in the oven until still slightly underdone. A sauce is made from the pan juices.

Cut the potatoes into long, triangular finger-length pieces. Place in a pan with the dill (keeping back a few sprigs to garnish) and simmer gently in salted water.

Preheat the oven to 400°F. Clarify 2 tablespoons of the butter by melting it gently in a small pan, then leaving it for 4–5 minutes until the solids fall to the bottom. Pour the clear butter off into a frying pan. Season the salmon steaks with salt and pepper. Heat the clarified butter, add the salmon and brown on both sides. Remove the pan from the heat and leave for 30 seconds. Pour over the wine, place the pan in the oven and cook for about 5 minutes.

Remove the salmon steaks from the pan and keep warm while you make the sauce. Pour the stock into the pan, bring to a boil and add the remaining butter. Boil rapidly to reduce the volume by half, then add the parsley.

Serves 4

Arrange the salmon, watercress and the potatoes on four warmed plates. Mix together the olive oil, wine vinegar and 1/2 teaspoon salt and spoon over the watercress. Pour the sauce over the fish and serve. *Serve a crisp Muscadet or other dry white wine.*

1¹/₂	pounds potatoes
1	small bunch fresh dill
6	tablespoons unsalted butter
4	salmon steaks, about 7 ounces each
4	tablespoons Muscadet or other dry white wine
1/2	cup *Fish Stock* (see p. 36) or *Chicken Stock* (see p. 37)
1	tablespoon chopped fresh parsley
3	ounces watercress
2	tablespoons virgin olive oil
1	teaspoon white wine vinegar
•	Salt and freshly ground black pepper

Horseradish and Mustard Sauce

This is the perfect accompaniment to the Salmon Marinated in Dill *(opposite). It also goes well with smoked salmon.*

Mix together all the ingredients except the cream. Whip the cream to stiff peaks, then fold in the rest of the ingredients and chill.

2	teaspoons grated horseradish
2	teaspoons grated onion (grated on a cheese grater)
1	teaspoon Dijon mustard
1	teaspoon sugar
2	tablespoons white wine vinegar
•	A good pinch of salt
1	cup heavy cream

Salmon en Croûte

No fish cookery book would be complete without a recipe for salmon cooked in puff pastry. I have always thought that tarragon has a great affinity with salmon and so I've put a lot of it in this recipe. This is quite a rich and filling dish, so you don't need a tremendous amount of salmon per person. I've allowed just over 5 ounces.

Put 2 tablespoons of the butter in a pan, add the vegetables, half the white wine and 1 teaspoon of the tarragon. Season with the salt and white pepper. Cover and cook very gently for about 5 minutes. Remove the lid and cook for another 2 minutes, gently driving off the moisture. Remove from the heat and leave to go cool.

Preheat the oven to 450°F. Roll out the puff pastry about ⅛ inch thick. It should be the same shape and larger than your fillet of salmon so it can contain both the fish and vegetables. Trim the edges to neaten. Place half the cooked vegetables in the center of one-half of the pastry so that it covers an area the same size as the salmon. Lay the salmon on top, season and top with the remaining vegetables.

Brush the edges with some of the beaten egg and chill for 30 minutes. Lift up the other half of the pastry and fold it over the salmon and vegetables and pinch the two edges together to seal. Seal the two ends in the same way.

Place on a lightly greased baking sheet and brush liberally with the beaten egg. You can decorate the top of the parcel with leaves cut from the leftover pastry and brush these with the egg. Bake for 20 minutes. Remove from the oven and leave to rest for at least 5 minutes before serving.

Serves 6

Meanwhile, make the sauce. Put the fish stock, the rest of the white wine, the cream and 2 tablespoons of the butter into a pan and boil to reduce it in volume by two-thirds. Make sure the sauce does not boil over when you begin the reduction. About 30 seconds before finishing the sauce, add the remaining tarragon, the lemon juice and a pinch of salt. Finally, cut the remaining butter into cubes and whisk into the sauce.

Slice the salmon at the table and serve the sauce separately.

A rich Chardonnay would go well with this.

½	cup unsalted butter
1	carrot, cut into matchsticks
1	leek, cut into matchsticks
⅔	cup thinly sliced fresh button mushrooms
4	tablespoons white wine
2	teaspoons roughly chopped fresh tarragon
1	teaspoon salt
•	Freshly ground white pepper
1½	pounds puff pastry, preferably made with butter
2	pounds salmon fillet, skinned
1	egg, beaten
2½	cups *Fish Stock* (see p. 36)
¾	cup heavy cream
•	Juice of ¼ lemon

Escalopes of Salmon with a Sorrel Sauce

The thin escalopes of salmon are cooked so quickly that they are almost raw inside. I find salmon and salmon trout, which you can use equally well in this recipe, disappointing when cooked right through, as they become dry.

Remove any bones from the fillet with tweezers, long-nosed pliers or by trapping them between the point of a small vegetable knife and your thumb.

With a sharp filleting knife or carving knife, cut the salmon into 12 slices about ¼ inch thick. Cut on the slant down to the skin, angling your knife at about 45 degrees to get wider slices. Brush a broiler pan with oil and arrange the salmon on it. Brush lightly with oil and season with a little salt.

Preheat the broiler and put four large plates in the oven to warm. Place the fish stock, half the cream and the vermouth in a pan and boil rapidly to reduce by three-quarters. Meanwhile, slice the sorrel leaves very thinly. When the fish stock has reduced, add the rest of the cream, the butter and the lemon juice. Reduce a little more, then stir in all but a pinch of the sorrel.

Serves 4

Broil the escalopes for about 1 minute. Pour the sauce over the warm plates. Carefully lift the escalopes from the broiler pan with a spatula and lay them on the plates, slightly overlapping. Sprinkle over a little sorrel and serve.

A slightly off-dry white wine is excellent with this, such as good Sauvignon or Chenin Blanc.

1½	pounds salmon fillet, from a good-sized salmon
2	tablespoons peanut oil
2½	cups *Fish Stock* (see p. 36)
¾	cup heavy cream
4	tablespoons dry vermouth
1	cup sorrel leaves
6	tablespoons unsalted butter
•	Juice of ¼ lemon
•	Salt

Smoked Salmon with Scrambled Eggs

Smoked salmon with scrambled eggs is for the sort of breakfast at which you will also be drinking champagne with one of those euphoric hangovers after an evening that was quite special. On reflection, you'd better get somebody else to make it!

Toast the brown bread slices, spread thinly with butter and then cut off the crusts. Now cut each piece of buttered toast into six triangles by cutting off each corner of the square midway between one corner and the next. Cut the small square of toast that remains in half. (Eating the scrambled egg is much easier when it's resting on neatly cut small pieces of toast.)

Break the eggs into a bowl and whisk together with the salt and pepper. Melt the butter in a pan and add the eggs. Stir with a wooden spoon, scraping the cooked egg away from the bottom of the pan all the time until the degree of firmness that you like is achieved; I prefer the eggs to be a little runny.

Remove the pan from the heat and stir in the cream. Fold the smoked salmon into the scrambled eggs and serve on the buttered toast.

4	thin slices brown bread
1/2	cup unsalted butter
12	eggs
1/2	teaspoon salt
•	Freshly ground black pepper
2	tablespoons heavy cream
4	ounces thinly sliced smoked salmon

⦚ **Serves 4**

Panfried Trout with Garlic and Bacon

This is one of the straight-out-of-the-river-into-the-pan recipes that reminds me of a passage from Mark Twain's Tom Sawyer:

They fried the fish with bacon and were astonished; for no fish had ever seemed so delicious before. They did not know that the quicker a fresh fish is on the fire after he is caught, the better he is.

Gut and scale the fish (see p. 20). Season inside and out, then dust with flour shaking off any excess. Melt the butter with the oil in a frying pan. Add the bacon and then the trout and fry for about 5 minutes on each side. Remove the trout and bacon from the pan and keep warm. Turn down the heat, add the garlic and cook gently until soft. Pour the vinegar into the pan and bring to a boil. Add the chopped parsley, stir and pour over the fish. Serve immediately.

4	trout or sea trout (steelhead), about 8 ounces each
•	All-purpose flour, for dusting
•	Small knob of butter
2	tablespoons vegetable oil
6	slices bacon, cut into thin strips
4	garlic cloves, chopped
2	tablespoons *Shallot Vinegar* (see p. 53)
1	teaspoon finely chopped fresh parsley
•	Salt and freshly ground black pepper

⦚ **Serves 4**

Poached Sea Trout with Mayonnaise, New Potatoes and Cucumber Salad

The fish in this recipe should be served warm, not hot.

Place all the court bouillon ingredients in a fish poacher and bring to a boil. (See p. 35 for alternative ways of cooking if you don't have a fish poacher.) Simmer for 10 minutes. Add the fish, bring back to a boil and simmer very gently for 5 minutes. Remove the fish poacher from the heat and set aside to cool for about 20 minutes.

Boil the new potatoes with 1 sprig of mint in salted water until soft. Drain and keep warm.

Peel the cucumber and slice it as thinly as possible, preferably with a mandoline (see p. 35). Chop the leaves of the remaining mint sprigs and mix them together with the sliced cucumber and white wine vinegar.

Serves 4

Remove the fish from the fish poacher and serve with a bowl of new potatoes, the mayonnaise and the cucumber salad.

Serve with a Chardonnay.

1	sea trout (steelhead), about 3½ pounds
1½	pounds new potatoes, preferably freshly dug
3	fresh mint sprigs
1	cucumber
1	tablespoon white wine vinegar
1	quantity *Olive Oil Mayonnaise* (see p. 43)

For the Court Bouillon

½	lemon, thinly sliced
2	bay leaves
3½	quarts water
⅔	cup white wine vinegar
1	carrot, thinly sliced
1	onion, thinly sliced
12	black peppercorns
5	tablespoons salt

Seared Smoked Sea Trout with Chive Dressing

Smoked sea trout is cured in the same way as salmon: brined and then smoke-cured without heating. There is no need to cook the fillet through; it should be seared on the outside and just warm in the center. Use a ribbed grill pan to get the sear marks. You can also use smoked salmon for this dish.

Finely slice all but 4 chives. Mix the chives and shallot with the oil, vinegar and salt.

Heat the ribbed pan until smoking hot. Brush the fillets with olive oil and cook on each side for 30–60 seconds, depending on thickness. The center should be just lukewarm.

Serves 4

Divide the dressing among four warmed plates and lay the fillets on top. Drape a chive over each fillet and serve.

1	small bunch fresh chives
1	small shallot, finely chopped
6	tablespoons extra-virgin olive oil
1	tablespoon white wine vinegar
½	teaspoon salt
•	12–16-ounce piece smoked sea trout (steelhead), skinned and cut into 4 pieces

(ABOVE) Escalopes of Salmon with a
Sorrel Sauce (*see page 95*),
(TOP RIGHT) Marinated Sea Trout with
Lime and Pink Peppercorns
(*see page 100*), and (RIGHT) Salmon
Marinated in Dill (*see page 92*)

Braised Fillet of Sea Trout with Basil, Celeriac and Chambéry

Any dry white vermouth will do for this recipe if you can't get hold of Chambéry.

Melt the butter in a heavy pan, big enough for the fillets to be cooked side by side without overlapping too much. Add the celeriac and onion and soften for 2 minutes. Add the vermouth and half the chicken stock and simmer gently, covered, for about 10 minutes, then remove the lid.

Season the fillets with the salt and white pepper and place them in the pan on top of the vegetables. Pour in the rest of the stock and sprinkle all but a final pinch of the basil over the top of the fish. Cover and braise very gently until the fish has just cooked.

Remove the fillets from the pan and keep warm on a serving dish. Concentrate the flavor of the braised vegetables by turning the heat to high and boiling

rapidly to reduce the volume by about half. Pour the contents of the pan around the fillets and garnish with the remaining basil.

Accompany with some fine beans and boiled potatoes.

The best wine to accompany this rich and slightly sweet dish is a full-flavored Chardonnay.

½	cup unsalted butter
1¼	cups matchstick-cut celeriac
½	medium onion, finely chopped
½	cup dry white vermouth
2½	cups *Chicken Stock* (see p. 37)
4	sea trout (steelhead) fillets, about 7 ounces each
6	fresh basil leaves, thinly sliced
·	Salt and freshly ground white pepper

Serves 4

Marinated Sea Trout with Lime and Pink Peppercorns

This is a wonderful way of serving steelhead trout. Pink peppercorns are available nowadays in good delicatessens.

Place the fillet, skin-side down, on a chopping board, take a very sharp, thin-bladed knife and cut thin slices on the diagonal toward the tail. Cut enough to cover four dinner plates. Flatten the fish by pressing a second plate briefly down onto the slices. Allow plenty of time to slice the fish as it is quite tricky.

Mix together all the dressing ingredients in a bowl or shake together in a screw-top jar. Five minutes before serving, pour the dressing over the fish, spreading it with the back of a teaspoon. Serve immediately.

8 ounces sea trout (steelhead) fillet

For the Dressing

½	cup peanut oil
1	tablespoon finely chopped fresh ginger
1	teaspoon pink peppercorns
·	Juice and grated zest of 1 lime
½	teaspoon salt

Serves 4

Deviled Smelt with Ravigote Sauce

In this dish of powerful flavors, smelt are brushed with mustard and coated with the bread crumbs, then grilled. You can make this dish with sardines, too.

Preheat the broiler. Brush the smelt with some of the mustard. Mix together the rest of the mustard, sugar, bread crumbs, cayenne pepper and salt in a wide, flat dish. Roll the smelt in the coating, dab with vegetable oil and place on a broiler pan. Grill for about 2 minutes on each side. Mix together all the ingredients for the sauce. Serve with the fish accompanied with boiled potatoes.

Serves 4

3 tablespoons Dijon mustard
1 teaspoon dark soft brown sugar
1½ cups fresh bread crumbs
¼ teaspoon cayenne pepper
½ teaspoon salt
16 whole, gutted smelt (sprats)
• Vegetable oil for brushing

For the Ravigote Sauce
2 teaspoons Dijon mustard
1 tablespoon red wine vinegar
³/4 cup peanut oil
1 tablespoon capers, coarsely chopped
2 fresh tarragon sprigs, finely chopped
1 tablespoon finely chopped fresh flat-leaf parsley
1 tablespoon finely chopped onion
• Salt and freshly ground black pepper

Deep-fried Whitebait with Lemon and Persillade

The action of chopping parsley with garlic to make persillade *actually removes a lot of the hot taste of the garlic. The chlorophyll in the parsley neutralizes the powerful aroma in garlic, which is why chewing parsley is good for getting rid of garlic on the breath.* Persillade *gives a very pleasant savory herb taste that I use a great deal in my cooking.*

Peel the garlic and chop fairly finely. Remove the stems from the parsley. Continue to chop the garlic, gradually chopping the parsley leaves and incorporating with the garlic until you have a very fine mixture.

Put the flour, cayenne pepper and salt into a bowl and mix together. Wash the whitebait under cold running water and shake them out vigorously in a colander.

Heat the oil to 375°F. Coat the whitebait with the seasoned flour, shaking off any excess. Deep-fry the fish in

batches until they are crisp (about 3 minutes per batch). Remove from the fryer and drain on paper towels. Place in a large bowl and sprinkle with the *persillade*. Serve with lemon wedges.

2 garlic cloves
1 small bunch fresh parsley
²/3 cup all-purpose flour
½ teaspoon cayenne pepper
1 teaspoon salt
1¼ pounds whitebait
• Oil for deep-frying
1 lemon, cut into wedges

Serves 4

6 Mediterranean Fish

BREAM, SEAROBIN

3IN MULLET AND SEA BASS

This chapter is devoted to those fish that are neither oily nor non-oily. But another way of grouping them is to consider them as the sort of fish you might cook on a barbecue or with Mediterranean ingredients like olive oil, garlic, aromatic herbs, olives and anchovies.

BREAM

You can usually expect to find two types of bream in the waters around the British Isles: red bream or black. Occasionally, you will find the gilt-head bream or the ray's bream on sale, too. Red snapper and John Dory are good substitutes for the European bream.

GURNARD (SEAROBIN)

Most fish is expensive if you consider the actual price per pound of fillet. So it is a great pleasure to find a fish of real quality that costs very little. But like travel writers who extol the virtues of some hitherto unknown paradise only to have it overrun, so I have a slight feeling of regret in telling you how wonderful gurnard is, as it will inevitably push the price up. But it is good; the fillets are firm and sweet. So if you see one on a fishmonger's slab, go ahead and buy it. Not only is the fillet exceptional but the bones add an essential taste to Mediterranean fish soup.

MULLET

People often ask me "What is your favorite fish?" Well it's a bit like being asked "Which is your favorite child?" The obvious answer to both questions is "I love them all." But mullet has a special place in my affections, with its beautiful pink and yellow tinges and its firm flaky texture and taste somewhere between fish and shellfish. The smell of mullet cooking on a grill evokes memories of Greek tavernas at the beginning of the season, before the crowds have arrived.

Red mullet, or goatfish, is a fairly common fish in the Southwest of England, particularly in October and November when they are caught off the north Cornish coast. I don't know why it is, but I have a real problem selling goatfish at the restaurant. Maybe it is because people have bought it in other restaurants and found it inferior. There is quite a trade in indifferent frozen red mullet, but all I know is that I have to work extremely hard to persuade people to eat them by saying things like "this utterly delicious fish" beside the description of the dish. To me it is incredibly good, full of flavor and aroma. The only problem with red mullet, though, is that in the Southwest of England it is usually only caught as a by-product of trawling for other fish; this means that only one or two will turn up in the nets at a time.

SEA BASS

It is generally true that mature, fully grown fish taste better than immature undersized fish, and this is particularly so with bass. A fillet from a large fish brushed with butter, seasoned with salt and pepper and roasted in the oven with maybe a simple *beurre blanc* or hollandaise will be a revelation if you have never tried it before.

However, bass, even in its small form, is a delicious fish that easily justifies its high price. Soft in texture with a sweet delicate flavor, it never fails to delight people, particularly when it's cooked in a way that crisps up the skin.

The flesh of sea bass is moist and fresh with a soft texture that is slightly flaky. The skin, however, is quite oily and indeed bass is richer in oil than might be expected of a fish often described as delicate. But because of the balance between richness and delicacy, bass is a fish capable of being successfully cooked in a myriad of different ways.

What you're liable to see mostly in fish markets these days is rather small bass because they are being successfully farmed.

No doubt, in time, fish farmers will grow their bass to much larger sizes. But at present, they're all coming out at about 1¼ pounds. The quality of these farmed fish is perfectly acceptable, though I still have mixed feelings about fish farming. There is no doubt, if we wish to continue to be able to buy fish like bass, salmon and, probably, turbot, which is also being farmed, we will have to supplement the supply of wild fish with farmed. However, the wild fish will always taste better.

I never serve farmed fish at the restaurant because I feel that my reputation relies on serving seafood straight from the sea, but it is perfectly acceptable at home.

Baked Red Snapper and Fennel with Orange and Provençal Herbs

In this dish, fennel and onions are cooked with olive oil, orange and herbs until soft. The fish is then baked with the fennel. The baking times are for fish weighing about 18 ounces each. If using bigger ones, bake for a little longer. This dish also works very well with parrot fish, goatfish, mullet and sea bass. Accompany with Grilled Vegetables (see p. 104). If making fresh herbes de Provence combine chopped thyme, fennel, savory, sage, hyssop and marjoram.

Pare the zest from half the orange with a potato peeler and cut into short, thin strips, like pine needles. Juice the orange. Put all the ingredients except the fish in a heavy-bottomed pan and cook gently, covered, for about 15 minutes or until the fennel is soft.

Preheat the oven to 400°F. Remove any scales from the fish, then wash and dry thoroughly. Slash the fish three times diagonally on both sides cutting right down to the bone. Season generously with salt and pepper both inside and out.

Place half the fennel and onion mixture in the bottom of a shallow baking dish, place the fish on top and spoon the rest of the fennel and onion over it. Cover with foil and bake for 20 minutes.

Serves 4

Remove the foil covering the fish and bake for a further 5 minutes.

1	teaspoon dried or 1 tablespoon fresh *herbes de Provence*
1	orange
3	anchovy fillets, chopped
2	tablespoons Pernod or Ricard
3	bulbs fennel, outer leaves removed
1	teaspoon salt
1	large onion, chopped
2	fresh bay leaves, cut into thin strips, or 2 dried bay leaves, crushed
3	garlic cloves, thinly sliced
2	tablespoons white wine vinegar
4	tablespoons olive oil
1	teaspoon sugar
4	whole red snapper, about 4½ pounds total
•	Salt and freshly ground black pepper

Grilled Vegetables

Preheat the broiler or ready the charcoal grill.

Put all the ingredients in a bowl and stir to coat evenly with the oil, marjoram and seasoning. Broil or grill the vegetables until cooked through.

1 eggplant, sliced
2 zucchini, sliced
2 red onions, cut into quarters lengthwise
1 bulb fennel, sliced lengthwise
2 red bell peppers, cut into 8 pieces
2 tablespoons olive oil
• A pinch of marjoram
• Salt and freshly ground black pepper

Poached Quenelles of Searobin with Shrimp Sauce

Gurnard makes a good quenelle *because of its firm texture and positive flavor.* Quenelles *are a kind of fish forcemeat, molded in dessert spoons and poached in water. Here, they are served with a shrimp sauce. Reserve a few shrimp removed from making the sauce to garnish.*

To make the *quenelles*, melt the butter and add to the milk and bread crumbs to form a coarse paste; chill. All the ingredients for the *quenelles* must be completely cold. Place the paste and all the ingredients except the cream in a food processor and blend until smooth. With the processor still running, pour in the cream taking no more than 10 seconds to add it.

To make the shrimp sauce, heat the *Shellfish Reduction,* then stir in half of the heavy cream and all of the *beurre manié.* Leave the sauce to thicken, then remove from the heat, set aside and keep warm.

Fill a shallow pan of lightly salted water deep enough to immerse the *quenelles* (about 2 inches). Bring to a boil, then reduce the heat until the water reaches a slow simmer.

Mold all the fish forcemeat into lozenge-shaped quenelles using 2 tablespoons or teaspoons. Dip the spoons in a jug of hot water between making each quenelle to make it easier to achieve a smooth shape. As you form each quenelle, drop it into the lightly simmering water. Leave to poach for about 5 minutes.→

For the Quenelles
2 tablespoons butter
2/3 cup milk
1 cup fresh white bread crumbs
12 ounces searobin (gurnard) or sea bass, skinned and boned
1/8 teaspoon ground nutmeg
• Juice of 1/4 lemon
1 egg
1/2 cup heavy cream
• Freshly ground white pepper
1 teaspoon salt

For the Shrimp Sauce
1 quantity *Shellfish Reduction* made with shrimp (see p. 37)
6 tablespoons heavy cream
1 teaspoon unsalted butter mixed with all-purpose flour (*beurre manié*)
1 egg yolk

Remove from the water with a slotted spoon and dry on a clean tea towel or paper towel. This will prevent the excess water from weakening the sauce. Place the *quenelles* in a warm gratin dish. Preheat the broiler.

Whisk together the egg yolk and the remaining cream and add to the sauce. Reheat the sauce over low heat without boiling, then pour over the *quenelles*. Place the dish under the broiler to glaze until the surface starts to turn brown. Serve piping hot.

Serves 4

Searobin with Bouillabaisse Sauce and Harissa Potatoes

I have taken the flavors of the classic bouillabaisse—saffron, garlic, olive oil and herbes de Provence—*and reduced them to a sauce. It is served with grilled fish fillets and boiled potatoes tossed in fiery* harissa, *a Moroccan blend of chili and coriander.*

Heat the oil in a pan and add the leek, fennel, garlic, onion, orange zest, saffron and cayenne pepper. Fry for 2–3 minutes to soften, then add the stock, white wine and tomato. Bring to a boil and boil rapidly to reduce the volume by three-quarters.

Cut the salt cod into tiny squares (about 1/8 inch). Add to the reduced stock and vegetables and simmer for another couple of minutes. Set the sauce aside and keep warm.

Peel the potato and cut it into pieces the size of matchsticks. Poach in salted water until just cooked. Drain thoroughly and mix with the *harissa.* Set aside and keep warm.

Preheat the broiler. Brush the fish fillets with olive oil and sprinkle with salt and peppercorns. Broil, skin-side up, for 4–5 minutes. Place the fillets on four warmed plates. Place a pile of potatoes on each plate and pour the sauce beside each fillet.

Serve with a good robust white or rosé wine.

Serves 4

4	tablespoons olive oil
1/2	cup finely chopped white of leek
1/2	cup finely chopped fennel
3	garlic cloves, finely chopped
1/2	cup finely chopped onion
1	strip of orange zest
•	A good pinch of saffron
•	A pinch of cayenne pepper
2 1/2	cups *Fish Stock* (see p. 36)
4	tablespoons dry white wine
1	tomato, chopped
2	ounces *Salt Cod* fillet, skinned and boned (see p. 54)
1	small potato, almost 4 ounces
1	tablespoon *Harissa* (see p. 45)
2	pounds searobin (gurnard) or sea bass fillets, skin on
1	teaspoon green peppercorns, roughly chopped
•	Salt

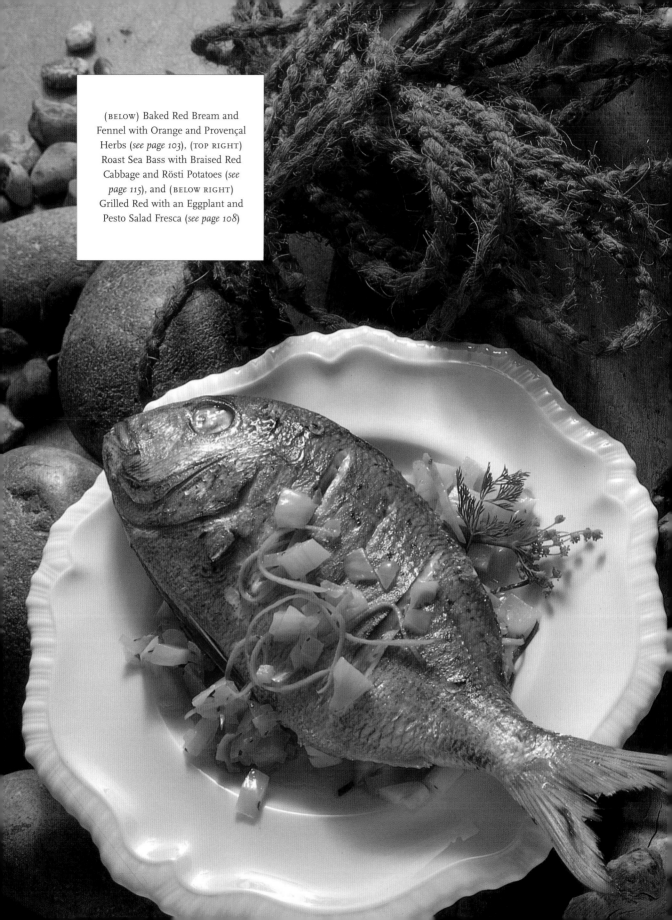

(BELOW) Baked Red Bream and Fennel with Orange and Provençal Herbs (*see page 103*), (TOP RIGHT) Roast Sea Bass with Braised Red Cabbage and Rösti Potatoes (*see page 115*), and (BELOW RIGHT) Grilled Red with an Eggplant and Pesto Salad Fresca (*see page 108*)

Broiled Goatfish with an Eggplant and Pesto Salad

What could be better than fish fillets with some grilled eggplant, pesto and salad? A perfect combination of flavors. This dish has its roots in the cooking of Simon Hopkinson, who used to be the chef at Bibendum restaurant in London. I'd rate him as about the best cook in the country.

Put all the pesto ingredients in a blender, blend for about 10 seconds, then remove half the mixture and set aside; it should be fairly coarse at this stage. Blend the remaining pesto until it is smooth.

Preheat the broiler. Cut the eggplant into 4 slices each ½ inch thick. Brush liberally with olive oil and season with salt. Broil until just cooked through.

Brush the fish fillets with olive oil and season with salt and pepper. Grill for about 4 minutes, 2 minutes on each side.

Meanwhile, spread the eggplant slices with the coarse pesto and place under the broiler until the pesto has warmed through. Place an eggplant slice on each of four warmed plates and arrange the fish alongside them.

Toss the salad greens with the tomato, olive oil and salt and put a small pile on each plate. Pour the smooth pesto around each plate, making sure that some, but not all, trickles over the fillets, and serve.

Serves 4

½ eggplant
· Olive oil for brushing
4 goatfish (red mullet) or bass fillets, 3–4 ounces each

For the Pesto
½ cup fresh basil leaves
2 large garlic cloves
¾ cup olive oil
2 tablespoons freshly grated Parmesan cheese
2 tablespoons pine nuts

For the Salad
3 ounces mixed salad greens
1 tomato, peeled, seeded and chopped
1 teaspoon *Lemon Olive Oil* (see p. 51)
· Salt and freshly ground black pepper

Deep-fried Goatfish with Lemongrass, Chili, Garlic and Ginger

This dish is quite spicy and hot. The flavors are inspired by Thai cooking, making this a wonderfully aromatic way to cook fish. If you would prefer the dish to be a little less hot, remove the seeds from the chilies before chopping them.

Serve with the Stir-fried Spinach with Garlic, Ginger and Chili *on p. 112.*

To make the marinade, mix the arrowroot with the water in a small pan. Place over moderate heat and bring to a boil until clear and thick. Remove from the heat and leave to cool before mixing with the rest of the marinade ingredients.

Heat the oil in a deep-fryer or large pan to 350°F.

Scale and gut the fish and snip off the fins. Cut three 1-inch pockets in each side of the fish. Insert ½ teaspoon of the marinade into each pocket and the gut cavity of the fish. Dip the fish in the batter and deep-fry in the hot oil for about 5 minutes. Remove and drain on paper towels. Place the fish on a serving dish and sprinkle over the rest of the marinade.

Serve the fish with the stir-fried spinach (see following recipe) and boiled rice, preferably jasmine, which you can buy in most supermarkets now.

Serve with a Chardonnay, Gewürztraminer or beer.

Serves 4

- Oil, for deep-frying
- 4 goatfish (red mullet), 10–12 ounces each
- 1 quantity *Tempura Batter* (see p. 53)

For the Marinade
- 2 teaspoons arrowroot or cornstarch
- ½ cup water
- 2 lemongrass stalks, outer leaves removed, finely sliced
- 3 small red chilies, finely chopped
- 4 cloves garlic, finely chopped
- 2-inch piece fresh ginger, peeled and finely chopped
- Juice and zest of 1 lime
- 3 tablespoons Thai fish sauce (*nam pla*)
- ½ cup fresh cilantro leaves, roughly chopped

(ABOVE) Deep-fried Red Mullet with Lemon Grass, Chili, Garlic and Ginger (*see page 109*), (TOP RIGHT) Grilled Sea Bass with Straw Potatoes and Salsa Verde (*see page 116*), and (RIGHT) Grilled Sea Basee with Beurre Blanc and Marsh Samphire (*see page 108*)

Stir-fried Spinach with Garlic, Ginger and Chili

If you are lucky enough to be able to get fresh water spinach, known also as ong choy or kankong, from a Chinese or Thai supermarket, it is even better than the spinach.

Heat the oil in a wok and add the garlic and ginger. Stir-fry quickly until they start to brown. Add the spinach and turn in the oil for about 30 seconds. Add the chili and fish sauce. Reduce the heat to low, cover and cook for about 1 minute, then serve.

Serves 4

2 tablespoons vegetable oil
1 teaspoon finely chopped garlic
1 teaspoon finely chopped fresh ginger
8 ounces spinach leaves
• A pinch of pure ground chili
1 teaspoon Thai fish sauce (*nam pla*) or anchovy paste

Broiled Mullet with Garlic, Lemon and Thyme

The mullet are slashed and marinated in olive oil, garlic and thyme. The marinade is made into a sauce with orange and anchovies.

Slash the fish three times on each side, cutting down to the bone. Place in a dish that is not much bigger than the fish itself. Mix together all the marinade ingredients and pour over the fish. Leave to marinate for 1 hour, turning occasionally.

Preheat the broiler and broil the fish for 6 minutes on each side, basting with the marinade twice on each side.

Transfer the fish to a warmed serving dish and add any cooking juices to the marinade. Pour the marinade into a small pan. Add the anchovy, grated zest of 1/2 orange and juice of the whole orange and the water. Bring to a boil, whisk a little and pour over the fish before serving.

Serves 4

4 mullet, about 12 ounces each

For the Marinade
• Juice of 1 lemon
2/3 cup olive oil
2 teaspoons very finely chopped fresh thyme
1 teaspoon sea salt
1 garlic clove, finely chopped
• Freshly ground black pepper

For the Sauce
2 anchovy fillets, drained and finely chopped
1 orange
4 tablespoons water

Steamed Mullet with Garlic, Ginger and Green Onions

I consider this to be a perfect combination of flavors; it was the first Chinese fish dish that I really raved about. See pp. 35 and 205 for details on steamers and how to make them.

During the filming of the TV series we came up with the idea of a list of five or six fish recipes that have been the most influential in forming my style of seafood cooking, a sort of Desert Island Dishes. Steamed Mullet with Garlic, Ginger and Green Onions wasn't on it because we hadn't got any mullet on the day, and with all the costs and shortage of time in filming, we had to make a decision not to do it. However, this is one of those dishes.

Sprinkle the ginger over the fish. Bring the water in the steamer up to a fast boil, put the plate in and cover. Steam the fish for 15 minutes, then transfer it to a warmed serving plate. Scatter the green onions over the fish.

Pour the juice from the plate into a small shallow pan and add the soy sauce and water. Heat and pour over the fish and green onions.

Serves 4

Heat the sesame oil in a small pan. When it is very hot, add the garlic and let it fry for 5 seconds. Pour the oil and garlic over the fish and serve.

- · 1-inch piece fresh ginger, peeled and finely chopped
- 4 mullet, about 12 ounces each
- 4 green onions, finely sliced
- 2 tablespoons soy sauce
- 4 tablespoons water
- 2 tablespoons Asian sesame oil
- 4 garlic cloves, finely chopped

Charbroiled Mullet with Slivers of Garlic, Chili and Virgin Olive Oil

This is such an amazingly simple dish that one is left wondering whether there is ever any point in doing anything more complicated with fish. It's a perfect dish for serving outside on a summer's evening. You need either a barbecue grill or a heavy-ribbed grill pan (see p. 35) to make it.

The garlic in this dish must be cut into very thin slivers so that it loses its rawness when the sauce is warmed through. The easiest way to cut it is to slice it in half, place the cut edge on the chopping board, then cut it into long, thin slices.

Brush the mullet with a little olive oil and sprinkle lightly with ordinary salt.

Soak the chili in the vinegar for 20 minutes. Drain the chili in a small sieve and discard the vinegar. The object of this is not only to make the chili less hot than it would normally be but also provide a slight tartness to the sauce. →

- 4 mullet fillets, skin on, 7–8 ounces each
- 4 tablespoons virgin olive oil
- · Salt
- 1/2 red chili, seeded and very finely chopped
- 2 tablespoons white wine vinegar
- 1 garlic clove, cut into very fine slivers
- 1 lemon, cut into wedges
- 1 teaspoon coarse sea salt

Ready the charcoal grill or preheat the ribbed grill pan to hot. Grill the fillets for 2–4 minutes on each side depending on their thickness. Cook them skin-side down first.

Meanwhile, gently warm the remaining olive oil, garlic and chopped red chili in a small pan. Do not allow the sauce to heat too close to the boiling point as this will destroy the flavor of the oil.

Serves 4

When the fish is cooked, pour the sauce onto four warmed plates. Place the fish on top with a wedge of lemon, sprinkle the sauce with the coarse sea salt and serve with a simple green salad and potatoes fried in their skins.

For the potatoes fried in their skins, wash, but don't peel, some new potatoes, then cut them into wedge shapes, lengthwise, and deep-fry until tender.

Broiled Sea Bass with Beurre Blanc and Marsh Samphire

First of all, don't put off cooking this dish if you can't get marsh samphire. Bass with beurre blanc *is a classic. The samphire has been included because it is a highly fitting vegetable to serve with fish and is especially good with sea bass.*

Marsh samphire grows on sandy mud in salt marshes and on muddy seashores all round the British Isles. It has a fresh, salty taste and a firm texture. Having unusual fleshy, light green joined branches rather than leaves and growing little more than 9 inches high, it is easy to identify, so, if you have the opportunity, try to find some to serve with the sea bass.

Snip the fins off the bass, being careful to avoid spiking yourself, then scale the fish and remove the guts. Wash inside and out and slash the flesh of the fish two or three times on each side.

Preheat the broiler. Brush the fish with some melted butter and season inside and out with salt and black pepper. Broil the bass for about 10 minutes on each side.

Wash the samphire thoroughly, then pull off the fleshy leaves and discard the thicker stalks with their woody centers. Bring a pan of unsalted water to a boil and boil the samphire for 2 minutes. Drain, set aside and keep warm.

Serves 4

Pass the *beurre blanc* through a sieve into a clean warm serving pitcher.

Serve the fish whole and fillet it at the table onto four warmed plates. Hand round the marsh samphire and *beurre blanc* separately.

- 1   sea bass, about 3 pounds
- ·   A little melted butter, for brushing
- 8   ounces fresh marsh samphire
- 1   quantity *Beurre Blanc* (see p. 42), made with fish stock
- ·   Salt and freshly ground black pepper

Roast Sea Bass with Braised Red Cabbage and Rösti Potatoes

Here, rösti pancakes are cooked with braised red cabbage sauce and a whole sea bass, which is roasted until the skin is crisp – an ideal dish for the cooler months.

Preheat the oven to 400°F.

To cook the braised red cabbage, remove the outer leaves of the red cabbage and cut out the thick white core. Slice the cabbage as thinly as possible then cut the slices into the smallest possible pieces. Place in an ovenproof dish with ¼ cup of the butter, half the stock and the remaining cabbage ingredients. Cover and place in the oven for about 1¼ hours. Stir occasionally. Remove from the oven, add the remaining stock, bring to a boil and stir in the rest of the butter. Keep warm.

To make the rösti, peel the potatoes and shred them on the largest holes of a grater onto a clean tea towel. Gather the edges of the tea towel and squeeze as much moisture out of the potatoes as you can. Don't rinse the potatoes or you will remove the starch that binds the potatoes into a pancake. Season the potato with salt and pepper and add the bacon. Divide into four portions and mold into balls with your hands.

Pour the clarified butter into a small nonstick or well-cured frying pan and add one ball of potato and bacon. Flatten it over the base of the pan to about 4 inches in diameter using a spatula. Fry over gentle heat for about 5 minutes. Work the spatula under the pancake to free it, then turn it over to cook on the other side for 5 minutes. Toward the end of the cooking time, press out then pour off the excess butter. Place the rösti on some paper towels to remove any remaining greasiness.

Serves 4

To cook the fish, preheat the oven to its highest setting. Brush the bass inside and out with the melted butter, then season inside and out with the salt and pepper. Place in a roasting pan and roast in the oven for about 25 minutes, basting a couple of times with the juices from the pan.

Place the fish on a large oval plate and pour over the juices from the pan. Serve at the table with the rösti potatoes and the braised red cabbage.

Serve with a sprightly Pinot Noir or a Merlot.

- 1   sea bass, about 3 pounds
- •   A little melted butter, for brushing
- ½   teaspoon salt
- •   Freshly ground black pepper

For the Red Cabbage
- 1   head red cabbage, about 10 ounces
- ¾   cup unsalted butter
- ⅔   cup *Fish Stock* (see p. 36) or *Chicken Stock* (see p. 37)
- 1   cup diced onion
- ⅔   cup red wine
- 2   tablespoons wine vinegar
- 1   teaspoon salt
- 1   tablespoon sugar

For the Rösti Potatoes
- 14   ounces potatoes
- 1   ounce bacon or pancetta, cut into thin strips
- ¼   cup clarified butter, for frying
- •   Salt and freshly ground black pepper

Broiled Sea Bass with Straw Potatoes and Salsa Verde

This is the sort of recipe that is very popular in restaurants in Sydney, Los Angeles and San Francisco. I have borrowed ideas from various cooking cultures, the grilled bass with the olive oil from the Mediterranean and the Kachumber Salad from India. Sometimes the result of this kind of mixing and matching leads only to pretentious rubbish. But here, the contrast of textures is very satisfying and the salad, with its chili and cilantro, seems to complement the flavor of the bass. For the best results, all the ingredients must be very fresh.

To make the straw potatoes, cut the potato into pieces the size of matchsticks. This is most easily done on a mandoline, if you have one (see p. 35). Wash in cold water.

Preheat the oil in the deep-fryer to 375°F. Fry the potatoes until crisp, then drain, season with salt and set aside. Keep warm.

Preheat the broiler. Brush the bass with olive oil and season with salt and pepper. Broil on both sides, taking care not to overcook. If cut from a small 1–2 pound fish allow about 2 minutes on each side but up to 5 minutes on each side if the fillets are thick.

Place the bass on four warmed plates and serve with *Kachumber Salad,* a tablespoon of *Salsa Verde* and a pile of the straw potatoes.

Serves 4

1½ pounds sea bass fillet, skin on, divided into 4 equal portions
- Olive oil for brushing
- Salt and freshly ground black pepper

- *Kachumber Salad* (see p. 53)
- 1 quantity *Salsa Verde* (see p. 48)

For the Straw Potatoes
6 ounces white potatoes
- Oil for deep-frying

Broiled Whole Sea Bass with Pernod and Fennel

The anise flavors of Pernod and fennel have an exceptional affinity with sea bass, especially when it is cooked over charcoal. The fennel-flavored mayonnaise that the fish is served with has a pleasing, slightly bitter alcoholic bite. When the whole fish is served in this way with some freshly dug new potatoes it makes a tremendous combination.

You can either cook the fish on a barbecue or under the broiler. If you cook the fish on a barbecue, make sure you light it at least 40 minutes before beginning to cook. It is important that all the flames have died away leaving hot ash because cooking a large fish or, indeed, a large piece of meat on a barbecue that is still flaming will result in a very burnt and charred exterior.

Ideally, the fish can be slipped into some sort of hinged grill basket. This is because the best flavor is achieved when the fennel is laid along the outside of the fish so that it chars and flavors it. If you don't have a grill basket, lay the fish on a bed of fennel sprigs directly on the grill rack.

Ready the charcoal grill. Trim and scale the bass, then slash it three times on each side, cutting down to the bone. Brush the fish liberally with olive oil both inside and out, then season with salt and pepper. Push several fennel sprigs into the gut cavity. Lay more sprigs on a grill basket and lay the fish on top, placing more on the other side of the fish before closing the basket. Grill carefully over charcoal for about 12 minutes each side, taking great care to avoid overcharring the fish. If it seems to be blistering too much, move it to a cooler part of the barbecue. Just before turning the fish to cook the second side, sprinkle it liberally with Pernod. Repeat just before taking the cooked fish off the grill.

Serve the bass with the *Fennel Mayonnaise* and a large bowl of boiled new potatoes.

The ideal wine for this magnificent dish is a full-bodied dry white or even a bottle of Greek retsina.

Serves 4

1	large sea bass, 3½–4 pounds
2	tablespoons olive oil
•	Salt and freshly ground black pepper
1	large bunch fresh fennel sprigs
2	teaspoons Pernod; pastis or Ricard
1	quantity *Fennel Mayonnaise* (see p. 44)

7

Round Fish

MONKFISH AND JOHN DORY

The great thing about members of the cod family is that they yield thick, suc-culent, relatively boneless fillets. What they lack a little in taste they more than make up for in texture, and lend themselves to baking and roasting with plen-ty of robust flavors. Like the cod family, monkfish and John Dory are both nonoily fish. Monkfish suits grilling and barbecuing very well, as does John Dory, which has the added bonus of being suitable for any flat fish recipes.

COD

It is a source of great satisfaction to me that we can now sell cod at the restaurant as easily as bass or salmon. I have always thought it a shame that such a beautiful fish was relegated as being suitable only for fish and chips (good though they are) or fishfingers. Cod doesn't have such a good flavor as other, more expensive, fish, but there are some serious compensa-tions for this. First, it has a satisfying chewy texture, second, it comes in enormous milky flakes and, third, with large cod, the bones are not a problem because they are too large and obvious to be eaten accidentally and to get stuck in your throat.

I like the occasional whole codling—a small cod weighing up to 11/2 pounds—if they have jumped straight out of the sea onto the plate, but if they are not this fresh they become dull. Fillets from large cod, cooked so that the skin is crisp and browned, are what delight me most about cod. I think the quotation on the first page of Keith Floyd's *Floyd on Fish* sums up the cod's superlative qualities.

What on earth is this?
A piece of cod sir.
The piece of cod which passeth understanding.
(Attributed to Sir Edward Lutyens, speaking to a wait-er at Brook's Club.)

A piece of perfectly fresh cod, chewy, flaky, moist and white—it's beyond description.

I was once asked by a leading supermarket chain to do a blind tasting of fish to prove how difficult it is to tell the difference between fresh and frozen fish. I, and the other tasters, sat in little booths bathed in eerie blue light and small lumps of fish on saucers were passed to us through hatches. Everything was deadly quiet, our total concentration was required. The fish had been carefully boiled in unseasoned water. By depriving us of any extraneous sensory influence (including taste, to my mind), we were expected to make a decision about the qualities of fresh over frozen fish. I was incapable of making any sensible critical judgment and concluded that all the fish tasted the same.

The judges were delighted, not only because my reac-tion was identical to everyone else's, but also because they thought it proved that frozen food is indistin-guishable from fresh. That, I say, may well be true if you choose to boil your fish.

The staff running the test were quite well-informed about fish. They told me that, on death, a fish goes through the same sort of enzyme changes as meat, only much faster, so the longer you keep fish the more tender it becomes. They actually aged cod before selling it. I remarked at the time that the piece of cod we had tried seemed to be extraordinarily soft. I was told that this was what customers wanted. Market research had shown that any suggestion of toughness in fish would not be tolerated. Interesting that what I consider to be one of the most glorious attributes of fresh cod, its delightful chewiness, is the one thing that most people apparently don't like.

HADDOCK
Faced with a fillet of haddock the heart doesn't sing.
Jane Grigson

I know why. Haddock is one of the best-flavored fish of all the cod family, but it doesn't look as exciting as cod. Cod has a gleaming steely-gray skin with flashes of yellow and green and sings loud. Haddock is a rather wan gray and black and is a bit limp looking. Don't be put off. Haddock has a sweet, soft flavor and it suits smoking better than all the other fish in the cod family.

Try and buy undyed smoked haddock because it indicates that the fish is of a higher quality. Finnan haddock has an incomparable flavor and is never dyed. But any haddock, if it comes undyed, is likely to have been well looked after.

Haddock can be easily identified because it has a black smudge, rather like a thumb print, near the head; a feature that it shares with John Dory. Both fish are said to have the thumbprint of St. Peter on them.

HAKE
Hake fetches by far the best price of all the fish in the cod family at European markets. The reason for this is that the Spanish, who buy the majority of hake caught in the British Isles, are passionate about it and ensure that, because of great demand, the price is always high. I must say I share their enthusiasm and can't understand why we in Britain don't eat more of it. Hake has a fine flavor and a soft, milky texture. It is easy to buy steaks that are ideal for anyone who has

a fear of fish bones because, like cod, the bones are large enough to be easily spotted. Like all the cod family, hake also takes well to salting.

LING
Ling is one of those underrated fish that, in addition to being reasonably flavored, is also firm in texture—a cheap version of monkfish, if you like. It is an extraordinary-looking fish that, though a member of the cod family, could easily be mistaken for an eel, so long and sinuous is it in appearance.

POLLACK
I used to think that pollack was just plain dull, it being about the least-flavored of all the cod family. But all fish have their uses and pollack, being very cheap, and coming in large bone-free fillets, is excellent for fish pies (see p. 72).

WHITING
Whiting can be a bit on the bland side, but small fresh fish brushed with butter and grilled are very good, especially if accompanied by *Noisette Butter* (see p. 50) and capers.

When I was at cookery college we used to do an excellent deep-fried dish with small whiting called *Merlan en Colère,* which means something like Whiting in a Temper. You bent the whiting round and inserted its tail into its mouth as if it were in such a state that it was trying to bite its tail off. The fish was dusted with flour, dipped in egg and bread crumbs, then deep-fried. We used to serve it with a tomato sauce like the one on p. 178.

JOHN DORY
An excellent fish, John Dory is firm-textured, well-flavored and suited to any form of cooking. The only drawback is that they are expensive and you don't get a lot for your money; only about a third of the total weight of the John Dory is edible fillet.

John Dory has a massive head, impressive fins and a fine bone structure. The fillets come away from the fish bone-free, and there are few greater pleasures than a really thick grilled fillet of John Dory. Because it's flat in appearance people tend to regard it as a flat fish but it's not. Flat fish live on the bottom of the sea, but John Dory swims like a round fish. It is rather a slow swimmer but an inability to outswim its prey is compensated by an almost invisible shape when viewed head on and an enormous mouth with which to gobble up smaller fish. With its long fins, great head and lugubrious eyes, it looks like something straight out of a nightmare!

John Dory is often named the St. Peter fish in most other European languages because they have a round black mark on their side that looks like a thumbprint, which is traditionally held to be that of St. Peter.

MONKFISH

I find monkfish an interesting phenomenon. Fifteen years ago nobody had ever heard of it. When we sold monkfish in the restaurant then, often as not we'd call it "other white fish" in some mixed fish dish. Now it is extraordinarily popular. Is this because of the lack of bones in the flesh, I wonder, and because of its texture, which has more similarity to meat than fish? It is not, in fact, particularly well-flavored, but it does have the most marvelous texture, making it one of the best fish for barbecuing. It is excellent for a raw sashimi and very thinly sliced as in the *Carpaccio of Monkfish* recipe on p. 138. The larger tails fetch more money than the smaller ones. But the smaller tails make the best eating because they are sweeter.

A very fine purple membrane covers the fillet of monkfish and if your fishmonger has not removed it, you should take as much of it off the fillet as possible or it will cause the fillet to twist rather unattractively as it cooks.

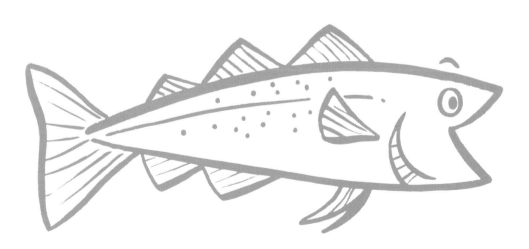

Roast Cod with Aïoli and Lima Beans

This is a hot version of the classic Provençal dish Aïoli Garni. Here, a fillet of cod is served roasted with sea salt and is accompanied by garlic mayonnaise, lima beans, eggs, fennel and a fish fumet flavored with basil.

To make the sauce, cook the mixture of carrot, leek, celery and onion in a large pan over medium-low heat with half the butter until soft. Add the cognac and let it boil, then add all the rest of the sauce ingredients, except the remaining butter and basil leaves. Simmer for 30 minutes, then pass through a fine sieve. Bring the sauce back to a boil and simmer until it has reduced to about ²/₃ cup.

Bring the lima beans to a boil in a large pan of salted water. Simmer gently until very soft. Remove from the heat and keep warm in the cooking liquid.

Place the eggs in boiling water and boil for 8 minutes. Drain, remove the shells and keep warm.

Remove the outer leaves of the fennel but don't cut off the tops. Slice into thin sections, then cook in salted water until just tender. Drain and keep warm.

Preheat the oven to 450°F. Roast the cod in the oven until just cooked through. This will take 10–15 minutes depending on the thickness of the fillets. Place the cod on four warmed plates. Drain the lima beans and divide among the plates. Add the fennel, then cut the eggs in half and put one-half on each plate, then add a spoonful of *Aïoli* to each serving.

Bring the sauce to a boil and whisk in the last 2 tablespoons of butter, then add the basil leaves. Pour the sauce over the beans, eggs and fennel and serve.

I would suggest a gutsy, robust white or rosé wine to go with this dish.

Serves 4

¹/₂	cup dried lima beans
2	eggs
1	bulb fennel, tops intact
4	cod fillets, skin on, 6–7 ounces each
•	Melted butter, for brushing
6	fresh basil leaves, thinly sliced
1	teaspoon sea salt
•	Freshly ground black pepper
1	quantity *Aïoli* (see p. 44)

For the Sauce

8	ounces chopped mixed carrot, leek, celery and onion (almost 2 cups)
¹/₄	cup unsalted butter
1	tablespoon cognac
¹/₄	ounce dried mushrooms
1	tablespoon balsamic vinegar
¹/₄	red chili
2	tablespoons olive oil
1	teaspoon Thai fish sauce (*nam pla*)
2¹/₂	cups *Fish Stock* (see p. 36)
¹/₂	teaspoon salt
4	fresh basil leaves, thinly sliced

Classic Cod in Parsley Sauce

If you tried to think of one of the most mundane-sounding English dishes, it would probably be cod in parsley sauce. Most of us have childhood memories of cod with parsley sauce, and it was with this in mind that I decided to make the dish to see if it really is as boring as it is made out to be. I took the trouble to make a good, but not complicated, parsley sauce to go with a very fresh piece of cod. It was like a sunny day proving that with English food, as long as the raw materials are the best, simplicity is everything.

Put the water, lemon and salt in a large pan. Bring to a boil then simmer for 5 minutes. Add the cod and simmer for 2 minutes. Remove the pan from heat and leave to finish cooking gently in the cooking liquid.

Melt 2 tablespoons butter in a heavy-based pan and sprinkle over the flour. Stir continuously with a wooden spoon to mix, then cook until the mixture smells nutty. Gradually pour in the milk, stirring all the time, to make a smooth sauce. Add 1¼ cups of the fish cooking liquid and leave to simmer for at least 20 minutes.

Drain the cod and cut into 4 portions. Place on 4 warmed plates. Stir the chopped parsley and the rest of the butter into the sauce and coat the fish liberally with it. Serve with some potatoes boiled in salted water and a sprig of mint.

2½ quarts water
1 lemon, sliced
1 tablespoon salt
1½–2 pounds thick cod fillet, skin on
6 tablespoons unsalted butter
1½ tablespoons all-purpose flour
2½ cups milk
1 cup fresh parsley sprigs, stems removed and leaves chopped (½ cup)

Serves 4

Kedgeree

There's a hint of Indian spice in my kedgeree; not enough to put you off your breakfast but just enough to serve as a faint reminder of where this dish came from.

Heat the court bouillon to the simmering point in a large pan. Add the haddock and cook for 8–12 minutes, depending on the thickness of the fillet. Remove from the pan and drain. Remove the skin and break up the fish into finger-sized pieces. Keep warm.

Preheat the oven to 400°F. Cook the butter, turmeric, clove and cardamom together in a flameproof pan, stir in the rice and cook for 1 minute then pour in the stock. Add the salt and bring to a boil. Cover and cook in the oven for 17 minutes. →

Remove the rice from the oven and gently fold in the fish, parsley and eggs to avoid breaking them up. Season with salt and serve immediately.

Serves 4

1 quantity *Court Bouillon for Poaching Smoked Fish* (see p. 38)
12 ounces smoked haddock fillet
2 tablespoons chopped fresh parsley
3 hard-boiled eggs, chopped into 4 rounds
• Salt

For the Rice
3 tablespoons butter
• A large pinch of ground turmeric
1 whole clove
1 cardamom pod
1½ cups long-grain rice
2½ cups *Chicken Stock* (see p. 37) or *Fish Stock* (see p. 36)
½ teaspoon salt

Smoked Haddock with Savoy Cabbage, Lemon and Noisette Butter

This recipe comes from one of my favorite cookery books, Bistro Cookery *by Patricia Wells. It is full of the sort of French cooking that we all really love to eat as opposed to the three-star cuisine that is more a matter of impressing us than filling us with love and affection. I love this dish.*

Trim the outer leaves of the cabbage, then quarter it and remove the thick central core. Thinly slice each quarter and cook in a large pan of boiling, salted water for 10 minutes. Drain and refresh in cold water. Drain again.

Heat the court bouillon to the simmering point in a large pan. Add the haddock and cook for 8–12 minutes, according to the thickness of the fillet. Remove from the heat and set aside without draining to keep the fish warm.

Melt half the butter in a large shallow pan over medium heat. Add the cabbage and cook gently for about 2 minutes to drive off the excess water and concentrate the flavor. Season with salt and pepper. Transfer to a shallow serving dish.

Carefully drain the haddock and remove the skin. Place the fish on top of the cabbage and keep warm.

In a small pan melt the remaining butter over medium heat until it turns a pale brown. Remove from the heat, stir in the lemon juice and season with salt and pepper. Spoon the sauce over the haddock, sprinkle on the parsley and serve immediately.

1 head savoy cabbage
1½ pounds smoked haddock fillets
1 quantity *Court Bouillon for Poaching Smoked Fish* (see p. 38)
¾ cup unsalted butter
• Juice of 1 lemon
2 tablespoons chopped fresh parsley
• Salt and freshly ground black pepper

Serves 4

Haddock Boulangère

For this dish, you need a good, thick chunk of haddock. This old French recipe, like all boulangère dishes, was made at home then taken down to the local bakery to be cooked. I have slightly altered the traditional method because the time taken to cook the potatoes is too long for the fish, so I cook them separately and only bring them together in the oven for 12 minutes.

Preheat the oven to 400°F.

Grease the bottom of a shallow baking dish with butter. Build up layers of potato, onion, bay leaf and thyme, seasoning each layer with the salt and ground black pepper as you go. Pour over the stock, dot with three-quarters of the butter and bake in the oven for 20 minutes.

While the potatoes and onions are baking, melt the rest of the butter in a frying pan, season the haddock and fry on both sides to brown the fish and to caramelize the outside.

Place the fish on top of the potato and onion. Cover and return to the oven for a further 12–15 minutes, depending on the thickness of the fish.

Serves 4

Serve with a green salad, tossed with the *Mustard Dressing* on p. 51.

2½	pounds potatoes, thinly sliced
8	ounces onions, thinly sliced
3	fresh bay leaves, finely chopped
1	fresh thyme sprig
2½	cups *Chicken Stock* (see p. 37)
½	cup unsalted butter
1½	pounds haddock fillet, skin on
	or
2	pounds haddock steaks
•	Freshly ground black pepper
2	teaspoons salt

Baked Hake with Lemon, Bay Leaf, Onion and Garlic

The original recipe for this dish came from a cook who influenced me a great deal in my early days of cooking, Sonia Stevenson, who ran a restaurant at Gullworthy near Tavistock, Devon. I used to eat there a great deal and thought it the most civilized and exciting place in the world. It looked out over the Tamar Valley and, as you sat in the light dining room on a fine summer evening with a copy of the menu, it seemed to achieve an unattainably high style. Although the recipe has been altered over the years, the idea remains the same: a simple treatment of a great fish.

Gently fry the onions and garlic in half the butter until they are soft. Add the white wine, lemon juice, salt, half of the lemon zest and half the bay leaves. Cover and leave to cook gently for 40 minutes, until the onions are very tender. You can prepare this garlic and onion *confit* some time in advance.

Preheat the oven to 450°F. Take a flameproof casserole dish large enough to hold the fish in a single layer. Place the onion *confit* with half the stock in the bottom. Place the steaks of hake on top. Sprinkle the fish with salt and pepper, the rest of the bay leaves and the rest of the →

lemon zest. Cover with foil and bake for 13 minutes. Remove the foil and bake for a further 4 minutes.

Remove the fish from the dish and place on four warmed plates. Sprinkle again with salt and black pepper. Add the rest of the stock to the casserole dish and bring to a boil on top of the oven. Add the rest of the butter and reduce to a thick sauce.

Pour the sauce around the fish and serve. The best accompaniments are new potatoes sprinkled with chopped parsley and mint, and thinly sliced spring cabbage cooked in boiling, salted water for just 3 minutes, then drained and tossed in a sauté pan with some butter.

Serves 4

8	ounces onions, chopped
4	garlic cloves, chopped
1/2	cup unsalted butter
6	tablespoons white wine
•	Juice of 1/2 lemon
1/2	teaspoon salt
•	Zest of 1 lemon, cut into long, paper-thin slices
2	bay leaves, very thinly sliced, or 2 dried bay leaves, crushed
1 1/4	cups *Fish Stock* (see p. 36)
4	hake steaks, about 8 ounces each
•	Salt and freshly ground black pepper

Hake with Clams in Green Sauce

This recipe comes from the Basque region of Spain. You will need a large frying pan so that all the fish can be cooked together.

Season the fish steaks with salt and freshly ground black pepper, then dust with flour, shaking off any excess.

Heat the olive oil in a large frying pan, then sauté the garlic and chili until the garlic begins to color. Remove the garlic and chili from the pan and reserve. Return the pan to the heat and sauté the hake in the oil for about 1 minute on each side. Add about one-third of the parsley and let it fry a little. Then add the stock, white wine and the reserved garlic and chili. Simmer for about 4 minutes, then add the clams and cook for a further 3 minutes, or until the fish is cooked and the clams have opened. Remove from the pan and keep warm.

Serves 4

Concentrate the stock and pan juices by rapid boiling, then season with salt, if necessary. When you are happy that the sauce is strong and thickening, add the asparagus, peas and the rest of the parsley. Pour the sauce over the fish and clams and serve with boiled potatoes and a salad.

4	hake steaks, about 8 ounces each
•	All-purpose flour, for dusting
4	tablespoons olive oil
4	garlic cloves, chopped
1	green chili, seeded and finely chopped
4	tablespoons fresh parsley leaves, roughly chopped
1/2	cup *Fish Stock* (see p. 36)
1/2	cup dry white wine
24	small live clams, in the shell
12	asparagus spears, blanched in salted water
1/2	cup cooked English peas
•	Salt and freshly ground black pepper

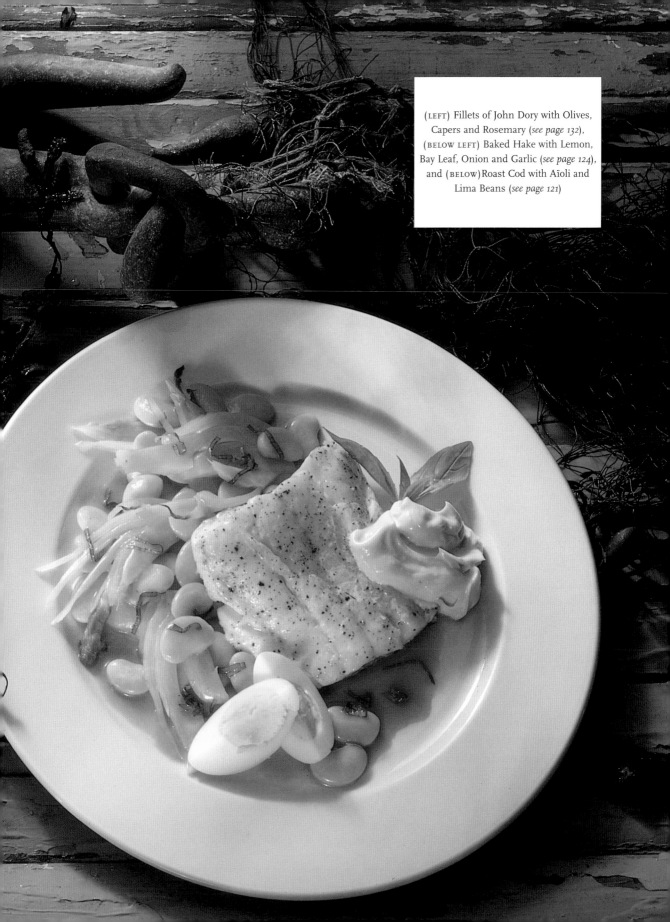

(LEFT) Fillets of John Dory with Olives, Capers and Rosemary (*see page 132*), (BELOW LEFT) Baked Hake with Lemon, Bay Leaf, Onion and Garlic (*see page 124*), and (BELOW) Roast Cod with Aïoli and Lima Beans (*see page 121*)

Grilled Hake with Green Onions, Mashed Potatoes and Morels

The important ingredient in this dish is an Islay malt whisky like Laphroaig. The smoky flavors of the whisky blend subtly with the dried morel mushrooms to produce an unusual but exciting combination of flavors.

Finish the dish off with celery herb, which has a strong celery taste. If you can't find it, use celery tops instead.

Get thick hake fillets that have been cut from a large fish.

To make the sauce, melt half the butter in a shallow pan and add the chopped mixed onion, leek, carrot and celery. Cook briskly until the vegetables start to caramelize (this gives the sauce an appetizing light brown color), add the whisky and let the alcohol boil off. Then, add the vinegar and let it reduce. Finally, add all but a small cupful of the stock and the dried mushrooms. Bring to a boil and simmer for 30 minutes. Put the remaining stock in a small pan and add the dried morels, bring to a boil, remove from the heat and leave the morels to soften. When they are soft, slice them into rounds. Strain and reserve the liquor.

To make the potatoes, scrub the potatoes but do not peel. Place in a large pan and cover with cold water. Bring to a boil and cook until very soft. Drain and leave to cool for 5 minutes. Peel off the skins with a small knife and mash with a fork or masher. Add the butter and milk and season with the salt and pepper. Keep warm. Cut the green onions into thin rounds and add to the mashed potato just before serving.

Preheat the oven to 400°F.

Brush the hake with melted butter and season with ground black pepper and coarse sea salt. Brush the roasting dish with more melted butter and place the fillets in it. Roast in the oven for 12 minutes.

Meanwhile, pass the simmered stock through a sieve into a shallow pan and add the liquor from soaking the morels. Boil on high heat until reduced to about 1¼

cups. Cut the rest of the unsalted butter into a few pieces and whisk into the sauce. Remove from the heat and add the celery herb and the sliced morels.

Arrange the fish on four warmed plates. Pour over the sauce and divide the mashed potatoes among the plates. Serve immediately.

4 hake fillets, about 8 ounces each
· Melted butter, for brushing
· Coarse sea salt

For the Sauce
6 tablespoons unsalted butter
2 cups chopped mixed onion, leek, carrot and celery
1 tablespoon Islay malt whisky or other malt whisky
1 tablespoon balsamic vinegar
5 cups *Fish Stock* (see p. 36)
½ ounce dried mushrooms
¼ ounce dried morels
½ teaspoon celery herb (see p. 12), finely chopped (or celery tops)

For the Mashed Potatoes
2 pounds potatoes
¼ cup butter
1¼ cups milk
6 green onions
· Salt and freshly ground black pepper

Serves 4

White-cooked Ling with Green Onions, Chili and Sichuan Pepper

I have adapted this recipe from a Chinese chicken dish that I often cook at home. The fish is gently poached in water, flavored with ginger, left to cool in the water and served with rice and a series of hot or salty dips. Both the fish and the rice are unsalted, but the dips add plenty of seasoning. This is a simple dish that I hope you will want to cook often. Sichuan pepper is available in Chinese markets and some well-stocked supermarkets.

You will need three tiny bowls to hold the condiments that go with the ling and the rice.

Place the rice in a large pan and pour in enough cold water to cover it by 1 inch. Bring to a boil, then simmer gently until all the water has been absorbed by the rice. Remove from the heat and set aside, covered.

Bring the water to a boil with the sliced ginger and simmer for 10 minutes. Put the fish fillet into the water and simmer for exactly 2 minutes, then remove from the heat and leave to cool (this will take about 40 minutes). When cool, slice the fillet into pieces 1 inch thick and arrange neatly on a serving dish.

Coarsely crush the black peppercorns, Sichuan peppercorns and sea salt together using a spice grinder or mortar and pestle, or by wrapping the spices in a tea towel and beating with a rolling pin.

Put the coarsely ground pepper and salt into one of the bowls and the soy sauce, chopped ginger and the green onions in the second bowl. Finally, put the chopped chili and the white wine vinegar in the third bowl. Pile the rice into a serving dish. Sprinkle the fish with some of the cilantro and put the sliced iceberg lettuce and the rest of the cilantro in a salad bowl (without any dressing).

To serve, each person takes a mound of rice, some of the fish and a pile of salad and dots the three condiments, i.e. the pepper and salt, the soy sauce and green onion, and the vinegar and chili, around their plate. The combination is totally satisfying.

2/3	cup long-grain rice
5	cups water
2	tablespoons fresh ginger, unpeeled, thinly sliced
1½	pounds ling fillet, skinned and boned
1	teaspoon black peppercorns
1	teaspoon Sichuan peppercorns
1	teaspoon sea salt
½	cup soy sauce
1	teaspoon fresh ginger, finely chopped
2	green onions, thinly sliced
1	red chili, seeded and finely chopped
2	tablespoons white wine vinegar
1	bunch fresh cilantro, leaves picked from the stems
½	iceberg lettuce, sliced

Serves 4

Salt Pollack with Mayonnaise, Chili and Cannellini Beans

Cannellini beans take on flavors exceptionally well and are available in Italian delicatessens and some well-stocked supermarkets. To make salt pollack use the recipe for salting cod on p. 53. Salting greatly improves the flavor of pollack.

Soak the cannellini beans for 8 hours in plenty of cold water. Soak the pollack in plenty of cold water for 2 hours.

Discard the water from soaking the cannellini beans. Put the beans in a large pan, then add the water, salt, diced chili and vinegar. Bring to a boil and simmer until the beans are very soft, like baked beans. Drain off the cooking liquor into a separate pan and reduce it down to about 2 tablespoons. Add to the beans and keep warm.

Poach the pollack in plain water for 10 minutes, strain, remove the skin and any bones, and add to the beans.

Stir in the chopped tomato and the garlic. Finally, stir in the mayonnaise just before serving. Sprinkle with the parsley and serve.

1³/₄	cups cannellini beans
12	ounces salt pollack
5	cups water
1	teaspoon salt
1	red chili, seeded and chopped
2	tablespoons balsamic or sherry vinegar
2	tomatoes, peeled, seeded and chopped
2	garlic cloves, very finely chopped
1¹/₄	cups *Mustard Mayonnaise* (see p. 43)
1	teaspoon fresh parsley leaves, roughly chopped

Serves 4

Whiting and Potato Bhaji

This bhaji recipe comes from Goa and is completely different from the normal deep-fried bhaji we know in this country. Here finely diced potato is cooked with some oil, mustard seeds, onion, tomato and spices to produce a very mild vegetable curry. In Goa I am very fond of eating this bhaji with fried eggs but have discovered how well it also goes with a delicate fish like whiting. So here it is.

Peel the potatoes and cut them into ¹/₂-inch (almost 5 ounces) dice, then boil in salted water. Heat the vegetable oil in a pan and fry the mustard seeds, turmeric and onion until the onion has softened. Drain the potatoes and add to the pan. Season and continue to cook gently. Add the tomato and simmer for a further minute, then add the chopped cilantro.

Preheat the broiler. Brush the fillets with a little melted butter and season. Broil for 4–5 minutes, then serve with the *bhaji* and slices of lemon.

12	ounces potatoes
2	tablespoons vegetable oil
¹/₂	teaspoon mustard seeds
•	A good pinch of ground turmeric
³/₄	cup finely chopped onion
²/₃	cup chopped, peeled tomato
1	teaspoon roughly chopped fresh cilantro
1	pound whiting fillet, skin on
•	Melted butter, for brushing
•	Salt and freshly ground black pepper
1	lemon, sliced, to serve

Serves 4

Charbroiled John Dory with Cilantro, Saffron and Kumquats

The charbroiled John Dory fillets are served on a citrus-dressed salad smelling of lemon and surrounded by a deeply-flavored citrus dressing.

Prepare the charcoal grill at least 45 minutes before cooking the fish (gas grills take about 20 minutes to heat or you can use a ribbed grill pan instead).

If using a whole fish, fillet the John Dory (see p. 24) but leave the skin on, then cut the fillets into four equal portions. Brush with a little olive oil and season with salt and black pepper.

To make the dressing, put the stock, white wine and saffron in a small, wide pan and bring to a boil. Simmer to reduce the volume by half.

Thinly slice the kumquats and remove the seeds. Assemble and prepare all the other dressing ingredients so that you can make the hot dressing at the last minute.

Grill the fillets of John Dory, skin side first for 3 minutes on each side. When the fish is cooked, keep warm while you make the dressing and toss the salad.

Place the salad greens in a mixing bowl and add the chopped preserved lemon, the tomato, the lemon olive oil and a pinch of salt. Mix carefully with your hands, taking care not to bruise the leaves, then arrange in the center of warmed plates.

Bring the reduced saffron stock to a boil then add all the remaining dressing ingredients, except the cilantro. Boil rapidly for 2 minutes, then add the cilantro.

Place the fish fillets on top of the salad, spoon some of the hot dressing over the fish and drizzle the rest around the plates.

Serves 4

1	John Dory, about 4 pounds, or 1½ pounds fillet, skin on
•	Olive oil, for brushing
•	Salt and freshly ground black pepper

For the Dressing

5	cups *Fish Stock* (see p. 36)
½	cup dry white wine
•	A pinch of saffron strands
4	kumquats
4	tablespoons extra-virgin olive oil
•	Juice of 1 orange
½	teaspoon salt
1	tablespoon balsamic vinegar
2	anchovy fillets, finely chopped
1	teaspoon chopped fresh cilantro

For the Salad

5	cups loosely packed salad greens (about 5 ounces)
¼	*Preserved Lemons*, cut into small pieces (see p. 52)
1	large tomato, peeled, seeded and cut into dice
1	tablespoon *Lemon Olive Oil* (see p. 51)
•	Salt

Fillets of John Dory with Olives, Capers and Rosemary

This dish is very much in the light Mediterranean style. The fish is filleted but the skin left on. Once grilled, it is served with olives, capers, tomato, flat-leaf parsley, waxy potatoes and rosemary, all carefully warmed through in the very best olive oil. It makes a perfect first course.

If you have small fillets of John Dory cut each in half lengthwise. If they are from a larger fish, cut each fillet into three, again lengthwise. Brush each piece of fillet with olive oil, then place on a baking sheet and season with salt and black pepper.

Cut each new potato into four long pieces. Simmer in salted water until just cooked, then drain and keep warm.

Cut each anchovy fillet in half lengthwise, then in half again to make thin slivers. Remove the skin from the tomatoes by either spearing the tomato on a fork and turning it around over a gas flame (you will hear the skin pop as it splits, which takes about 10 seconds) or by briefly immersing in boiling water until the skin splits. Cut the tomatoes into quarters and remove the seeds. Slice each of the quarters into three long segments.

Cut the sun-dried tomatoes into long, thin strips. Remove the pits from the olives and slice them. Take the stems off the parsley and cut up very roughly so that the leaves are still almost intact.

Preheat the broiler. Grill the John Dory until only just cooked. Put the extra-virgin olive oil, new potatoes, anchovy fillets, tomatoes, sun-dried tomato, olives, capers and rosemary into a shallow pan and warm through gently, but don't overheat the oil. Very gently, mix the ingredients around so that they are all coated with the oil then add the parsley. Avoid losing the shape of any of the ingredients.

Divide the fish among four warmed plates and arrange the contents of the pan over, under and around the fillets. Try to make the ingredients look as attractive as possible, making sure that each plate has roughly the same quantity of all the ingredients.

1	John Dory fillet, about 1 pound, skin on
4	tablespoons extra-virgin olive oil
4	small, waxy new potatoes
2	anchovy fillets
2	medium-sized tomatoes
3	sun-dried tomatoes
4	black olives
•	A small bunch fresh flat-leaf parsley
12	capers, preferably the tiny *non pareil*
10	rosemary needles
•	Salt and freshly ground black pepper

Serves 4

Panfried Fillet of Monkfish with the New Season's Garlic and Fennel

I thought up this dish to make use of the very tender-skinned fresh garlic that arrives in May and June and, if you can get hold of some of this, you don't have to actually peel the garlic. However, the dish is very good made with any garlic.

Put the semolina and two of the cloves of garlic and all but one sprig of the fennel in a food processor or blender. Blend until the garlic and fennel have all amalgamated with the semolina to produce a pale green aromatic powder. It is a good idea to slice the cloves of garlic a little to make it easier for them to be blended.

Cut the remaining cloves of garlic lengthwise, then place in a pan with half the butter and the sliced fennel. Fry the garlic and fennel until both start to brown, then add half the stock, salt and black pepper. Cover the pan and leave to simmer until the garlic and fennel are soft. This will take about 15 minutes.

Preheat the oven to 400°F. Coat the fillets generously with the semolina, fennel and garlic mixture. Heat the peanut oil in a dutch oven or flameproof baking dish with a small knob of butter. Add the fish and fry over moderate heat until golden brown, then turn and transfer the pan to the oven. Cook for 10 minutes.

Remove the monkfish fillets from the pan, place them on a chopping board and slice them carefully on the diagonal so that each slice rests pleasingly against the next. Transfer to a warmed dish and keep warm.

Finish the sauce by adding the garlic, fennel and butter, lemon juice, pastis and the remaining sprig of fennel, finely chopped.

Reduce the sauce a little by rapid boiling. Add the rest of the butter. Lay the sliced fish on four warmed plates and surround them with the sauce.

3/4	cup semolina flour
16	large garlic cloves
1/2	cup fennel sprigs
1/2	cup unsalted butter
1	pound fennel, thinly sliced
2	cups *Fish Stock* (see p. 36)
2	pounds monkfish fillet, cut into 4 equal pieces
4	tablespoons peanut oil
•	Juice of 1/4 lemon
•	Splash of pastis
•	Salt and freshly ground black pepper

Serves 4

(BELOW) Monkfish with Saffron and
Roasted Red Pepper Dressing
(*see page 136*), (TOP RIGHT) Salt Pollack
with Mayonnaise, Chili and
Cannellini Beans (*see page 130*), and
(BELOW RIGHT)White-cooked Ling
with Green Onions, Chili and
Sichuan Pepper (*see page 129*)

Monkfish with Saffron and Roasted Red Pepper Dressing

Like many of my recipes there's not a lot to this dish really. But that is all to the good, providing you have the very freshest of fish.

To make the roasted pepper sauce, put the fish stock, vermouth and saffron in a small pan and simmer to reduce the volume by three-quarters. Roast the red peppers by putting them on a broiler pan (you don't need to coat them with any oil) and charring them under the broiler, or in a hot oven, until the skins are blistered. Leave to cool, cut in half, remove the seeds, take off the skins and finely chop the flesh. Mix together the virgin olive oil, vinegar, salt and pepper.

Light the charcoal grill 30–40 minutes before you intend to grill the monkfish. (You can, as with all my charbroiled recipes, use a ribbed grill pan instead.)

Brush the fillets of monkfish with a mixture made up of the olive oil, thyme, salt and pepper, then grill them. They will take about 10 minutes to cook. Turn them over frequently to prevent burning.

Return the fish stock and saffron back to the heat, add the chopped red peppers and the olive oil dressing and bring to a brisk boil. Check that the sauce is pleasantly strong; it should taste tart but not too tart, salty but not too salty and generally round and pleasing. If it has not reached this stage, continue to reduce by rapid boiling to concentrate the flavor. Once you are satisfied that a suitably concentrated taste has been achieved, whisk in the teaspoon of butter to give the sauce a light amalgamation and remove from the heat.

Mix the salad greens with the lemon olive oil and sea salt. Place the salad greens on four plates. Slice the 4 monkfish fillets into four thick pieces on the slant so that the slices fall together against each other pleasingly. Place each sliced fillet on top of a pile of lettuce and pour the sauce around it. Serve immediately.

Serves 4

4	monkfish fillets, about 7 ounces each
2	tablespoons olive oil
1	tablespoon finely chopped fresh thyme
1/2	teaspoon salt
•	Freshly ground black pepper

For the Roasted Red Pepper Sauce

5	cups *Fish Stock* (see p. 36)
6	tablespoons dry vermouth
•	A large pinch of saffron
2	red bell peppers
6	tablespoons virgin olive oil
1	tablespoon balsamic vinegar or sherry vinegar
•	Salt and freshly ground pepper
1	teaspoon unsalted butter
5	cups loosely packed salad greens (about 5 ounces)
1	tablespoon *Lemon Olive Oil* (see p. 51)
•	A good pinch of sea salt, preferably coarse

Tandoori Monkfish with Tomato and Cilantro Salad

For this dish you need small monkfish tails that have a sweet and delightful flavor and are ideally suited to cooking in a tandoori style.

We can never quite capture the taste of tandoori food because we don't possess, most of us anyway, such a spectacular piece of equipment as a tandoor. But fairly convincing results can be achieved using a barbecue grill. Alternatively use your broiler or oven.

You need to be a bit careful when charbroiling fish or meat marinated in tandoori spices. While you do need the barbecued flavor, you don't want to burn the marinade too much, otherwise it tastes bitter. This is an occasion to use one of those hinged grill baskets. Cooking in a tandoori oven is done using long spears on which the food is impaled so that it doesn't touch anything in the oven.

I'm afraid this is one of those rare occasions when food color has to be used. You can make tandoori without, but it just doesn't look right.

Slash the monkfish tails 3–4 times right down to the central bone on either side to allow the marinade to permeate right into the fish. Place in a small dish with the lemon chili marinade ingredients and leave to marinate for 1 hour, turning occasionally and rubbing more marinade into the cuts. Make the tandoori marinade, add to the dish, and leave for a further hour.

Light the charcoal grill 30–40 minutes before you start cooking. Cook the monkfish over the coals, turning frequently to prevent burning. They will take about 10–12 minutes to cook.

While the fish is cooking, prepare the two salads. For the raita simply mix all the ingredients together. Serve the tandoori monkfish with the salad, some wedges of lemon and some fresh naan bread.

Serves 4

4   small monkfish tails, 10–12 ounces each
1   quantity *Kachumber Salad* (see p. 53)
•   Lemon wedges to serve

For the Lemon Chili Marinade
1   teaspoon pure ground chili powder or cayenne pepper
1   teaspoon salt
•   Juice of 1 large lemon

For the Tandoori Marinade
1/4   cup plain yogurt
1/4   cup heavy cream
1   tablespoon finely chopped fresh ginger
1   tablespoon finely chopped garlic
1   teaspoon garam masala
3/4   teaspoon ground cumin
1   teaspoon red food color

For the Raita Salad
6   tablespoons plain yogurt
1/2   cucumber, thinly sliced
1   teaspoon chopped fresh mint
•   A pinch of salt

Carpaccio of Monkfish with Lemon Olive Oil

This recipe was given to me by our sous chef, Paul Ripley. He has taken the idea of thinly sliced raw fillet of beef and transferred it to fish; in this case monkfish, which is excellent for such treatment. Being very firm in texture, monkfish slices thinly very easily, so it is perfect as carpaccio. *You can make your own lemon olive oil (see p. 51), but it's quite easy to buy in good delicatessens.*

The best *carpaccios* are made from very thin slices of meat or, in this case, fish. To slice the monkfish very thinly you will need to part-freeze it. Freeze the fillet for about 1 hour, then thinly slice with your sharpest, thinnest knife. Lay the slices neatly onto four cold plates. Pour over the lemon olive oil and dust lightly with salt and a little freshly ground white pepper.

Lay the arugula leaves on top. Make shavings of the Parmesan from a block of cheese by using a potato peeler. Lay about 6–8 shavings of Parmesan over the arugula. Serve at once.

Serves 4

8   ounces monkfish fillet
4   tablespoons *Lemon Olive Oil* (see p. 51)
·   Salt and freshly ground white pepper
2   ounces arugula leaves
2   tablespoons freshly grated Parmesan cheese

8 Flat Fish

BRILL, HALIBUT, PLAICE, SOLE AND TURBOT

The recipes in this chapter include some of my all-time favorites. They are ideal for anyone who doesn't like bones in fish. We have, in our waters, the greatest range of flat fish anywhere in the world. From the regal turbot down to the humble dab, the recipes here reflect that range and are a mixture of quick and easy and more elaborate dishes.

BRILL

Whenever you read about brill it is always classed as being a second-division turbot, a sort of brother of the more famous turbot! It is not quite so sweetly flavored as turbot but brill is still extremely good and quite often can be half the price. Large brill cut into small steaks and served with hollandaise sauce in the same way as the roast turbot on p. 157, are stupendous. As with all flat fish, if you're going for fillets, go for the larger fish. In the case of brill these should be 3–8 pounds.

It is quite difficult to distinguish large brill from large turbot, but the former are more oval in shape and turbot have little lumps on their skin. Running your finger over the skin of either one will soon tell you which is which.

In the United States, petrale sole would be a good substitute.

HALIBUT

Sadly, halibut is not a fish caught off the Southwest of England so we only occasionally get one, but it is a marvelous fish. The fillet is firm and white and well-flavored but prone to dryness if at all overcooked. It is one of the most spectacular-looking fish because it can come as large as 2 yards long and 1 yard wide. A dark browny-green in color, it is by far the largest of the flat fish and tremendously speedy looking.

PLAICE

Of all sea fish, plaice has the closest flavor to freshwater fish, a taste I find irresistible. For this reason I normally cook my *meurette* of sea fish with plaice (see p. 66-7). This fish stew, made with a good Beaujolais or Burgundy, was originally created for fish caught in the Rhône and the Loire rivers. Plaice is a most attractive fish with almost fluorescent orange and red spots. In the United States, any one of the flounders are good substitutes.

DOVER SOLE

Some of the world's best fish are caught off Padstow between February and April in a rich fishing ground off Trevose Head about twelve miles out to sea called the Trevose Bank. For those three months, not only Dover sole (sometimes called English sole in the United States), but superb large cod, brill, haddock, turbot, monkfish, hake, pollack and skate are caught in great abundance. But the prize catch is Dover sole—from large 3- to 4-pound fish the fishermen call tombstones down to the little tiny soles, no more than 6–8 inches long, that they call tongues.

The great attraction of this bounty from the sea is that the weather is so appalling at that time of year, with gales coming from every direction, that the price of fish everywhere in the British Isles is high. Dover sole will fetch high prices. Fishing for sole is extremely uncomfortable; I know, I've been there. I was sick most of the time. I stood there on a pitching deck in the freezing cold with green mountains of sea powering over me and tons of rusty iron chains and beams crashing against the metal sides of the trawler, a point of impact where most fishermen lose their fingers. All around me was the howl of wire hawsers hauling a bulging bag of net over onto the deck with fish heads poking through it grotesquely. Then one of the crew pulled open the cod end and everything flopped down into a stainless steel trough and I was amazed by the freshness of it all: the ozone smell, the brightness of all those different fish and the lumps of coal in among them. There was an old fisherman's glove, star fish, some crabs, whelks (conchs), scallops, the dark fearful mouth of a large monkfish, a couple of enormous cod, a haddock, an octopus, a beautiful pink gurnard (searobin), a large brill, some little chicken turbot, the fluorescent orange and red spots of plaice and flounder and, above all, everywhere the brown flatness of Dover sole. The crew looked after its fish, everything was hand-washed after being gutted and placed carefully in ice, but none more carefully than the Dover sole; the prize catch. In spite of constant nausea and a feeling of anxiety about the howling wind and the enormous seas, I was filled with a cook's enthusiasm for the beautiful raw material of those Dover soles. I wanted to take them home and simply grill them knowing nothing on this planet could taste better.

LEMON SOLE

I'm particularly fond of the skin of lemon sole and never serve it without, even though people may fastidiously set it aside. It has a very soft but well flavored flesh. A lemon sole brushed with plenty of butter, sprinkled with salt and freshly ground black pepper and cooked under a broiler is a delight, but it is also well suited to serving with sauces. It seems to have a particularly sweet affinity with cream, fish stock and white wine.

As with all flat fish, go for the bigger ones. For serving whole lemon sole, I would suggest a weight of around 1 pound.

TURBOT

To me turbot is in the same class as lobster and inevitably, I'm afraid, very expensive. It has firm, sweet flesh, white and moist. Of all fish it is the densest and therefore loses least of its precious liquor when resting, particularly when cooked on the bone. There is an added advantage in that the flesh near the bone is imbued with a sort of gelatinous moistness after having been cooked, which is lost when the fish is filleted.

Turbot served simply with hollandaise sauce is always a great success. Large turbot about 10–15 pounds in weight make much better eating than small ones but, if you can get hold of a perfectly fresh small turbot that is up to about 11/4 pounds in weight (called a chicken turbot) and grill it, you'll have a splendid meal, though it won't quite aspire to the luxury of a *tronçon* (steak) cut from a big fish.

A Casserole of Petrale Sole with Shallots and Wild Mushrooms

You can use either petrale sole, brill, turbot or flounder for this dish if your budget won't run to the pricier fish. But this recipe is definitely only for large fish, so you need a good thick fillet for its success. Some people feel that partnering fish with rich dark sauces like this one is a mistake. I disagree. You don't lose the taste of the fish as long as it's good and fresh. Also, flat fish and wild mushrooms go very well together. If you can't get wild mushrooms, go for ordinary field mushrooms and maybe some shiitake and oyster mushrooms to provide variety. You can get these in any supermarket these days. Dried cèpes, on the other hand, are usually only available from good delicatessens.

Soak the cèpes for 30 minutes in ²/₃ cup warm water.

Use a shallow pan large enough to take the fish fillets side by side. Melt 2 tablespoons of the butter with the sugar, then add the shallots and garlic and cook until lightly browned. Barely cover them with some of the stock and add ¼ teaspoon salt and the black pepper. Add the diced ham and simmer gently until both shallots and garlic are tender. Turn up the heat and reduce the stock to a thick syrupy glaze so that both the onions and garlic are coated with it and become dark. Remove from the pan and keep warm. (Use the same pan, unwashed, to finish the dish so the syrupy juices combine with the rest of the sauce.)

To make the stock, fry the carrot, leek, celery and onion in 2 tablespoons of the butter. Allow the vegetables to catch a little to create a rich brown finish to the sauce. Strain the soaking water from the dried mushrooms and add it to the rest of the chicken stock, the balsamic vinegar, 1 sprig of thyme and the red wine. Simmer for 20–30 minutes, then pass through a conical sieve into another pan.

To cook the fish, heat a frying pan, then melt a small piece of the butter. Quickly brown the skin side of the fillets, season with salt and pepper and remove. Place the fillets side by side in the pan used to cook the shallots and garlic, and pour on the rest of the stock. Add the second sprig of thyme. Cover the pan and braise until the fish is just cooked.

While the fish is braising, take the frying pan in which you browned the skin of the fish, add 1 tablespoon butter and fry all the mushrooms, seasoning with a little salt and pepper.

Remove the fish from the pan and keep warm. Reduce the cooking liquor a little then add the remaining butter. Add the mushrooms to the sauce, place the pieces of fish on four warmed plates, add the glazed shallots and garlic and pour over the sauce and mushrooms.

½	ounce dried cèpes (porcini)
7	tablespoons unsalted butter
½	teaspoon sugar
12	small shallots
8	garlic cloves
4	cups *Chicken Stock* (see p. 37)
¼	teaspoon salt
•	Freshly ground black pepper
1	slice cooked ham, finely diced
1	carrot, chopped
1	leek, chopped
1	celery stalk, chopped
½	medium onion, chopped
2	teaspoons balsamic vinegar
2	sprigs fresh thyme
4	tablespoons red wine
1½	pounds petrale sole fillet (see above), skin on, divided into 4 equal portions
4	ounces wild mushrooms, sliced

Serves 4

(LEFT) Broiled Scored Plaice with Garlic, Oregano and Lemon Juice (*see page 148*), (BELOW LEFT) Escalopes of Halibut with Dill, Carrots and Celery (*see page 147*), and (BELOW) A Casserole of Petrale Sole with Shallots and Wild Mushrooms (*see page 141*)

Fillets of Petrale Sole with Stir-fried Spinach and Cilantro

The sauce which accompanies this is rather an interesting combination of West and East. Fish stock, butter and tomato on one side and soy sauce and cilantro on the other.

Wash the spinach in plenty of cold water and remove the stems. Tear into small pieces if the leaves are big. Thinly slice the snow peas. Remove the outer leaves of the fennel bulb and thinly slice. Cut the fennel slices into thin strips.

Pour the stock and soy sauce into a small pan and bring to a boil. Reduce the volume by half by rapid boiling.

Preheat the broiler. Brush the brill with olive oil and season with salt, then cook under the broiler for 5–8 minutes, depending on the thickness of the fillets.

Heat a wok and pour in the olive oil.

Add the snow peas and fennel and turn in the hot oil. Add the spinach, basil, fish sauce and lemon juice and stir briefly. Cook long enough to allow the spinach to wilt, then divide the contents of the pan among four warmed plates.

Add the butter to a boiling stock and soy sauce and as soon as it has blended in, add the tomato and cilantro. Remove from the heat.

Place the fish on top of the stir-fried vegetables and pour over the sauce. Serve.

Serves 4

4   petrale sole or brill fillets, 7–8 ounces each

For the Stir-fried Spinach
4   ounces spinach
1   ounce snow peas
½   bulb fennel
6   fresh basil leaves, thinly sliced
•   A splash of Thai fish sauce (*nam pla*)
•   Juice of ¼ lemon

For the Sauce
5   cups *Fish Stock* (see p. 36)
2   tablespoons soy sauce
1   tablespoon virgin olive oil
¼   cup unsalted butter
2   tablespoons peeled, seeded and diced tomato
1   teaspoon chopped fresh cilantro

Fillets of Petrale Sole in Madiran with Young Broad Beans

The title of this recipe was partly chosen because I love the name Madiran. It's a little-known red wine from an adventurous wine maker in southwest France called Alain Burmont, who is responsible for a collection of unusual and delicious wines including the sweet and dry Pachérenc du Vic-Bilh whites and the dark rich red Madiran. I don't expect you to go to the expense of buying a bottle just to cook with, so use a good deep Côtes du Rhône or other full-bodied red wine instead; the results will be quite similar. This is a seasonal dish using young fresh fava beans. You can, of course, use frozen beans, but if you wait till spring and make the dish one time of the year only, you'll enjoy it much more.

Prepare a steamer (see pp. 35 and 205) for cooking the fish. Season the skinned fish fillets lightly with salt.

Shell the fava beans and bring a pan of salted water to a boil. Cook the beans for 4–5 minutes. Drain, remove the gray skins and discard.

Bring the stock to a boil, together with all but a tablespoon or so of the red wine and the sugar and simmer until the volume has reduced by three-quarters.

Arrange the fish fillets in the steamer and steam until just cooked—there should be a slight suggestion of translucency right in the center of the fillet when you part it with a small knife.

Arrange the fish on four warmed plates. Bring the reduced red wine and stock to a final boil. Add the rest of the red wine and whisk in the butter. Pour the red wine sauce over the four fillets of fish. Mix the chopped mint with the beans and place in neat piles beside the fish.

Serves 4

4	petrale sole or brill fillets, about 4 ounces each, skinned
•	Salt
2	pounds fava beans, weighed in the pod
1¼	cups *Chicken Stock* (see p. 37)
1¼	cups Madiran, Côtes du Rhône or other full-bodied red wine
½	teaspoon sugar
½	cup unsalted butter
½	teaspoon finely chopped fresh mint

Ceviche of Brill

In this South American dish, fillets of fish are cured in fresh lime juice. I like the fish a little under-cured; most recipes call for the fish to be left for some hours. I think 2 hours quite enough when the fillets are cut into finger-sized slices. It tastes much fresher this way. The accompanying salsa is extremely hot as it contains lots of chili.

Cut the fish into strips the length of your finger but half as thick. Cover with lime juice. Turn over and marinate for 2 hours. Drain and sprinkle with the fennel and salt.

Cut the avocado into quarters, remove the skin and thinly slice lengthwise. Sprinkle the avocado with some lime juice and a little sea salt and arrange on four plates.

Mix all the salsa ingredients just before you serve the dish, then put a pile on each plate with the fish. Serve immediately.

Serves 4

- 1 pound petrale sole (brill) fillet
- · Juice of 2 limes
- 1 teaspoon finely chopped fresh fennel sprigs
- · A good pinch of sea salt
- 1 avocado

For the Salsa
- 8 ounces tomatoes, peeled, seeded and chopped
- 1/2 green bell pepper, diced
- 2 green onions
- 2 garlic cloves, finely chopped
- 2 chilies, seeded and finely chopped
- 1 tablespoon roughly chopped fresh cilantro
- 1 tablespoon virgin olive oil
- 1/2 teaspoon sea salt

Spinach with Butter

The standard way of cooking spinach is just to wash it and then let it cook gently in its own juices adding plenty of butter. It is then left to stew for some time, producing a rich, satisfying and smooth green flavor. However, much as I love this way of cooking it, I think this recipe is ideal for partnering

Pick over the spinach leaves and wash in at least two changes of water. Bring a pan of salted water to a boil, drop in the spinach leaves, bring back to a boil and strain. Give the colander you strain the leaves through a good shake to get as much moisture out of the spinach as possible, then return the leaves to a clean pan with the butter. Cook very gently for about 2 minutes, driving off the steam and concentrating the flavor slightly. Season with salt and pepper.

Serves 4

For the Spinach
- 8 ounces spinach leaves
- 2 tablespoons unsalted butter
- · Salt and freshly ground black pepper

Escalopes of Halibut with Dill, Carrots and Celery

These are thin slices of the fish that are cooked very quickly in a little vegetable oil—so quickly, in fact, that they are still very underdone in the middle when they're served and therefore moist.

Cut the halibut into thin escalopes with a sharp, thin-bladed knife. Cut the fish on the slant so that you get a few, wide pieces. It doesn't really matter if you don't do it neatly, providing the pieces are no more than about 1/4 inch thick.

Peel the carrots and cut into fine neat dice by first slicing the carrot lengthwise into 1/8-inch slices, then cutting into 1/8-inch sticks and finally cutting into 1/8-inch dice. Repeat with the celery.

Melt 2 tablespoons of the butter in a pan and start to fry the carrot and celery over gentle heat. Just as they are beginning to soften, add the white wine and all but a generous pinch of the dill (keep some back to garnish the dish). Cook gently with a lid on the pan for a further 5 minutes. Season with salt.

In a separate pan, boil the stock until the volume has reduced by three-quarters, then pour into the carrot and celery. Whisk in the remaining butter and lemon juice.

Serves 4

Heat the peanut oil in a frying pan. When the oil is hot, add only enough escalopes to cover the base of the pan. Sprinkle with salt and pepper and turn over almost immediately, then remove from the pan to a warm plate after only 20 seconds of cooking. Cook the rest of the escalopes.

Take a long, elegant serving dish and pour all the sauce onto it. Layer the escalopes of halibut down the middle and sprinkle with the pinch of dill. Serve with a few potatoes cut into triangular, finger-length pieces and boiled with dill (see p. 93).

1 1/2	pounds halibut fillet, preferably a single piece cut from a large fish
2	carrots
2	tender celery stalks
3/4	cup unsalted butter
4	tablespoons white wine
1	tablespoon finely chopped fresh dill
5	cups *Fish Stock* (see p. 36)
•	Juice of 1/4 lemon
1	tablespoon peanut oil
•	Salt and freshly ground black pepper

Broiled Scored Plaice with Garlic, Oregano and Lemon Juice

The fish, scored and marinated with olive oil, garlic, oregano, chili and sea salt, is good served with a bowl of chips and a soft lettuce salad with mustard and chive dressing. I have never forgotten the wonderful earthy flavor of some chips eaten in a taverna in Paxos, Greece, caused by not being too fastidious with the peeling. Just roughly peel some potatoes, leaving on some of the peel, then cut into large, irregular chips and deep-fry in hot oil.

Cut off the fins with a pair of scissors and trim the tail. Make a deep cut down the back of each fish from head to tail. Then make a series of diagonal cuts across from this cut to the sides so that the slashes look like the veins of a leaf. Turn the fish over and do the same on the other side.

Roast the red pepper by placing it in a hot oven for 10 minutes or by putting it under a hot broiler and turning it as it blackens. Cut in half, remove the seeds and skin and chop the flesh very finely, into 1/8-inch dice. Put in a bowl with the olive oil, garlic, oregano, salt, black pepper and lemon juice to make the marinade.

One hour before cooking, coat both sides of the fish with the marinade, making sure that it spreads right into the slashes.

Turn on the broiler and heat it until it's very hot. Broil the fish for 5 minutes on each side, starting with the light side. Serve with chips and a salad of soft green leaves with its *Mustard Dressing* made with chives (see p. 51).

Serves 4

4	whole plaice or flounder, about 1 pound each
1	small red bell pepper
1/2	mild red chili, seeded and finely chopped
4	tablespoons virgin olive oil
1	large garlic clove, finely chopped
1	teaspoon chopped fresh oregano or 1/2 teaspoon dried
1	teaspoon salt
•	A pinch of freshly ground black pepper
•	Juice of 1/4 lemon

Charbroiled Whole Dover Sole with Sea Salt and Lime

The skin of the sole is very pleasant to eat when crisply cooked, as it is here. The fish can be cooked on a barbecue or under a very hot broiler. Good-quality flounders can be substituted.

Scale the soles and cut off the fins. Dry the fish with paper towels.

To make the sauce put the stock and fish sauce in a small pan. Grate the zest of 1 lime and add to the pan with its juice.

Preheat the broiler until it's very hot.

Just before cooking the fish, dry them one more time, then brush with vegetable oil and sprinkle the dark side with sea salt. Brush the broiler pan with oil and immediately put the fish on, dark (top) side down. Cook for about 5 minutes then sprinkle the light side with sea salt, turn and cook for 5 minutes on the other side. Remove the fish from the broiler and sprinkle with more sea salt. You may find that, in spite of all you've done, the fish will stick a bit. Don't worry, they will still taste wonderful and they don't look bad with some of the top skin pulled off.

Place each fish on a warmed plate then finish the sauce.

Bring the ingredients in the pan to a boil and add the butter. Whisk until it has all melted, then add the chopped red onion and the parsley. Pour the sauce around the fish immediately and garnish with the remaining limes cut into wedges and sprigs of parsley.

Serves 4

4   Dover soles, 14–16 ounces each, skin on
•   Vegetable oil, for brushing
•   Sea salt

For the Sauce
1¼   cups *Fish Stock* (see p. 36)
1½   teaspoons Thai fish sauce (*nam pla*)
3   limes
1   tablespoon unsalted butter
¼   small red onion, finely diced
1   bunch fresh flat-leaf parsley, roughly chopped, a few sprigs reserved for a garnish

Dover Sole à la Meunière

Dover sole à la meunière or "miller's wife style" gets it name from the light dusting of flour it is given before frying. The flour should be just a dusting and not a thick layer. I don't actually fry the fish in a pan on top of the stove because I never have enough stove-top space. Instead, I paint the fish liberally with melted butter and put it under the broiler. I think it works better this way and is equally helpful in the domestic situation as well. Frying large fish at home is a near impossibility. The same dish done in a broiler becomes easy and something you will probably want to do at least once a week—if you can afford the fish, that is!

The success of this dish lies in making sure there is ample noisette butter and plenty of lemon juice. How often have I had soles cooked like this in restaurants where, by the time I've got in the second two fillets, I've run out of the delicious butter and wedges of lemon. So make sure you serve plenty of butter and plenty of lemon juice and, if you can be troubled, some preserved lemon as well to add little bites of piquancy as you eat the fish. Serve with Grilled Potatoes (see below) and a salad of soft green leaves tossed with Mustard Dressing (see p. 51).

Preheat the broiler. Put the seasoned flour in a tray and drop the fish into it, one side at a time, then smack them sharply to remove all the excess flour. Melt the butter in a small pan and use it to brush the soles, then season them on both sides with salt and freshly ground white pepper.

Broil the fish for 5 minutes on each side.

Place the soles on four large warm plates. Season again with salt, then sprinkle with the juice of 1 of the lemons, the parsley and the finely chopped preserved lemon (if using). Pour over the *noisette* butter and serve with the other lemon cut into wedges.

For this dish, you need to splash out on a top-notch Sauvignon Blanc.

¹⁄₃	cup all-purpose flour seasoned with 1 teaspoon salt
4	Dover soles, 14–16 ounces each, skinned
3	tablespoons unsalted butter
2	lemons
1	tablespoon finely chopped fresh parsley
¹⁄₄	*Preserved Lemon* (see p. 52) (optional)
1	quantity *Noisette Butter* (see p. 50)
•	Salt and freshly ground white pepper

Serves 4

Grilled Potatoes

Preheat the broiler.

Peel the potatoes and cut them lengthwise into ¹⁄₄-inch slices. Boil in salted water until tender then drain. Lay on a broiler pan and brush liberally on both sides with olive oil. Season with black pepper and grill until beginning to turn brown.

1	pound large potatoes
4	tablespoons virgin olive oil
•	Salt and freshly ground black pepper

Serves 4

Grilled Fillets of Dover Sole with Cilantro, Cumin and Chili

This is a dish which makes the most of Moroccan flavors. I first went to Morocco on my honeymoon and I recall it as not being a total success in culinary terms because we arrived during Ramadan, a time of fasting in the Muslim calendar and so we couldn't get anything to eat between sunrise and sunset, or not much anyway.

But, despite this drawback, I began to become aware of the richness and variety of the cuisines of North Africa, especially the clean, fresh-tasting mix of strong herbs and spices—very exciting. I wouldn't like to suggest that this dish is authentically Moroccan, but I don't think a Moroccan would disapprove of it. I've tried various combinations for the marinade, charmoula, but this one from Robert Carrier is, I think, the best. The sole fillets don't need to be marinated for very long because they're so thin. They should, ideally, be cooked in a ribbed grill pan (see p. 35).

Put the couscous in a bowl, pour over the boiling water and add a good pinch of salt. Stir a little, then leave for a couple of minutes so the grains can absorb the water. Heat the olive oil and butter in a frying pan, add the couscous and cook gently for 4 minutes then add the mint, set aside and keep warm.

Mix the preserved lemon with the arugula or salad greens, 1 tablespoon of virgin olive oil and a little salt.

Heat the ribbed pan until very hot. Brush the sole fillets with some of the *charmoula* and cook for about 2 minutes on each side. Arrange a pile of arugula or greens, the sole fillets, couscous and a tablespoon of *charmoula* on each of four warmed plates. Serve immediately.

Serves 4

1¼ pounds Dover sole fillets
1 quantity *Charmoula* (see p. 45)

For the Couscous
²/₃ cup couscous
6 tablespoons boiling water
2 tablespoons virgin olive oil
2 tablespoons unsalted butter
· A good pinch of salt
1 tablespoon chopped fresh mint

For the Salad
¼ *Preserved Lemon*, finely chopped (see p. 52)
1 cup arugula leaves or mixed salad greens
1 tablespoon virgin olive oil
· Salt

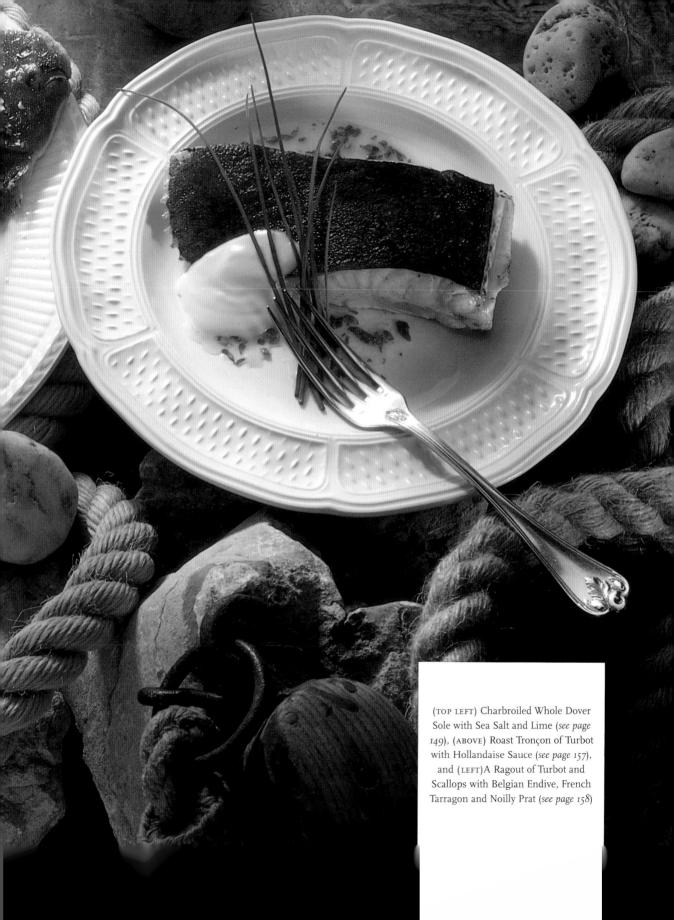

(TOP LEFT) Charbroiled Whole Dover
Sole with Sea Salt and Lime (*see page
149*), (ABOVE) Roast Tronçon of Turbot
with Hollandaise Sauce (*see page 157*),
and (LEFT)A Ragout of Turbot and
Scallops with Belgian Endive, French
Tarragon and Noilly Prat (*see page 158*)

Deep-fried Goujons of Lemon Sole with Tartare Sauce

Goujons are small pieces of fish fillet, cut to about the size of your little finger, coated in bread crumbs then deep-fried. We use Japanese bread crumbs called panko; *they fry much crispier than any other coating. At the time of writing, I am fairly certain that you cannot get* panko *in most supermarkets. But when writing a cookery book, one has to look into the future slightly as far as new products are concerned, and I am certain that within a short time* panko *bread crumbs will be more widely available because they are so extremely good. In the meantime, look for them in Japanese food shops. Also, you can still get perfectly acceptable results making* goujons *with ordinary fresh bread crumbs; they make a perfect first course and are universally popular.*

To cut the lemon sole into *goujons*, slice the fillet diagonally to make long pieces of about the size of your little finger. Put the flour in a small shallow dish or tray. Beat the eggs together and put in a second dish or tray and put the bread crumbs in a third. Set the deep-fryer to 375°F, or heat some oil in a large pan to the same temperature or until a cube of bread browns in about 30 seconds.

Serves 4

Dip the *goujons* first in the seasoned flour, then the egg and finally the bread crumbs and deep-fry until golden brown. Drain on paper towels and serve with the lemon cut into wedges and the tartare sauce.

12	ounces lemon sole fillet, skinned
1½	tablespoons seasoned all-purpose flour
2	eggs
1	cup *panko* or fresh bread crumbs
1	lemon
1	quantity *Tartare Sauce* (see p. 44)

Fillets of Lemon Sole with a Vermouth Sauce and Whole-grain Mustard

The fillets of lemon sole are accompanied by a variation of the classic sauce beurre blanc *(made with dry vermouth instead of white wine) and thinly sliced cucumber flavored with Thai fish sauce (*nam pla*), which I use as a subtly flavored substitute for salt, so if you can't get it, use plain salt instead.*

First, prepare the cucumber by cutting into sections about 2 inches long, then slice into matchsticks.

Pass the *beurre blanc* through a sieve into a clean pan. Add the mustard and a small pinch of salt. Keep warm.

Preheat the broiler. Brush the fillets with butter, then season with salt and freshly ground white pepper. Cook under the broiler for 4 minutes.

Put the cucumber in a small pan and add a tablespoon of fish sauce (or a good pinch of salt) and the cilantro.

Serves 4

Cover and cook gently for 2 minutes. Stir, then divide among 4 warmed plates. Arrange the lemon sole fillets neatly beside the cucumber so they overlap each other on the plates and pour the vermouth sauce all around. Serve immediately.

½	cucumber
1	quantity *Beurre Blanc* (see p. 42) made with 4 tablespoons dry vermouth
1	teaspoon whole-grain mustard
1½	pounds lemon sole fillets, skin on
1	tablespoon Thai fish sauce (*nam pla*)
1	teaspoon roughly chopped fresh cilantro
•	Salt and freshly ground white pepper

Roast Tronçon of Turbot with Hollandaise Sauce

The tronçon, *a steak cut from a big fish, is accompanied by not only the hollandaise but also a thin, very well-seasoned liquor that is flavored with chopped fresh parsley, tarragon, chervil and chives.*

Preheat the oven to 450°F. Heat a frying pan and melt a small piece of butter. Add the *tronçons* and quickly brown them before transferring to a roasting pan. Season with salt and pepper, then roast in the oven for about 15 minutes.

To make the sauce, combine the stock, the *fines herbes*, the Thai fish sauce or salt, the lemon juice and the remaining butter in a small pan and bring to a boil.

Arrange the *tronçons* on four warmed plates and just cover the top of each *tronçon* with the *fines herbes* sauce. Spoon the hollandaise sauce onto the plate against one side of each *tronçon*. Serve with some plainly boiled new potatoes and a simple green vegetable such as spinach, French beans or snow peas.

I would suggest a medium-body Chardonnay to go with this.

Serves 4

2	tablespoons unsalted butter
4	steaks or *tronçons* of turbot, 8–10 ounces each
6	tablespoons *Fish Stock* (see p. 36)
1	teaspoon chopped fresh *fines herbes*: parsley, French tarragon, chives, chervil
¼	teaspoon Thai fish sauce (*nam pla*) or a pinch of salt
•	Juice of ½ lemon
•	Salt and freshly ground black pepper
1	quantity *Hollandaise Sauce* (see p. 40)

A Ragout of Turbot and Scallops with Belgian Endive, French Tarragon and Noilly Prat

The turbot and scallops are braised on top of some sliced vegetables with white vermouth and a splash of fish stock. It is important not to overcook the scallops, which is easily done given the difference in size between the turbot and the scallops.

Slice the turbot into 3/4-inch slices across the fillet. Strip off enough tarragon leaves to make about a teaspoonful of roughly chopped tarragon. Cut each scallop into three rounds. Put half the cream and all of the stock in a pan with the remaining tarragon. Bring gently to a boil to avoid boiling over and simmer until the volume has reduced by three-quarters.

While the sauce is simmering, place the butter and the Noilly Prat in a wide shallow, heavy-based pan. Add the Belgian endive and leek, cover and cook gently for about 5 minutes. Add the sliced mushrooms and cook for a further 1 minute. Place the turbot and scallops on top of the vegetables, add half a teacup or so of the reduced fish stock and cream, lightly season and simmer, covered, for 3 minutes when the fish will be just cooked. Carefully lift out the fish and vegetables with a spatula and keep warm. Add the rest of the cream and the chopped tarragon to the pan and boil vigorously for 3–4 minutes to concentrate the flavor.

Return the fish and vegetables to the pan, sprinkle with the chopped chervil, add a little lemon juice to taste and serve on four warmed plates.

12	ounces turbot fillet
1	ounce French tarragon, weight including stems
12	scallops
3/4	cup heavy cream
5	cups *Fish Stock* (see p. 36)
6	tablespoons unsalted butter
4	tablespoons Noilly Prat or other vermouth
1	head Belgian endive, thinly sliced
4	ounces white of leek, thinly sliced
4	ounces fresh button mushrooms, thinly sliced
1	tablespoon roughly chopped fresh chervil
•	Juice of 1/4 lemon
•	Salt and freshly ground white pepper

Serves 4

9 Large Fish

SKATE, SHARK, SWORDFISH, TUNA AND CONGER EEL

Most of the recipes in this chapter are fairly exotic, reflecting the fact that these fish also swim in warmer waters—except the conger eel, which is a cold water fish. It can grow up to $6\frac{1}{2}$ yards in length, though, so I've included it among the large fish here.

SKATE

Lots of people and lots of cookery books say that the smell of ammonia in skate is perfectly acceptable and that it is driven off by cooking. If you are offered a piece of skate that smells strongly of ammonia, do not buy it. You will never get rid of the taste, and even if you can't smell it when you eat it, it will come back into your mouth as an aftertaste and haunt you for at least the rest of that day, if not the next.

Skate, when it is very fresh, is inedible because it's so tough and after about a week it is inedible because of its taste of ammonia. The gradual build up of ammonia in the flesh is also the process by which the fish is tenderized. You have a window of about five days to buy the fish when it will be both tender and delicious. Fortunately, it freezes very well and you can extend its shelf-life in this way. To all intents and purposes, although they are different species, skate, thornback ray, starry ray and spotted ray are normally sold by the fishmonger as skate. The wings of skate are the only parts sold and are normally skinned before sale. I would suggest that if possible you should go for skate wings weighing 1–2 pounds. Larger than that the skate becomes rather coarse; smaller and they can be a bit fiddly to eat. Skate has no bones, just cartilage, and it is not necessary to fillet it. The best eating of all the skate or rays is the thornback ray. Be a bit careful if you happen to get hold of a whole fish, though, because they're called thornback rays for a reason.

SHARK

All sharks are good for eating—well flavored, lemony, slightly sweet and oily. But some are better than others. The porbeagle, closely related to the great white, is the best. Would a large porbeagle ever turn nasty I wonder? The mako also makes good eating and is very similar in flavor to the porbeagle and probably, though I have never tasted it, the great white. Some have likened porbeagle to veal. It has a similar pink color and is meaty in texture. Try dusting with flour, egg and bread crumbs and frying it like a veal escalope.

The blue shark is less good but still worth charbroiling or making into curry (see p. 163) as are most of the dogfish. The angel shark tastes more like skate than anything else. The other name for angel shark is monkfish, which is rather confusing as it in no way resembles the more common monkfish in flavor or, apart from a passing similarity in shape, in appearance. The monkfish or angler fish, with its enormous teeth, looks like something out of hell; the monkfish or angel shark looks like a benign Labrador.

Like skate, other members of the shark family also smell of ammonia after death, as they use urea in their bloodstreams to counteract the salinity of the sea. Without it, they would dehydrate through osmosis. The urea breaks down after death and is responsible for tenderizing the flesh but after a week it becomes too powerful. Give a fillet of shark a good sniff before you buy.

DOGFISH AND TOPE

Dogfish and tope are both members of the shark family. The best dogfish to eat is the spurdog. That's the one with a sort of thin spike or spur just in front of the dorsal fins. Next, in order of good eating, comes the lesser-spotted dogfish and lastly the starry smooth hound and the smooth hound. I'm not passionate about dogfish; maybe if they had always been known by their popular names of huss, flake and rigg it would have been different. I do think a certain amount as a fillet with other seafood makes a good contrast—you can use it in the seafood salad on p. 163. It smokes extremely well though. If you ever have a chance to smoke fish or meat, make a brine of 5 tablespoons salt to $2^1/_2$ cups of water, soak a fillet for a couple of hours, then cold smoke it for 4–5 hours. Serve it sliced with the horseradish and mustard sauce on page 93. Like all the sharks, dogfish suits cooking on a barbecue very well. I would combine it with some other fillets of fish, perhaps sea bass, John Dory or red mullet (goatfish) and serve say three grilled fillets with a *sauce vierge* (virgin olive oil sauce) of tomato, garlic, shallot, lemon juice, salt and basil. Tope, on the other hand, should be kept only for soup in my opinion.

SWORDFISH AND TUNA

Elsewhere in the book I have purposefully confined the fish used in the recipes to those that can be bought fresh and, in particular, those landed in Cornish fishing ports, because they are familiar to me. This is now the case with swordfish and tuna; they are both caught out in the Bay of Biscay and landed at Newlyn and are delicious.

The flesh of both fish is compact and swordfish is ideal for cutting into thin steaks and grilling. Tuna is better when cut into thicker steaks and left a little underdone in the center. If you don't want to go to the (not enormous) trouble of making *Grilled Swordfish Steaks with Salsa Fresca* on p. 164, just broil some steaks of swordfish or tuna and serve them with a pool of extra-virgin olive oil.

CONGER EEL

There are some signs today that conger eel is not going to remain the abundant cheap fish that it always has been. The price is beginning to edge up, a fact that I regard with some consternation. Conger eel is one of the main constituents of our fish soup, but large eels also provide beautiful, firm, bone-free fillets. I have put conger eel in this chapter because they can be enormous—the largest I've had delivered was 12 feet long—quite fearsome at that size.

Skate with Black Butter

This is one of my favorite dishes. I'll never drop it from my repertoire at the restaurant. It's always popular. One of those perfect combinations that I'm always looking for when producing recipes myself. Skate, being one of the shark family, has a flavor that is what I would call insistent. The first few mouthfuls are delicious, but after a while you sort of feel that maybe you've had enough unless, that is, you partner the fish with some strong and sharp sauce like black butter where lots of red wine vinegar is used. For the same reason, the Indians tend to use shark for their most aromatic fish curries. (See the recipe for shark curry on p. 163.)

Bring all the court bouillon ingredients to a boil in a large pan. Remove from the heat and leave to cool before using to complete the infusion of flavors.

Cut the skate into four portions and place in a wide, shallow pan. Pour the court bouillon over the fish, bring to a boil and simmer very gently for 15–20 minutes, depending on the thickness of the skate. Drain the fish and keep it warm on a serving dish. Sprinkle with the capers.

Melt the butter in a frying pan. When it foams, begins to go really dark and smells nutty, pour in the vinegar.

Serves 4

Add the parsley, and let it boil down for a minute or so, then pour over the fish. Serve at once with plainly boiled potatoes.

Serve with a bottle of young Sauvignon Blanc.

1	quantity *Court Bouillon* (see p. 38)
2	pounds skate wings
1	tablespoon capers

For the Black Butter

3/4	cup salted butter
4	tablespoons red wine vinegar
1	tablespoon finely chopped fresh parsley

Skate, Leeks and Wilted Lettuce with a Cider Vinegar and Butter Sauce

I based this recipe around an old Cornish farmhouse cider that a friend gave me. It had an unusual nutty flavor, in some ways similar to, but then again quite unlike, a good sherry vinegar.

Preheat the oven to 400°F. Brush the skate wings with a little melted butter, season with salt and roast in the oven for 15 minutes. Remove and keep warm.

Remove the outer leaves from the leeks, thinly slice and wash carefully in a colander. Top and tail the snow peas and cut into long thin strips. Put 1/4 cup of the butter in a pan, then cover and soften the leeks and the snow peas over gentle heat for 3–4 minutes. →

Serves 4

. 4	skinned skate wings, 10–12 ounces each
3/4	cup unsalted butter
2	leeks
4	ounces snow peas
1	head butter lettuce
2½	cups *Fish Stock* (see p. 36)
½	cup good-quality hard cider vinegar
1	tablespoon roughly chopped fresh parsley
•	Salt and freshly ground black pepper

Remove and discard the outer leaves from the lettuce, then wash, dry and slice the rest. Add the lettuce to the leeks and snow peas and cook for a further 4–5 minutes. Season with salt and pepper.

Put the vinegar and fish stock in a small pan and boil rapidly to reduce the volume by three-quarters. Add the rest of the butter and simmer until it coats the back of a spoon.

To serve, divide the leek and lettuce mixture among four warmed plates and place a skate wing on top of each. Pour the vinegar and butter sauce over the fish and scatter with parsley. Serve with boiled potatoes.

Skate Mayonnaise with a Vegetable Salad

Having no bones and a firm texture, skate is an ideal fish for poaching and serving cold in a salad.

Bring the court bouillon to a gentle simmer, add the skate and poach for 15–20 minutes. Leave to cool in the liquid.

Cut the celery, carrot and leek into 2-inch matchsticks. Heat the oil in a shallow pan and gently cook the vegetables for 1 minute. Add the white wine, salt and pepper and cook until the wine has boiled off completely. Turn out onto a plate and chill.

Top and tail the beans and snow peas. Cut the beans into lengths of about the same size as the rest of the vegetables; the snow peas can be left whole. Bring a pan of salted water to a boil and blanch the beans and snow peas for 30 seconds, then plunge them into the cold water. Drain through a colander and mix with the rest of the vegetables. Season with salt and black pepper.

Remove the skin and cartilage from the skate and mix with the olive oil mayonnaise, tomato, avocado and potato. Check and adjust the seasoning as necessary. Serve garnished with a couple of leaves from the heart of the lettuce and the vegetable salad.

1	quantity *Court Bouillon* (see p. 38)
1¹/₂	pounds skate

For the Vegetable Salad

2	ounces celery stalks
2	ounces carrot
2	ounces leek
2	tablespoons peanut oil
2	tablespoons white wine
•	Salt and freshly ground black pepper
2	ounces green beans
2	ounces snow peas
8	lettuce leaves and the heart of a lettuce

For the Mayonnaise

¹/₂	cup *Olive Oil Mayonnaise* (see p. 43)
¹/₂	cup peeled, seeded and roughly chopped tomato
1	avocado, peeled and chopped
³/₄	cup diced cooked potato

Serves 4

Goan Shark Curry

This curry is known in Goa as amo-tik, *which means sour-hot. The sourness comes from the tamarind and vinegar. It is particularly suited to any of the shark family, all of which have a rather sweet, oily flavor. I would suggest using porbeagle shark for the best flavor but any of the following would produce a good dish: blue shark, ray, angel shark or dogfish. These are all sharks native to the U.K., but shark or dogfish from other countries will work very well too.*

Sprinkle the shark with some of the salt and leave for 20 minutes before cooking.

Grind the garlic, ginger, tamarind, peppercorns, turmeric and chilies in a mortar or a blender. If using the latter, grind the peppercorns in a pepper mill first.

Fry the onions in the oil until translucent. Add the cumin seeds and fry for another minute, then add the dry masala ingredients. Cook for 2–3 minutes, then add the chopped tomatoes, wine vinegar, water and the rest of the salt. Bring to a boil and simmer for 2–3 minutes. Add the shark and simmer gently for 5 minutes. Sprinkle with the chopped cilantro and serve with boiled rice.

Serves 4

1¼ pounds shark or dogfish fillet, cut into 1-inch pieces

For the Masala
2 garlic cloves
• 1-inch piece fresh ginger, peeled
• A walnut-sized piece of tamarind, seeded
½ teaspoon black peppercorns
½ teaspoon ground turmeric
6 red chilies
2 onions, chopped
2 tablespoons vegetable oil
½ teaspoon cumin seeds
2 tomatoes, chopped
2 tablespoons wine vinegar
1¼ cups water
1 teaspoon salt
1 teaspoon chopped fresh cilantro

Shark, Conch and Octopus Salad with Lemon, Garlic and Olive Oil

This Italian salad has a simple dressing so that the flavors of the fish and shellfish are not smothered. I have purposely chosen cheap but unusual seafood for this dish because it is just as good using shark and conchs as the expensive monkfish and large prawns.

Simmer the octopus in lightly salted water for 1 hour. Cool, remove the dark brown skin and thinly slice.

Cook the shark by poaching it in salted water for about 5 minutes. Leave to cool in the water, then remove and slice into ½-inch pieces. →

1 octopus, prepared for cooking (see p. 28)
12 ounces shark fillet
4 cooked or uncooked conchs (whelks)
• Juice of ½ lemon
6 tablespoons extra-virgin olive oil
2 garlic cloves, finely chopped →

If you need to cook the conchs, bring them to a boil in seawater or water salted at the rate of 1½ teaspoons of salt to 2½ cups for 5 minutes. Remove the meat from the shells, taking care to cut away the little round "door" at the front of the shell. Cut off and discard the brown end, then thinly slice the meat.

Mix all the ingredients together in a large bowl and serve.

1	tablespoon roughly chopped fresh parsley
1	tablespoon white wine vinegar
4	ounces fresh button mushrooms, thinly sliced
1	teaspoon salt
½	iceberg lettuce

} **Serves 4**

Grilled Swordfish Steaks with Salsa Fresca

You can just as successfully use tuna or sea bass for this dish. The grilled fish steaks are served with a chili hot sauce and an ice-cold salsa with avocado, cucumber, tomato and green onions. It is dressed with a thin mayonnaise-based sauce from Mexico. Try to keep all the avocado, cucumber, tomatoes and green onion roughly the same size when chopping them.

Keep all the prepared *salsa* ingredients cold, and separate until just before serving, then quickly mix them together in a bowl and divide among 4 plates.

Cut the olive flesh from the pits in strips, then cut these strips into thin pine needle–sized shards. In a small pan, mix the mayonnaise, cream and warm water with the olive shards, then warm through. The sauce should be served warm not hot.

Ready the charcoal grill or heat a ribbed grill pan. Season the swordfish steaks with salt and pepper and brush with olive oil. Grill for about 3 minutes on each side.

Serve with a portion of salsa and some of the sauce spread over the steaks and around the plates.

Serve with a Mexican beer light in alcohol, so you can drink lots of it to combat the heat of the chili.

} **Serves 4**

4	swordfish steaks, about 6 ounces each
•	Olive oil, for brushing
•	Salt and freshly ground black pepper

For the Salsa

1	green chili, seeded and finely chopped
1	avocado, peeled and cut into ¼-inch dice
2	garlic cloves, finely chopped
3	green onions, thinly sliced
½	cucumber, cut into ¼-inch dice
•	Juice of 2 limes
2	underripe tomatoes, peeled, seeded and cut into ¼-inch dice
1	tablespoon fresh cilantro, roughly chopped

For the Sauce

4	green olives
4	heaped tablespoons *Olive Oil Mayonnaise* (see p. 43)
4	tablespoons heavy cream
½	cup water

Sashimi with Soya and Japanese Horseradish

Sashimi is raw, sliced fish served here with a Japanese horseradish called wasabi, *a green, fiery horseradish that is mixed with soy sauce and lime juice to make a hot dressing. If you can't get hold of any* wasabi, *use hot prepared horseradish sauce instead. Even if this recipe does not appeal to you at first, try it. You'll be amazed how full of flavor raw fish, particularly tuna, is.*

Buy the fillets of three or four different types of fish for this dish. The Japanese insist on absolute freshness—so fresh that the fish is still jumping around just before being cut up. But, as long as you can trust your fishmonger, the best fillets that he has will be perfectly adequate. All you need to do is just say to him that you don't mind what fish it is as long as it's the freshest that he's got. At the restaurant we tend to go for fish with differing textures and shades so, for example, there will normally be an oily fish like salmon or tuna for its color and two other oily fish, such as mackerel or herring, which are both excellent for sashimi. There may also be a fish like turbot, brill or plaice, which slice very satisfactorily and are always free from bones and perhaps, finally, a sliced scallop or some bass. Raw lobster is a particular delicacy for sashimi.

You need to buy about 12 ounces of fillet as a first course for four people. If you are not too adept at skinning fillet, then ask your fishmonger to do it for you.

To make the slicing of the fish easier, make sure it is well chilled. Cut the fillet slightly on the diagonal so that the slices lie against each other in an attractive way. The presentation of the dish is very important and no one does it better than the Japanese. The great thing with delicate presentation is not to fiddle around with things. It is far better to slice the fillets on a cutting board, pick them up on a spatula and put them confidently on the plate. Don't attempt to neaten them up. I find that it doesn't really matter if the slices are not totally neat as long as they're natural.

First, cut the fish fillets into four equal portions, then slice each portion of each fish as thinly as possible, slightly on the diagonal. Lay the fish around four cold plates. Place a teaspoon of the *wasabi* (or horseradish) on each plate. Lay a couple of chives and some sprigs of cilantro across the plates to garnish.

Mix together the ingredients for the lime and soy sauce and hand round separately.

Serves 4

12 ounces skinned fish fillet
1 tablespoon green *wasabi* powder mixed to a stiff paste with water or prepared horseradish sauce
• A few fresh chives
• A few fresh cilantro sprigs

For the Lime and Soy Sauce
2 tablespoons finely chopped fresh ginger
6 tablespoons soy sauce
6 tablespoons water
2 green onions, finely chopped
• Zest and juice of 1 lime

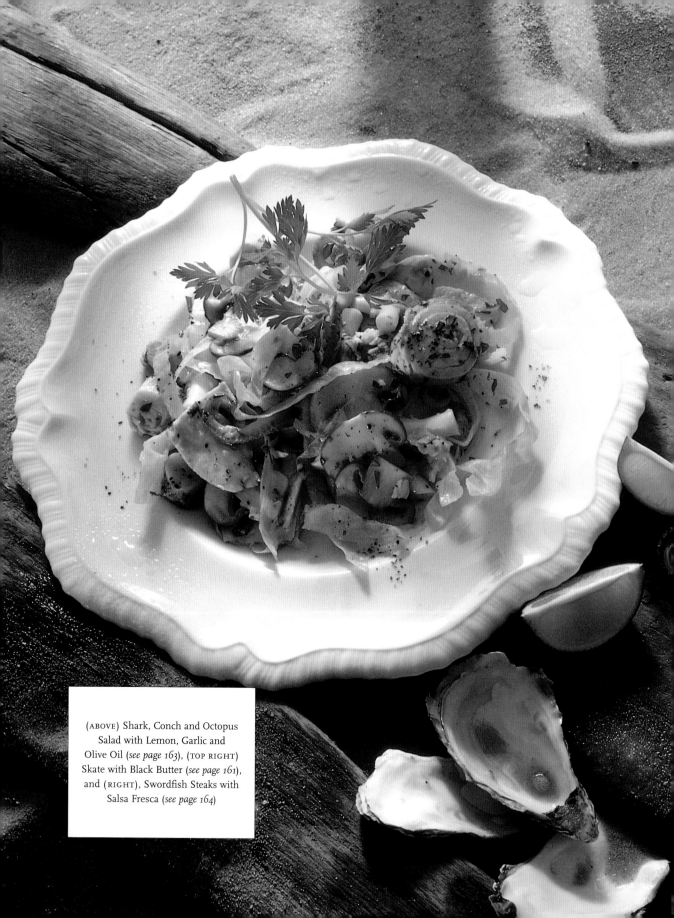

(ABOVE) Shark, Conch and Octopus Salad with Lemon, Garlic and Olive Oil (*see page 163*), (TOP RIGHT) Skate with Black Butter (*see page 161*), and (RIGHT), Swordfish Steaks with Salsa Fresca (*see page 164*)

Grilled Tuna with Olives, Lemon and Sorrel

This recipe comes from Gay Bilson, an inspired cook from Sydney. Her restaurant, The Berowra Waters Inn, produced one of the most memorable meals of my life. She has now moved on to running a restaurant in the Opera House.

The tuna fish steak is seared on the outside but left underdone inside; this is by far the best way to eat it. A cast-iron ribbed grill pan is the ideal utensil for cooking this dish, though a real charcoal grill imparts a superior flavor. The quantities are for a first course.

Remove the pits from the olives and cut into thin slivers. Wash the sorrel, remove the stalks and cut into long, fine strips.

Put the grill pan on the heat to get really hot. Cut the tuna fillet into four pieces and brush with a little olive oil and season well with salt and black pepper. Grill for 1 minute only on each side.

Put the fish sauce, lemon juice, 2½ teaspoons of the olive oil and water into a small pan. Bring to a boil then remove from the heat immediately and keep warm.

Warm the remaining olive oil in another small pan, add the olives and about three-quarters of the sorrel. Allow the sorrel to wilt but don't cook it any further or it will brown.

Divide the olive and sorrel sauce among four warmed plates, place the tuna on top and pour the other sauce over the fish. Sprinkle with the remaining sorrel and serve.

12	green olives
2	ounces sorrel
1	pound tuna fillet, skinned
4	tablespoons virgin olive oil
2	tablespoons water
½	teaspoon Thai fish sauce (*nam pla*)
•	Juice of ¼ lemon
•	Salt and freshly ground black pepper

Serves 4

Grilled Tuna Salad with Guacamole

This dish comes from the Fifth Floor Restaurant in Harvey Nichols Department Store in London. The idea that raw tuna is cooked on a charcoal grill so briefly that only the outside is colored and caramelized and the inside practically raw has been much copied and adapted, especially to meat like fillet steak. But I know from talking to the chef, Henry Harris, at the Fifth Floor, that he was the one that brought the dish to England from California, and jolly good for him. This is not his exact recipe. I much prefer to get enthusiastic about a dish in someone else's restaurant than attempt to copy it. By doing this, two surprisingly different versions of the same dish emerge; two for the price of one, if you like.

Prepare a charcoal grill or heat a ribbed grill pan until it is very hot. Brush the tuna with oil and sprinkle liberally with salt and freshly ground black pepper. Blacken the fillet on the grill for 2–3 minutes, turning to color it all over. Remember the center of the tuna should remain raw. Remove from the grill and season again. Leave to cool completely.

Blend all the guacamole ingredients in a food processor until smooth, then mix all the dressing ingredients together.

Slice the tuna into 1/4-inch slices and arrange on four cold plates. The slices should slightly overlap and be to the side of the plates. Put a spoonful of the guacamole on each plate, again slightly to the side (offsetting food on plates makes it look more natural). Add a generous pool of dressing and decorate the guacamole with a sprig of cilantro.

Serves 4

- 1   pound tuna fillet
- •   Oil, for brushing
- •   Sea salt and freshly ground black pepper
- 4   sprigs of fresh cilantro, to garnish

For the Guacamole
- 1   large avocado, pitted and peeled
- 1   green chili, seeded
- •   Juice of 1 lime
- 2   green onions, chopped
- 1   tablespoon chopped fresh cilantro plus 4 sprigs
- 3   tablespoons vegetable oil
- 1/2 teaspoon salt

For the Soy Sauce Dressing
- 4   tablespoons water
- 1   tablespoon soy sauce
- 1   green onion, finely chopped
- 1/4 green chili, seeded and chopped
- •   Juice and zest of 1/2 lime
- 1/2 stalk lemongrass, finely sliced
- 1   teaspoon chopped fresh ginger

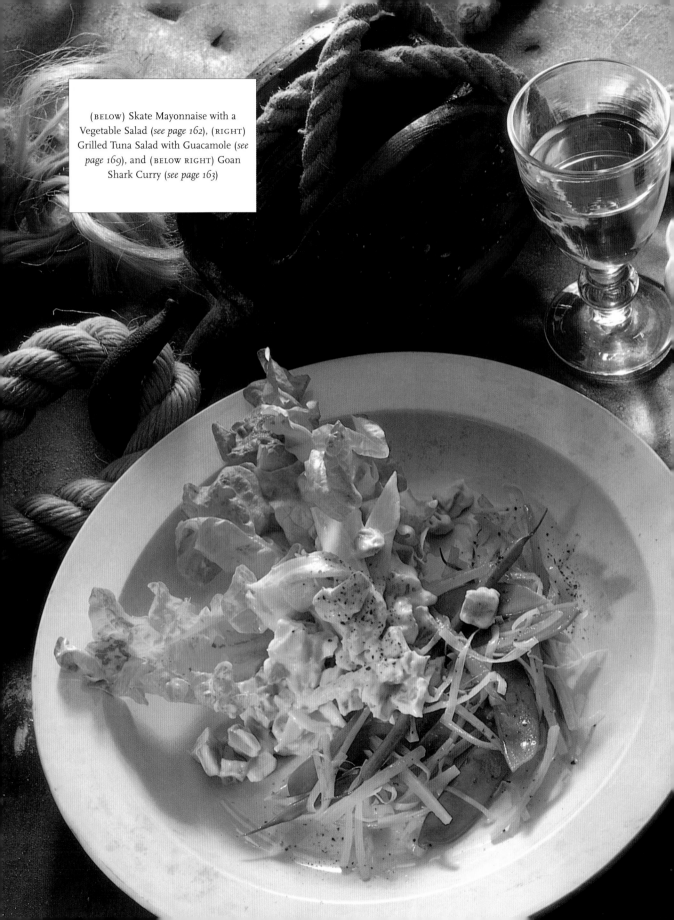

(BELOW) Skate Mayonnaise with a Vegetable Salad (*see page 162*), (RIGHT) Grilled Tuna Salad with Guacamole (*see page 169*), and (BELOW RIGHT) Goan Shark Curry (*see page 163*)

Conger Eel with White Beans, Smoked Ham and Garlic

One of my themes in fish cookery is to break down the barriers between fish and meat. You may think that the idea of fish in a sort of cassoulet is in poor taste, but the cubes of conger eel with smoked ham, Toulouse sausage, tomato and garlic with plenty of white beans works very well here. Try to use cold smoked ham in this recipe, something like Black Forest or any air-dried smoked ham.

Soak the beans for 8 hours and drain. Put them in a pan, add enough water to cover them generously and simmer for 25 minutes. Add the salt and simmer for a further 25–30 minutes until nearly tender.

Preheat the oven to 350°F. Place the parsley, white bread and half the garlic in a food processor and process until you have a bread crumb mixture. Season with salt and pepper. Add the remaining ingredients, except 5 tablespoons of the oil and the salt and pepper to the pan. Simmer for 20 minutes, then season with ground black pepper. Transfer the contents of the pan to a deep ovenproof pot, preferably earthenware. Pour over the rest of the olive oil and sprinkle with the bread crumb mixture. Bake in the oven for about 1 hour, pushing the bread crumbs down into the cassoulet three or four times during the baking to build up a crust.

Serve with a lightly dressed green salad.

I would suggest a young, fresh Cabernet Sauvignon to go with this.

Serves 4

2	cups dried large white (haricot) beans
1	teaspoon salt
2	tablespoons roughly chopped fresh parsley
4	slices fresh white bread
6	cloves garlic, chopped
2	ounces smoked ham, sliced and cut into 1/2-inch strips
3	Toulouse sausages or other wine-and-garlic-flavored pork sausages, cut into slices
1¼	cups chopped canned tomatoes
2½	cups *Chicken Stock* (see p. 37)
1/2	red chili, seeded and chopped
1	pound conger eel fillet, skinned, boned and cut into 1-inch cubes
2/3	cup extra-virgin olive oil
•	Salt and freshly ground black pepper

Crustaceans

CRAB, LANGOUSTINE, LOBSTER, PRAWNS AND SHRIMP

Crustaceans are some of the most highly prized species of the sea, and lobsters, langoustines, prawns, and the like often represent the ultimate treat for seafood lovers. The best way to appreciate their delicate, salty-sweet flavor is to serve them very simply, with just mayonnaise or salad. However, they are also the ideal choice for spectacular dishes such as *Lobster Ravioli with Basil and Spinach* (p. 189) and *Crab in Filo Pastry with a Rich Tomato Sauce and Basil* (p. 178).

CRAB

If the meat of crab came out of the shell in the same solid chunks as lobster, it would, without doubt, fetch the same sort of price. Crab is as sweet and full of flavor as lobster, but it comes out in small flakes. Even when lobster meat is taken from the shell it looks presentable, but crab, on the other hand, is just a pile. Many of my recipes for crab, therefore, include some sort of container to improve the appearance of the dish. Thus, the recipes in this chapter include crab quiche, crab in filo pastry and crab cakes.

Crab is delicate and a common error is to partner it with overpowering flavors so the taste is lost completely. When writing my own recipes I have kept that thought in mind.

Green Shore Crabs

"Where the hell am I supposed to get shore crabs from?" I hear you say. Well, you could go down to a nearby beach and turn over a lot of large stones, which is what I would do or, if you were in France, you could nip down the road to your local supermarket and buy a kilo or two. That is because in France they are aware of the great value of these tiny green crabs both for making bisques and for making shellfish *fumets*. Just as

important, though, is the fact that the back shell supplies a neat little container for crabmeat dishes.

One of the problems in writing a fish cookery book is that the supply of raw materials is limited to the more popular species. One feels a certain guilt in including recipes for things like fresh whelks (conchs), velvet crabs, razor clams, and garfish (a sleek silver fish with a small sword like beak and green bones with oily firm flesh) and even such very common species as spider crabs, because one knows that they are not going to be easily available everywhere. But one of my main reasons for taking up seafood cookery in the first place was to show everyone in Britain that seafood is rich and varied. Just because you can't readily get hold of a raw material, I still feel that you should share my enthusiasm for some dishes that require it because it may just make you go and demand them from your fishmonger—and it is customer demand that will, in the end, improve the variety available.

In the meantime, however, as far as green shore crabs are concerned, go and pick your own. Simply turn over rocks on a rocky beach and you will find plenty, or else dangle a net with a couple of fish heads inside it and a length of twine over any harbor quay side and the green crabs will jump onto the net trying to get at the fish heads and you haul them up. Why not get your children to do it! Velvet crabs can be bought anywhere near the sea where there is also lobster fishing, because they get caught in the same pots as lobsters. Most lobster fishermen now are aware of their value, having got good prices for them in France and Spain, and will gladly sell them to you.

LANGOUSTINE

Of all the raw materials that are used at our restaurant, langoustines, known as lobsterettes in the United States, cause the most trouble. Although they are in great abundance in the Irish Sea 100 miles northwest of the restaurant, no one in Britain seems inclined to go fishing for them. The French, on the other hand, are there in force. Consequently we have to get our langoustine from Scotland and suffer the same sort of problems of varying quality that everyone else in Britain seems to have to put up with as far as fish and shellfish are concerned if they can't buy fish straight from the quayside. We have to have langoustine because they are what any self-respecting fish restaurant sells. One day the fishing industry in the southwest may find a market for them but, meanwhile, we have to buy them from Scotland.

A couple of tips about the quality of langoustine that you get in fish markets these days. They are much more akin to lobsters than shrimp and look more like lobsters. Also, like lobsters their flesh deteriorates very quickly after death. Again, like lobsters, this is not due to any poisonous organism in them but because of a chemical change. The flesh becomes soft like cotton wool. It is easy to tell if they are fresh: pull back their tails; if they have a good degree of spring in them the meat inside will be firm. If the tail stays spread out when you pull it, the meat will be soft. Be governed by your sense of smell with langoustine, they should smell sweet and appetizing. If there is any suggestion of sourness or, worse still, ammonia, don't buy them.

Apart from serving them hot with a cream and garlic sauce (see p. 182-3) or with *Garlic Butter* (see p. 49), they are best served simply with a good mayonnaise such as the *Mustard Mayonnaise* on p. 43.

LOBSTER

Every country with a coastline thinks that their seafood is the best. We say that fish and shellfish from our colder waters have a finer flavor. Australians say theirs is best because the warmer waters of the Pacific produce abundant and therefore cheap seafood from unpolluted waters. They cite the Pacific shrimp as the best large prawn in the world and I would not disagree. But our lobsters are the best in the world. I have tried spiny lobsters in the Mediterranean, Southeast Asia and Australia and I have tried lobsters from the eastern seaboard of the United States and Canada, and I now know, without doubt, that ours are the sweetest and richest of all seafood.

I regard lobster as the same caliber of delicacy as caviar or truffles. For the amount of work that goes into catching them, I think they are astonishingly good value for money. Canadian or American lobsters, which are now available live and airfreighted into the U.K. are, however, a good buy for dishes where the meat is taken out of the shell and served with other ingredients like the *Special Salad of Lobster, Avocado, Green Beans and Duck Livers* on p. 185. But if it's a straight grilled lobster or a lobster with mayonnaise, it has to be one from the western seas of Britain and Ireland.

It is easy for me to tell the difference between our own lobsters and those from Canada and America. The New World lobster is a deep green when live and a fairly uniform orange red when cooked. The European lobster is blue when live and more of a pinky red with a lot of white mottling when cooked. The lobster from America has rounder claws than those from Europe. I must try eating Maine lobsters in Maine. It may be that they lose something in the journey. I suspect they will taste much better eaten right by the sea where they came from just as the only place to eat Cornish lobster is Cornwall.

Crawfish or Spiny Lobster

We are lucky in the southwest of Britain to be one of the only places in the world where both the blue cold-water lobster and the browny-red spiny lobster abound. Any farther north and the water is too cold for the spiny lobster, and the blue lobster becomes rarer farther south as the water becomes warmer. From a chef's point of view the spiny lobster is not as prized as the common lobster because it grows to a much larger size and is therefore difficult to get hold of in 1–2 portion sizes, i.e. weighing between 1 pound and 2^1/$_2$ pounds.

Serving slices from a bigger fish just doesn't have the same impact as giving someone half or a whole lobster. However, for cooking at home, they are ideal because of the impact achieved by bringing such stunning-looking seafood to the table. All recipes for lobster suit the spiny lobster as well. I don't, myself, think they have such a good flavor as ordinary lobster but others disagree. To me spiny lobsters should only be eaten freshly boiled because their flavor is more ephemeral than ordinary lobsters and disappears when they are left, particularly if they are chilled. No fresh seafood is as good as when served recently boiled and left to cool at ambient temperatures. Chilling removes some of that fragrant iodine flavor.

PRAWNS

It is almost impossible to get fresh prawns, which are called shrimp in the United States, in Britain. We get small quantities from time to time, a by-product of lobster fishing and caught up, unbelievably, in lobster pots. I have tried to persuade local lobster fishermen to have a go at using some creel pots and even offered to pay for the gear, but so far I have achieved nothing. The prawns you are likely to see everywhere at fishmongers and fish counters are not fresh but have been caught out in the North Atlantic and boiled at sea in sea water and then deep frozen. Fortunately the quality is excellent and while no one would mistake

the fragrance of fresh prawns for the rather obvious salty sweet and savory taste of frozen ones, they have an undeniably good flavor.

The situation as far as imported large prawns is concerned seems to be getting better and better. Frozen raw prawn tails can be very good and fresh whole prawns from Southeast Asia and best of all Australia are now quite common. In fact the supply of raw materials from all over the world is becoming ever more varied, thanks to airfreight. A fishmonger I know from Sydney, who runs a very upmarket business called the Flying Squid Brothers, has his seafood store not by the sea but by the airport, as most of the best fish from around Australia arrives in Sydney by plane.

SHRIMP

Why can't we get plenty of fresh shrimp? Occasionally someone comes to the back door with a bag of them. Once in a while we find a new supplier who produces a couple of 10-pound bags boiled in sea water. I try to tempt my children to nip out with a net and catch a few, but only occasionally does it work. In Brittany, there they are, in Britain there they aren't. One day we may find someone enterprising enough to maintain a supply. It isn't from any unwillingness on my part to pay good money for them. I love fresh shrimp; their taste reminds me of long-gone holidays as a child with a shrimping net bringing them back in buckets of sea water and having them for tea with thinly sliced bread and butter. I'd love to have the time to sail up the estuary in a small boat, fish for some myself and then bring them back to boil up and serve to the customers; that would be ideal.

The only drawback to the sweet, salty taste of shrimp is that there is such a lot of labor involved in peeling them. They are really of the same order of food as sunflower seeds: something to pick at. In Brittany they may give you a small bowl as an appetizer with your Muscadet and that's what I do when I can get them. If you do want to go to the trouble of picking them out to make a recipe, may I suggest mixing fresh shrimp with peeled langoustine (lobsterette) tails, salad greens and a simple dressing of olive oil, peeled, seeded and chopped tomato, lemon juice and basil.

Alternatively, fresh shrimp make an exquisite bisque. Follow the same recipe as for the *Crab Bisque* on p. 57, but use shrimp instead of crabs. Don't bother to buy frozen shrimp; they taste of bits of string.

FRESHLY BOILED CRAB

This needs to be served as a whole crab, straight from the pot, which means it is a dish for those who like eating with their fingers. It is not so much a recipe—since all it includes is the crab, some mayonnaise, new potatoes and a salad—as a set of instructions on the best way to cook and serve up whole crabs to make them easy to eat. I've also included some instructions for dressing crabs, removing the meat from a whole crab, if you prefer to serve it like this.

Crabs should be boiled in plenty of water, salted at the rate of ²/₃ cup salt to 5 quarts water. This is about the same salinity as seawater. Unlike lobsters, crabs can be killed by skewering (see the instructions on p. 25) or by immersing them in cold, salted water and gradually bringing them to a boil until they drown. It is never a good idea to drop live crabs into rapidly boiling water because they shed claws and legs in the process.

I believe in serving a big crab, say 2 pounds for one person, or an even larger crab, 3–4 pounds in weight, for two to three people. A 2-pound crab should be boiled for 15 minutes, while a 4-pound crab will take up to 20 minutes.

When they are cooked, take the crabs out of the water and run them under the cold tap to make them easier to handle. Remove the tail flap from underneath the crab and the two flaps that cover the mouth on the undershell beneath the eyes. Once you have removed these two flaps, you can separate the body from the main shell section (carapace). Place the crab face down on a chopping board and give its rear end a sharp thump with the heel of your hand. This will split the body from the back shell. Alternatively, you can do this with the point of a large knife inserted between the body and the back shell and twisted. Once you have removed the body from the carapace, pull off the gills, known as Dead Man's Fingers, which are popularly held to be poisonous but are just inedible, like feathers. If you look in the cavity of the carapace right in the center behind the eyes, you will see the stomach sac. Push the little piece of shell behind the eyes and you will hear a click. The piece of shell and the stomach sac can then be removed. Empty any excess water from the back of the shell.

Now cut the body section in half from front to back and then in half from side to side. Crack each of the claw sections with the back of a large knife. Try to do this without completely shattering the claws so that you can reassemble the crab to look much as it was. Take a large plate for each person, put the four sections of body back together, put the carapace on top, rearrange any legs that have fallen off so they are the right way round and put the claws back at the front of the crab as they were.

If you prefer to remove all the meat you will need a lobster pick or a teaspoon. Remove the white meat from the cracked claws. Pull off the legs, crack open the top joints and remove the meat from them. It is not normally worth removing the meat from the other leg joints unless the crabs are large. Push the thin end of the pick or the handle of the spoon into the knucklelike joints onto which the claws and legs were attached and twist them off. Remove all the meat from the cavities behind.

Remove any brown meat from the body, which you cut into four sections, and the back shell. Chop the brown meat. (Not all crabs contain brownish meat in the claws and/or body.) Pick out the white meat from the body sections, taking care not to remove the wafer-thin pieces of shell. Serve the dressed crab in the back shells. The traditional accompaniments are chopped hard-boiled egg yolks and whites and chopped parsley. These are placed in the back shell in lines separating the brown meat (if any) from the white. I always like to fold a little mayonnaise and some black pepper into the brown meat.

Serve with new potatoes, a green salad and *Mustard Mayonnaise* (see p. 43).

CRAB NEWBURG

I found this recipe in the Faber Book of Food edited by Colin Spencer and Clare Clifton, a marvelous anthology of eating. The recipe appealed to me as a period piece from the '30s and '40s; the sort of dish that may well have appeared on the menu at dinner on the Queen Mary or the Mauretania. We tried it out in the kitchen and it was delicious, but go easy on the sherry.

We boil the crabs immediately, 20 minutes in salted water. We like best to eat them just so, with home-made mayonnaise and Cuban bread and cold bitter ale. The meat comes from the shells in enormous flakes, snow-white and incredibly sweet and flavoursome...

When we have crab meat to spare, I make a crab Newburg so superlative that I myself taste it in wonder, thinking "Can it be I who has brought this noble thing into the world?"

It is impossible to give proportions, for I never twice have the same amount of crab meat to work with, and here indeed I have no mother, but only instinct, to guide me. In an iron skillet over a low fire I place a certain amount of Dora's butter. As it melts, I stir in the flaked crab meat, lightly, tenderly. The flakes must not become disintegrated; they must not brown. I add lemon juice, possibly a tablespoonful for each cup of crab meat. I add salt and pepper frugally, paprika more generously, and a dash of powdered clove so temporal that the flavor in the finished Newburg is only as though the mixture had been whisked through a spice grove. I add Dora's golden cream. I do not know the exact quantity. It must be generous, but the delicate crab meat must never become deluged with any other element. The mixture bubbles for a few moments. I stir in dry sherry, the quantity again unestimable. Something must be left to genius. I stir in well beaten eggs, perhaps an egg, perhaps two, for every cup of flakes. The mixture must now no more than be turned over on itself and removed in a great sweep from the fire. I stir in a tablespoon, or two, of the finest brandy, and turn the Newburg into a piping hot covered serving dish. I serve it on toast points and garnish superfluously with parsley, and a Chablis or white Rhine wine is recommended as an accompaniment. Angels sing softly in the distance.

We do not desecrate the dish by serving any other, neither salad nor dessert. We just eat crab Newburg. My friends rise from the table, wring my hand with deep feeling, and slip quietly and reverently away. I sit alone and weep for the misery of a world that does not have blue crabs and a Jersey cow.

Crab in Filo Pastry with a Rich Tomato Sauce and Basil

I have added a rich tomato sauce containing one of those secret ingredients beloved by chefs: a gastrique. It is simple: you boil vinegar and sugar together until very rich and concentrated and add a teaspoon or so to a tomato sauce to give it real muscle.

Preheat the oven to 375°F. Brush 1 side of 2 of the sheets of filo pastry with melted butter. Lay the other sheets on top to form 2 pairs. Cut each into 6 rectangles, giving you 12 pieces in all. Place on a baking sheet and bake for about 5 minutes until crisp.

Fry the onion and garlic in the olive oil until translucent. Add the chopped tomatoes and simmer for 30 minutes. Meanwhile, put the vinegar and sugar in a small pan and boil down to about 1 teaspoon. Add to the tomato sauce, then pass through a conical sieve, pushing as much of the debris through with the back of a ladle as you can. Return the sauce to the heat in the small pan, and simmer until the sauce coats the back of a spoon. Season with salt and white pepper.

Mix the crabmeat, the basil, the virgin olive oil and the lemon juice in a pan. Carefully warm through over low heat. Put 1 piece of filo on each of the 4 plates, a table-spoon or so of crabmeat and basil on top and add another layer of filo. On top of that add another table-spoon or so of crabmeat and basil and then the final layer of filo. Spoon the sauce around and serve.

4	sheets filo pastry, 12 by 16 inches each
2	tablespoons butter, melted

For the Tomato Sauce

1	medium onion, finely chopped
1	garlic clove, finely chopped
2	tablespoons olive oil
1	can (14 ounces) chopped tomatoes
4	tablespoons red wine vinegar
2	teaspoons sugar
8	ounces cooked white crabmeat, preferably fresh
10	fresh basil leaves, thinly sliced
1	tablespoon extra-virgin olive oil
•	Juice of ¼ lemon
•	Salt and freshly ground white pepper

Serves 4

Crab Cakes with a Tomato, Crab and Basil Dressing

This dish is designed to reinforce the delicate flavor of crab so, as well as there being a lot of crab in the crab cakes, there is also some crab oil. The oil is made by very gently cooking fresh crab debris with a light olive, not virgin, oil over a long period of time.

Use potatoes that are good for mashing.

Preheat the oven to 300°F.

Extract all the meat from the crab but reserve all the shells. You will need about 10 ounces of crabmeat.

Place the shells with the olive oil in a shallow roasting pan with the carrot, leek and onion. Bake in the oven for 2 hours to gently extract the flavor. Leave to cool, then strain the oil and discard the debris. →

Cook the potatoes in lightly salted boiling water until soft. Mash with a fork and mix in 7 ounces of the crab meat and one third of the crab oil. Correct the seasoning with salt. Divide the mixture into balls each weighing about 2 ounces. On a floured surface, shape into round flat patties. Pass the cakes first through the flour, then the egg and then the bread crumbs.

Put the remaining crab oil, the tomatoes, sliced basil, lemon juice and the rest of the crabmeat in a pan and warm through but do not boil.

Set the deep-fryer to 320°F, or heat some oil to the same temperature in a large pan. Add the cakes and fry for 3 minutes. Remove and drain on paper towels.

Serves 4

Divide the crab cakes among four warmed plates. Pour the dressing around the crab cakes. Garnish with a whole basil leaf placed on top of the dressing. Serve immediately.

1	cooked crab, weighing about 2½ pounds
1¼	cups olive oil
1	large carrot, chopped
1	leek, chopped
1	medium onion, chopped
2	pounds potatoes
•	All-purpose flour, for dusting
2	eggs, beaten
2	cups fresh bread crumbs
2	tomatoes, peeled, seeded and chopped
10	fresh basil leaves, 6 thinly sliced and 4 left whole
•	Juice of ¼ lemon
•	Salt and freshly ground black pepper

Fresh Crab Salad with Tarragon Mayonnaise, Cucumber and Frisée

This is based on a similar salad I ate in a restaurant in Dartmouth and is typical of the innovative cooking of the owner, Joyce Molyneux. The crabmeat is best picked from a freshly boiled crab (see instructions on p. 176).

For the tarragon mayonnaise, add the parsley, tarragon and star anise to the *Olive Oil Mayonnaise*.

To make the cucumber salad, peel the cucumber, cut it into segments lengthwise, remove the seeds and slice thinly. Mix the parsley, fish sauce, lime juice and zest, and water together in a small bowl. Pour over and mix with the cucumber.

To make the frisée salad, put the oil, vinegar, mustard, garlic, shallot, *quatre épices* and salt in a bowl. Whisk together and use to dress the frisée leaves. →

12	ounces crabmeat
	For the Tarragon Mayonnaise
1	teaspoon finely chopped fresh parsley
1	teaspoon finely chopped fresh tarragon
½	teaspoon ground star anise
½	quantity *Olive Oil Mayonnaise* (see p. 43)
	For the Cucumber Salad
½	cucumber
1	teaspoon chopped fresh parsley
1	teaspoon Thai fish sauce (*nam pla*)
•	Juice and zest of 1 lime
4	tablespoons water →

To serve, place a pile of crabmeat on each plate with a dollop of mayonnaise, and a portion each of the cucumber and frisée salads.

Serves 4

For the Frisée Salad

4	tablespoons peanut oil
1	tablespoon white wine vinegar
½	teaspoon English mustard
½	small garlic clove, finely chopped
½	shallot, finely chopped
1	teaspoon *Quatre Épices* (see p. 54)
½	teaspoon salt
2	handfuls frisée leaves

Snow Crab with Pasta, Parsley and Chili

Snow (spider) crabmeat takes more time to pick out than meat from other crabs. It doesn't come out so easily and the claws are smaller so you get less meat for your labor, but the flavor is so good, fragrant and sweet that it's worth the extra trouble. I would suggest using trenette, linguine, pasta or spaghetti. Trenette and linguine are long pastas, like spaghetti, but flat rather than round. Buy only 100 percent durum wheat pasta for this, the best you can afford.

If the crab has red roe in it, use equal quantities of brown and white meat. (The red roe of the snow crab is excellent.)

Boil the pasta in plenty of well-salted water, until tender but still firm with some bite to it. The best way to cook pasta until it is *al dente* is to keep biting until it feels right.

Warm the tomato, crabmeat, parsley, lemon juice, olive oil, chili and garlic over low heat. Let the mixture warm through but don't let it boil or you will alter the flavors. Spoon the pasta onto four warmed plates and spoon over the sauce.

I would drink an Italian Soave with this dish, to match its sweet garlicky flavors, or any other soft, fruity white wine.

Serves 4

12	ounces pasta (see above)
3	medium tomatoes, peeled, seeded and chopped
10	ounces cooked snow crabmeat or other crabmeat
1	tablespoon roughly chopped fresh parsley
•	Juice of ½ lemon
4	tablespoons extra-virgin olive oil
1	good pinch of dried, crushed chili
1	garlic clove, very finely chopped

Crab, Saffron and Leek Quiche

Crabmeat and creamed leeks are cooked here in a light savory custard flavored with Noilly Prat and saffron. You will need a deep 8-inch flan ring or flan case for this dish.

Preheat the oven to 375°F. Roll out the pastry and line an 8-inch tart pan with a removable bottom. Prick the pastry, cover it with parchment paper and fill with pie weights or baking beans. Bake for 10 minutes then remove the weights and paper and leave to cool.

Slice the leeks and boil them in lightly salted water for 10 minutes until really soft. Drain and place in a pan. Add the soaked saffron with the butter and drive off the excess moisture by stirring over high heat.

Boil the fish stock and Noilly Prat together to reduce it to about 2 tablespoons. Add the lemon juice, salt and cayenne pepper, then beat into the eggs and cream. Line the pastry shell with the leeks and sprinkle the crabmeat over the top. Pour over the eggs and cream

Serves 4

and bake in the oven for 20 minutes. You can serve this either hot or cold.

8	ounces shortcrust pastry dough
4	ounces leeks, outer leaves and top removed
•	A pinch of saffron strands soaked in 1 table-spoon warm water
1	tablespoon unsalted butter
1¼	cups *Fish Stock* (see p. 36)
2	tablespoons Noilly Prat or other dry vermouth
•	A little lemon juice and salt
•	Salt
•	A pinch of cayenne pepper
3	eggs
½	cup heavy cream
6	ounces cooked crabmeat

Deep-fried Soft-shell Crabs with Chili Sauce

This recipe came about after I read a Pulitzer prize-winning book called Beautiful Swimmers *by William Warner about "the pugnacious, succulent, Atlantic blue crab in its home waters, the salt water marshes and shoals on the Chesapeake Bay." It is a most unlikely book to win a major prize but has so much information about crab fishing that it is enthralling.*

The prize of the Chesapeake blue crab fishing industry is the soft-shell crab. The fishing of it is a real art. It is only for a few days, while changing from one shell to another slightly bigger one, that these crabs have soft shells and only then can the whole crab be eaten.

It occurred to me that the green shore crab, like all crustaceans, goes through a phase of being soft-shelled and so might also be good when deep-fried. I found a bait fisherman who said that he could get good quantities of these at low tide, because, and this is rather a sad part of the story, at night the soft-shell crabs move about from one hiding place to another under the body of a hard-shell crab for protec-tion. It is easy, with a strong flashlight, to see them scuttling about and pick off the soft-shell crabs. So I tried them and they were very good.

You could use frozen blue soft-shell crabs instead. You will need 12–16 for four people. →

To make the chili sauce, bring the water to a boil in a small pan and add the arrowroot, then remove from the heat and add the fish sauce, lemongrass, chili, sugar, lime zest and juice, green onions and half the cilantro. Pour into a small serving bowl.

Set the deep-fryer to 375°F, or heat some oil in a large pan.

Drop the crabs into the tempura batter and turn over to coat them well. Transfer to the fryer and fry for 4 minutes if they're small crabs, 6 minutes if they are larger. Remove from the fryer and drain on paper towels.

Arrange the crabs in one large pile on a serving plate. Sprinkle with the cilantro. Hand round the chili sauce separately.

Serves 4

20	soft-shell crabs
1	quantity *Tempura Batter* (see p. 53)

For the Chili Sauce

½	cup water
1	teaspoon arrowroot
2	tablespoons Thai fish sauce (*nam pla*)
½	lemongrass stalk, thinly sliced
½	red chili, seeded and finely chopped
1	teaspoon sugar
•	Juice and zest of 1 lime
1	green onion, chopped
1	tablespoon roughly chopped fresh cilantro

Grilled Lobsterettes with Creamed Garlic and Chives

I got this recipe from a restaurant in La Baule in Brittany. The restaurant was dreadful, damp and cheaply done out like lots of places by the sea in both Britain and France trying to make a quick buck in the summer. But this dish caught my imagination. It seemed a delightful way of grilling fresh langoustine with lots of cream and garlic. The langoustine can either be raw or cooked.

Remove the cloves of garlic from the head but don't peel them. Put them and the water in a small pan and cook very gently on low heat until soft. Squeeze the flesh out of the skins into a blender, add the cooking water and blend until smooth. Add this, the cream, fish sauce and lemon juice back to the pan, and warm through over gentle heat.

Preheat the broiler. Brush the lobsterettes with the garlic oil and broil until the shells begin to char. This will be long enough to heat them through, if you are using cooked ones. Raw ones will need a little longer, about 5 minutes in total. →

For the Sauce

1	large head garlic
⅔	cup water
⅔	cup heavy cream
1	tablespoon Thai fish sauce (*nam pla*)
•	Juice of ½ lemon
24	good-sized lobsterettes (langoustine)
2	tablespoons oil infused with 1 garlic clove, for grilling
1	tablespoon chopped fresh chives

Serves 4

When ready to serve, add the chives to the warm garlic sauce, arrange the shellfish on four plates, pour over the sauce and serve.

Serve with an ice-cold bottle of Greek retsina or a good dry white wine.

Lobster with Mayonnaise

In the end I regard this and the recipe for grilled lobster below as the best ways of eating lobster. This is the first way I ever tried it, and it just has the edge over the grilled lobster in my estimation. My wife, Jill, prefers them grilled. When eating whole lobster, remember that the body section contains plenty of meat, particularly in the joints where the claws and legs join the body. You remove the meat with a lobster pick in exactly the same way as picking out crabmeat.

Serve the lobsters with the mayonnaise, a salad of mixed greens dressed with a little Lemon Olive Oil _(see p. 51), salt and some minted new potatoes._

Fill a large pot with the water and bring to a boil. Add the salt. When the water is boiling fiercely, put in one lobster. Wait until the water comes back to a boil, then add the second one. Boil for 15 minutes. If you don't have a pan big enough, boil the lobsters one at a time as they must be fully immersed to cook properly.

Remove the lobsters from the water and leave to cool. To cut the lobster in half, place on a chopping board and drive a large knife through the middle of the cara-pace (the body section) and cut down toward and between the eyes, then, turn the knife around, place it in the original cut and bring the knife down right through the tail to split it in half. Pull off the claws and

cut off the rubber bands binding them together. Crack open each of the three claw sections with a short, sharp chop from the thickest part of your knife blade. Remove the stomach sac behind the mouth and the intestine that runs down the tail.

For a wine accompaniment it's got to be a bottle of good Californian Chardonnay or, if you can afford it, a Burgundy from the Côte d'Or such as Montrachet or Meursault.

6	quarts water
7/8	cup salt
2	live lobsters, 1½ –1¾ pounds each
1	quantity _Olive Oil Mayonnaise_ (see p. 43)

Serves 4

Broiled Lobster with Fines Herbes

This is the way we have cooked lobster at my restaurant ever since we opened: very simple and perfect. The herbs should be fresh and only cut up at the last minute. Parboil the lobsters as described below or simply split them in half while still alive and grill them. This is not as barbaric as you might think, since as long as you cleave them in two efficiently, they are quickly killed. For more general notes on killing lobsters see p. 25. →

Bring the water to a boil in a large pot. When it is boiling fiercely, put in one lobster, wait until the water comes back to a boil, then add the second one. Boil for 5 minutes.

Preheat the broiler. Remove the lobsters from the water. To cut in half, refer to the instructions in *Lobster with Mayonnaise* on p. 183.

Place the lobster, flesh side up, on a broiler pan, brush with melted butter and broil for about 10 minutes.

In a small pan, bring the stock, fish sauce and lemon juice to a boil and whisk in the butter. Add the herbs and pour over the lobster.

Serves 4

6	quarts water
2	live lobsters, 1½–1¾ pounds each
•	A little melted butter, for brushing
¾	cup *Fish Stock* (see p. 36)
½	teaspoon Thai fish sauce (*nam pla*)
•	Juice of ¼ lemon
¼	cup unsalted butter
1	teaspoon chopped fresh parsley
1	teaspoon chopped fresh chervil
1	teaspoon chopped fresh tarragon
1	teaspoon chopped fresh chives

Sautéed Lobster with Saffron and Chambéry

This dish is far easier to make than you might think. The flavor of the saffron, a little butter and a sweetish, spicy vermouth like Chambéry are very well suited to the lobster.

Bring the water to a boil in a large pan. Add the lobster, cover and cook for 5 minutes. Remove from the pan and leave until cool enough to handle. Place the lobster on a chopping board and refer to the instructions for cutting up lobsters in *Lobster with Mayonnaise* on p. 183.

Put 4 tablespoons of the butter in a large shallow pan and melt quickly over a fierce heat. Place all the lobster pieces in the pan and cook until they start to turn red. Pour in the Chambéry and three-quarters of the stock and add the saffron. Cover and leave to simmer gently for 10 minutes. →

Serves 2

6	quarts water
1	live lobster, about 1¾ pounds
	For the Sauce
5	tablespoons unsalted butter
4	tablespoons Chambéry or other sweet vermouth
1¼	cups *Fish Stock* (see p. 36)
½	teaspoon saffron strands
•	A few drops of lemon juice

Remove from the heat and take out the lobster pieces. Leave until cool enough to handle, then crack the claws and carefully extract the meat with a lobster pick. Remove the meat from the tail sections. Keep warm and slice into pieces 1 inch thick.

Add the remaining stock to the pan. Reduce the sauce a little, then whisk in the rest of the butter and finish with lemon juice to taste.

Arrange the lobster pieces on two warmed plates. Through a sieve, pour over the sauce and serve.

Special Salad of Lobster, Avocado, Green Beans and Duck Livers

Salads like this appear on the menu of virtually every three-star restaurant in France, but there the duck livers would be foie gras. *By cooking a simple duck liver terrine you can produce something surprisingly similar.*

Make the terrine the day before you want to eat the salad and keep it chilled. You will need some sort of mold. I would suggest using a mug if you have nothing better. Line the mold with well-buttered parchment paper.

Preheat the oven to 300°F. Place all the terrine ingredients, except the butter, in a blender and blend for 1 minute. Melt the butter in a pan, then pour into the blender and blend in thoroughly. Pour the mixture into the lined terrine, cover with the buttered paper and some sort of lid. Stand the mold on a cloth in the bottom of a roasting pan and pour in enough warm water to come about halfway up the terrine mold. Bring the water to a boil on the top of the stove, then transfer to the oven and cook for about 25 minutes. Remove and chill.

Slice each bean in half lengthwise. Blanch in boiling salted water for 30 seconds only, drain and refresh in very cold water. Drain well.

Cut the lobster in half and remove the meat from the tail. Crack open the claws and remove the meat. Slice the lobster tail into 1/2-inch slices. If you have a hen lobster with the bright red coral, add the coral to the lobster meat, cut into thin slices. →

3	ounces slender green beans, topped and tailed
1	ripe avocado
1	lobster, 1 1/2 pounds, cooked
4	tablespoons extra-virgin olive oil
1	tablespoon balsamic vinegar
1/2	teaspoon salt
•	A small bunch fresh chervil, leaves only

For the Duck Liver Terrine

4	ounces duck liver
1/4	teaspoon salt
•	A pinch of white pepper
1/2	small garlic clove
1	tablespoon port
2	teaspoons brandy
1/4	cup unsalted butter

} **Serves 4**

(BELOW) Broiled Lobster with Fines Herbes (*see page 183*), (RIGHT) Fresh Crab Salad with Tarragon Mayonnaise, Cucumber and Frisée (*see page 179*), and (BELOW RIGHT) Sautéed Lobster with Saffron and Chambéry (*see page 184*)

Cut the avocado in half, remove the pit then cut in half again, lengthwise. Peel and thinly slice.

Make little lozenge shapes out of the terrine using two teaspoons.

Put the beans, avocado, olive oil, balsamic vinegar and salt in a bowl and toss gently. Divide among four plates, add the lobster but do not put it all on top. Finally, place the lozenges of duck liver in the salad, again not all on top. The salad should be a contrast in flavor between the oily salad ingredients and the lobster and duck liver terrine. Garnish with a few leaves of chervil.

Serve with a slightly spicy, full-bodied white wine.

Lobster à L'Américaine

There has always been some doubt as to where this excellent lobster dish came from. Some say it should be Lobster Armoricaine, the old name for Brittany; others say it couldn't possibly have come from Brittany because most of the ingredients would suggest the Mediterranean and not Brittany. One thing is for certain, the dish came from France not America. I am a little wary of lobster served in sauces because I believe that fresh lobster needs very little accompaniment except some butter or mayonnaise and a few herbs, it having such a wonderful taste in its own right. However, I make an exception of this dish because the sauce, when made properly, is so fresh tasting.

It is traditionally made with live lobsters, but if you do not like the idea of cutting up lobsters alive, bring a large pan of boiling water to a boil and plunge the lobsters into it. Bring back to a boil and boil for 5 minutes to kill them.

Make sure the tomatoes you use in this recipe are good, sun-ripened, sweet ones.

Cut the live lobsters in half lengthwise; refer to the instructions on p. 183 in *Lobster with Mayonnaise*. Pull each tail section away from the head section and cut each section of tail into 4 or 5 pieces. Break the claw sections apart and crack each section so that the meat can be extracted easily later. The easiest way to do this is with the thickest part of a large knife.

Put the olive oil into a heavy-based pan big enough to hold all the pieces of lobster. Cook the onion and garlic in the olive oil until they are beginning to soften, then add all the pieces of lobster. Turn up the heat a little and turn the lobster pieces over until they are beginning to color red. Add the cognac and let the alcohol boil off. Add the tomatoes, chopped tarragon, white wine, →

2	live lobsters, 1½–2 pounds each
6	tablespoons olive oil
½	cup finely chopped onion
1	tablespoon cognac
2	garlic cloves, finely chopped
1½	pounds tomatoes, peeled, seeded and chopped
1	tablespoon roughly chopped fresh tarragon
6	tablespoons dry white wine
1	teaspoon sugar
2½	cups *Fish Stock* (see p. 36)

Serves 4

sugar and stock. Cover. Leave the lobsters to cook through for about 8 minutes.

Remove the lobster pieces and keep warm. Return the pan to the heat and reduce the sauce by half.

When the sauce has reduced, return the lobster pieces to the sauce, heat through, transfer to an attractive serving dish and serve with grilled potatoes as in the recipe for *Dover Sole à la Meunière* on page 152.

Lobster Ravioli with Basil and Spinach

This is a dish where the use of North American lobsters is perfectly acceptable. Most of the cooked lobster that you see in supermarkets and fishmongers in this country is from North America. This dish is designed to make a small amount of lobster go a long way, but it is still very much a luxury first course.

If you have a pasta machine, roll the dough to setting number 6. If you don't, roll out to no more than 1/8 inch thick. The ravioli are single large ones. Using a 4-inch round pastry cutter or a plate or bowl, cut out 8 discs. Allow the pasta to rest for 10–15 minutes.

Remove the meat from the lobster. Slice the lobster meat into 1/4-inch slices.

If there is any coral in the lobster or berries under the lobster's tail, cut the coral up and remove the berries and add with all the brown meat from the lobster's head.

Put the fish fillet, the egg, the lemon juice and salt and 2/3 cup of the heavy cream in a food processor. Blend until smooth, then pour in the rest of cream in a steady stream, taking only about 10 seconds; any longer and the mixture will curdle. Transfer to a bowl and fold in the lobster meat and the basil. Remember to remove the stomach sac.

Put a pile of filling in the center of each of four of the pasta disks, leaving a 1/2-inch border. You should be able to get most of the mixture into the ravioli. Moisten the outer edge of each disk with water, including the disks you will put on top. Put the four remaining disks on top, slide a spatula under the ravioli and place on →

For the Ravioli
1   quantity *Egg Pasta Dough* (see p. 54)
1   lobster, 1 1/4 pounds, cooked
12   ounces skinned fillets of cheap flat fish such as flounder or sand dabs
1   egg
•   Juice of 1/4 lemon
1 1/2   teaspoons salt
2 1/2   cups heavy cream
5   fresh basil leaves, thinly sliced

For the Sauce
2 1/2   cups *Fish Stock* (see p. 36)
6   tablespoons heavy cream
1/4   cup unsalted butter
6   tablespoons dry white wine
5   fresh basil leaves, thinly sliced
12   spinach leaves, preferably small ones

Serves 4

(LEFT) Shrimp Cocktail with Malt Whisky (*see page 192*), (BELOW) Lobster Ravioli with Basil and Spinach (*see page 189*), and (BELOW) Special Salad of Lobster, Avocado, Green Beans and Duck Livers (*see page 185*)

the palm of your hand. Gently crimp the edges together with your fingers, pulling the ravioli round as you do.

Drop each ravioli into a large pan of boiling salted water for about 40 seconds. Remove and drop into a bowl of cold water for 5 seconds before placing on a tray. You can make these ravioli a day in advance. Cover with plastic wrap and store in the refrigerator.

To serve, rapidly boil the stock, cream, butter and white wine together until the sauce has reduced to the point where it will coat the back of a spoon. Stir in the sliced basil leaves and keep warm.

Bring a pan of salted water to a boil, drop in the spinach leaves and blanch briefly for about 20 seconds. Remove and keep warm. Put the ravioli in the same water, reduce the heat and poach for 4–5 minutes. Take four warm plates and lay the spinach leaves out in the center of them. Put the ravioli on top and cover with the sauce. Serve immediately.

Serve with a good-quality Chardonnay.

Stir-fried Shrimp

This is a Sichuan recipe often characterized by plenty of chili. The chili bean sauce in the recipe can be easily bought at Chinese markets but, if you can't get hold of it, mix together yellow bean sauce and chili sauce. If you want to make the dish even hotter, put in a few finely chopped red chilies as well.

Grind together the Sichuan and black peppercorns. Put the peanut oil in a wok and stir-fry the white part of the green onions, the ginger and the garlic for 1 minute. Add the shrimp and stir-fry for another 1 minute, then add the sherry, soy sauce, chili bean sauce, tomatoes and sugar. Cover and cook for 3 minutes. Sprinkle with the green part of the onions and serve.

Serves 4

1	teaspoon Sichuan peppercorns
1/2	teaspoon black peppercorns
1	tablespoon peanut oil
3	green onions, white and green separated, thinly sliced
•	1-inch piece fresh ginger, peeled and finely chopped
4	garlic cloves, finely chopped
1	pound shrimp, peeled
1	teaspoon dry sherry
1	tablespoon soy sauce
2	tablespoons chili bean sauce
8	ounces tomatoes, peeled and sliced
•	1/2 teaspoon sugar

Shrimp Cocktail with Malt Whisky

There is no substitute for tomato ketchup for a shrimp cocktail, no fresh tomato sauce ever tastes so good. However, the other ingredients can make all the difference. The difference here is malt whisky, which gives the shrimp cocktail a subtle aftertaste of open log fires: just the thing for Christmas. →

In this recipe I have included a small amount of natural yogurt, which gives the sauce a subtle extra tartness. If, as I do, you love shrimp cocktails, make them big, particularly for a special occasion. Go to a glassware shop and buy some really voluminous glasses. The glasses we use are large and no attempt is made to fill them, although the portions in this recipe are generous.

Chill four large glasses.

Take a small bowl and whisk together the egg yolks, vinegar, pepper and salt. Continuing to whisk, gradually drizzle in the oil to make a mayonnaise. Add the tomato ketchup, malt whisky and yogurt.

Tear the salad greens into pieces no more than 2 inches across and divide among the chilled glasses. Place the shrimp gently on top so that they cover the salad, but leave a gap around the circumference of the glass.

Pour the sauce over the shrimp without totally covering all of either them or the salad. The dish looks much more appetizing if you can see a few pink pieces of uncovered shrimp and some uncoated leaves. Finally put a little pile of the sliced basil leaves in the center of each glass.

Serves 4

8 ounces large shrimp, cooked, peeled and chilled

For the Marie Rose Sauce
2 egg yolks
2 teaspoons white wine vinegar
· A pinch of ground white pepper
1/4 teaspoon salt
1 cup vegetable oil
5 tablespoons tomato ketchup
2 tablespoons single malt whisky
4 tablespoons plain yogurt

For the Salad
3 1/2 ounces mixed salad greens, including, if possible, some radicchio
4 fresh basil leaves, thinly sliced

Salad of Shrimp, Arugula and Prosciutto

The supreme strength of Italian cuisine is that the unique flavors of the ingredients are presented in such a way that they enhance but do not smother each other. All the flavors in this salad are interesting on their own, but drawn together with some good olive oil they produce an effect greater than the sum of their parts.

Tear the prosciutto into pieces about 2 inches across. Divide the arugula leaves among four cold plates and arrange the prosciutto among the leaves. Scatter over the shrimp then drizzle 1 tablespoon of olive oil over each salad. Finally, grind over some black pepper and serve.

Serve with a bottle of chilled white Pinot Grigio.

4 ounces large shrimp, cooked and peeled
6 very thin slices of prosciutto
2 ounces arugula leaves
4 tablespoons extra-virgin olive oil
· Freshly ground black pepper

Serves 4

Shrimp Terrine with Zucchini Salad

This terrine, which sells well in our delicatessen in Padstow, uses large shrimp in the shell, which have a far better flavor than the same type of shrimp sold out of the shell. Use any white fish such as cod, whiting, lemon sole or flounder. It makes a light first course. You will need a terrine mold about 6 by 3 by 3 inches in size.

Preheat the oven to 300°F. Peel the shrimp and reserve the shells. Melt the butter in a pan, add the carrot, onion and shells and cook gently for 5 minutes. Pour in the brandy and add the tomato paste. Cook for a few minutes longer, then add the stock and simmer for 20 minutes. Pour into a blender or food processor and blend for about 30 seconds.

Pass through a fine sieve into another pan, pushing against the debris with the back of a ladle to extract as much flavor as possible. Bring the sieved liquid back to a boil and simmer until there is only about 1 tablespoon of strong shellfish reduction.

Cool the concentrated stock, then place in a food processor with the fish fillet. Add the egg, lemon juice, salt and one-third of the cream. Blend together until smooth, then pour in the remaining cream, taking no more than 10 seconds or the mousse will curdle.

Brush the terrine mold with melted butter, then fill with the fish mousseline, adding the peeled shrimp as you fill the mold. Place some buttered parchment paper over the top and cover. Stand the terrine on a cloth in the bottom of a roasting pan and pour in enough warm water to come about halfway up the sides. Bring to a boil on the top of the stove, then transfer to the oven and cook for about 40 minutes.

Leave to cool, then refrigerate for at least 3 hours before attempting to remove the terrine from the mold. Slip a thin-bladed knife around the sides of the terrine and turn out onto a flat dish. Slice carefully with a serrated knife, holding each slice of terrine in place until it is cut right through.

Slice the zucchini into thin strips. Dress with *Olive Oil Dressing* and serve each slice of terrine with a little pile of zucchini.

A perfect wine for this rich and sweetly flavored dish would be a Sauvignon Blanc.

12	ounces shrimp in the shell
1	tablespoon unsalted butter
1	small carrot, chopped
1	small onion, chopped
1/2	tablespoon brandy
1/2	teaspoon tomato paste
2/3	cup *Fish Stock* (see p. 36) or *Chicken Stock* (see p. 37)
8	ounces white fish fillet, skinned
1	small egg
•	Juice of 1/2 lemon
1	teaspoon salt
1 1/4	cups heavy cream, chilled
4	zucchini
1	quantity *Olive Oil Dressing* (see page 51)

Serves 6-8

Shrimp Jambalaya

Jambalaya comes from New Orleans and is based on paella. But not being able to get saffron and olive oil, the Spanish settlers used what was available locally, and in using the combination of green peppers, celery and onions they produced what is now known as the "holy trinity," the flavor that most typifies Creole cookery.

For extra flavor in the jambalaya, fry the shells in about 4 tablespoons of vegetable oil, then pass the oil through a sieve into the dish just before adding the rice.

Heat the oil in a large frying pan or any other large, shallow skillet-type dish and gently fry the sausages. Add the paprika and stir to color the oil. Toss in the garlic and cook a little, then add the onion, green peppers, celery and the red chilies. Cook over medium heat until the moisture has been driven off and the vegetables are beginning to color. Add the chicken, shrimp, the bay leaves, thyme and the oregano and cook over medium heat for about 5 minutes.

Add the rice and stir for 2 minutes, then pour in the stock and add the salt. Bring to a boil and simmer gently for about 15 minutes, or until all the liquid has been absorbed by the rice. Stir in the chopped green onions and check the heat. If you like things hot, add some chili powder.

Serve with a green salad.

Serve with some ice-cold beer.

Serves 6

4	tablespoons vegetable oil
4	ounces Spanish smoked sausages or other smoked pork sausages, sliced
2	teaspoons paprika
8	garlic cloves, chopped
1	medium onion, chopped
2	green bell peppers, seeded and chopped
4	celery stalks, sliced
2	red chilies, seeded and finely chopped
1	pound boneless, skinless chicken, cut into 1-inch pieces
1	pound shrimp, peeled
2	fresh bay leaves, thinly sliced, or 2 dried bay leaves, crushed
1	fresh thyme sprig, chopped
1	teaspoon fresh oregano or 1/2 teaspoon dried
2 1/4	cups long-grain rice
5	cups *Chicken Stock* (see p. 37)
1	teaspoon salt
3	green onions, sliced
•	Chili powder to taste

Tiger Prawns with Lemongrass, Chili and Cilantro

Tiger prawns are now being farmed in large quantities in Thailand. You should be able to get all the ingredients to make this first course, including some bamboo skewers for a really authentic touch, at any Asian food shop. The lemongrass should be fresh rather than dried.

Fish sauce is one of the greatest introductions to Western cookery since soy sauce; its clean, salt and savory taste is ideal as a base for salad dressings instead of oil.

I use a large, relatively mild Dutch green chili; be wary of the small ones.

Ready the charcoal grill at least 30 minutes before you want to start cooking. (The secret of successful barbecuing lies in getting the grill bars so hot that anything you put on it sears and carbonizes quickly and so doesn't stick.)

Remove the shells from the prawns except the last small piece on the end of the tail. Cut them in half lengthwise, leaving them joined at the tail. Using a pastry brush, paint the prawns liberally with the seasoned oil. Thread five prawns onto each skewer and set aside while you make the dressing and salad.

Measure the fish sauce and water into a bowl. Remove the seeds from the chili and chop finely. Add it to the dressing. Remove the coarse outer leaves from the lemongrass and finely slice the more tender center; don't be too purist about this as all lemongrass is fairly stringy. Add it to the bowl with the lemon juice and sugar.

Pick off about 20 of the best cilantro leaves to use in the salad and reserve. Chop the rest finely. Set aside.

Slice the iceberg lettuce finely and arrange on four plates. Sprinkle with the reserved cilantro leaves.

Grill the prawns for exactly 5 minutes, turning them halfway through the cooking time. Meanwhile, warm the dressing through over gentle heat and add the chopped cilantro just before taking it off the heat.

Place the prawns, still on the skewers, on top of the lettuce. Spoon the dressing liberally over the prawns and salad and serve.

Gewürztraminer goes exceptionally well with Thai food. The wine is sufficiently spicy and powerful to stand up to the strong tastes of chili, cilantro and lemongrass.

20	tiger prawns, headless, or other large shrimp, about 1 ounce each
2	tablespoons peanut oil, seasoned with 1 teaspoon salt and freshly ground black pepper

For the Dressing

2	tablespoons Thai fish sauce (*nam pla*)
²/₃	cup water
1	green chili
1	lemongrass stalk
•	Juice of 1 lemon
½	teaspoon sugar

For the Salad

•	A small bunch fresh cilantro
½	head iceberg lettuce

Serves 4

Fruits de Mer

Fruits de mer, or plateau de fruits de mer *as it is called in France, is the spectacular creation of French seaside restaurants: lobsters, crabs, langoustines (lobsterettes), prawns, shrimp, mussels, oysters, clams, periwinkles, conchs, sea urchins and any other shellfish that are available are presented on a large platter, normally on a base of seaweed and crushed ice, sometimes with some big chunks of cork beneath them to give extra height. The dish is served with accompaniments of lemon wedges, mayonnaise and* Shallot Vinegar *(see p. 53).*

This dish is the centerpiece of all the dishes presented at my restaurant. Nothing induces good, lively conversation better than the fruits de mer.

There is something relaxing and animating about eating with your fingers, but the world is split evenly between those who enjoy it and those who regard the whole thing as a bore. It is this division, between those who enjoy the sensual side of eating and those who regard eating as something that must be got out of the way, which leads to some people being wonderfully enthusiastic and joyful customers and others frankly being a pain. I have a great affection for Jean-Anthelme Brillat-Savarin, whose book, The Philosopher in the Kitchen, *published in 1825, is as meaningful today as it was then and should be read by anybody interested in eating. He quite literally saw physical differences between those who do and those who don't enjoy eating and summed it up as follows.*

Individuals predestined to gourmandism are generally of medium height, they have round or square faces and bright eyes and small foreheads and short noses, full lips and well rounded chins. The women are buxom, pretty rather than beautiful with a tendency to run to fat. Such is the exterior beneath which to look for the most agreeable company for these are the guests who accept everything they are offered, eat slowly and savour each morsel thoughtfully. They are never in a hurry to leave the place where they have found true hospitality and they are invited to stay all evening because they know the games and pass times appropriate to gastronomical gatherings. Those on the contrary to whom nature has refused an aptitude for the pleasures of taste have long faces, noses and eyes, whatever their height there is something elongated in their proportions, their hair is dark and flat and they are never plump, it was they who invented trousers. The women whom nature has afflicted with the same misfortune are angular in body, are easily bored at table and only live for cards and scandal.

But back to the fruits de mer.... *It is a totally wonderful dish. The great thing about it is that it gives importance to all those little, unloved shellfish and crustaceans like periwinkles, conchs, shrimp and hermit crabs and even sea urchins. The sort of thing that you would never buy any amount of on their own together make up a meal that most are quite happy to pick at over a long, leisurely lunch with a bottle or two of wine and some convivial company.*

You might think that trying to assemble the ingredients for a fruits de mer is a little outside your scope, but you can make it out of as few or as many species as you like. It is one of those dishes, when on holiday by the seaside, that you can build up from a day's wandering around rocky beaches, picking mussels and periwinkles, fishing for shrimp in rock pools, turning over stones for shore crabs and digging in the sand for cockles and clams. By adding all these bits and pieces to, maybe, two lobsters, a large crab and a spider crab, you can make up a more than acceptable fruits de mer.

In France shellfish are usually opened and served raw, like oysters. There is quite a lot of skill

Fruits de Mer (*see page 197*)

involved in opening live shellfish like clams, cock-les and mussels, so you may find it easier to steam them briefly open, maybe with a little bit of white wine. The trick is just to remove them from the heat as soon as they pop open so that the meats are hardly cooked at all and will taste, to all intents and purposes, raw.

Sitting out here in the garden at Trevone Bay on this stunning April morning just before Easter, with the sound of the surf in the distance, I think I'll go and raid the restaurant's kitchen, get some friends over, plus half a dozen bottles of ice-cold Muscadet, and lose an afternoon to pure pleasure.

To Serve

2½	cups *Mustard Mayonnaise* (see. p. 43)
⅔	cup *Shallot Vinegar* (see. p. 53)
2	lemons, cut into wedges
½	bucket seaweed
•	Ice
3	lemons
2	or 3 lobster picks
•	A claw cracker

Serves 6

3	lobsters, about 1 pound each
3	crabs, about 1 1/2 pounds each
36	mussels
36	large shrimp in the shell
1	pound medium shrimp in the shell
18	oysters
36	periwinkles

Plus any of the following:
- Small crabs
- All types of clam
- Cockles
- Scallops
- Sea urchins
- Conchs (whelks)

Cooking and Assembling the Fruits de Mer

Blanch the seaweed in boiling water (unless it's from a clean beach), then rinse in cold water and chill.

LOBSTERS AND CRABS

Cook the lobsters and crabs in plenty of boiling water salted at the rate of 2/3 cup to 5 quarts. This is the salinity of sea water. The crabs should be pierced with a skewer once between the eyes and once under the tail flap, through the body and up to the eyes to kill them before boiling (see p. 25). Both crabs and lob-sters should be dropped into boiling water, brought back to a boil and simmered for 20 minutes, then drained and left to go cool. They taste better if they are not refrigerated, so cook them the same day you intend to eat them.

MUSSELS, CLAMS AND COCKLES

Wash and scrub the mussels, clams and cockles. Place separately in a large pan and add a splash of water or white wine. Cook on a fierce heat with the lid on and let the shellfish open in the steam produced by the splash of water. As soon as they open, remove from the heat and drain through a colander into a bowl. Keep the cooking liquor for another dish. Remove the beards from the mussels. →

LARGE AND MEDIUM SHRIMP

Place them in a pan of boiling, salted water, bring back to a boil and simmer for 1 minute for medium shrimp and 2 minutes for large shrimp.

OYSTERS

Open by inserting the blade of an oyster knife or short, thick-bladed knife between the hinge of the two shells. Protect the hand that holds the oyster by wrapping it in a tea towel.

PERIWINKLES, CONCHS AND SMALL CRABS

Place in a pan of boiling, salted water. As soon as the water comes back to a boil, drain immediately for periwinkles, simmer for 4 minutes for conchs and 5 minutes for shore crabs. Drain.

SCALLOPS

Clean the scallops as described on p. 29, but leave the scallop in the deep bottom shell. Discard the top shell. Steam the scallops in a perforated tray over boiling water until they turn white.

SEA URCHINS

Cut in half and drain off the water.

TO ASSEMBLE THE FRUITS DE MER

Use a large tray such as a circular tin tea tray or a wooden tray to display the seafood. Take the cubes from about four ice trays, place them in a polythene bag and crush with a rolling pin.

Place the ice and chilled seaweed on the tray and arrange the shellfish and lemons as naturally as you can. Carry the tray out to your guests and be prepared to receive the sort of rapturous reception that such a display must inevitably cause.

There are a few wines that are ideal to serve with this dish. A French Muscadet is best, but any light, acidic French or Californian wine would go well.

11 Shellfish

Mussels, clams, cockles and conchs are some of the best-loved and cheapest seafood to be found, and even scallops are not madly expensive. Oysters are a bit of a luxury and the recipes that use them reflect that. This chapter also contains recipes for squid, cuttlefish and octopus, which, unexpectedly, are classed as mollusks. The last two recipes are a bit of fun.

COCKLES

To me cockles are one of the best-tasting bivalves (two-shelled mollusks) and yet they are so cheap. I imagine this is because they're, thankfully, so abundant. I'm a great fan of eating raw cockles. When I dig for cockles, I can open them by forcing the base of one cockle against another, then twisting them until one opens to give me the sweetest and most delicious-tasting morsel to eat. I always include cockles in all the mixed shellfish dishes, like the *Mussel, Cockle and Clam Masala* on p. 210, the *Fruits de Mer* on p. 197 and the *Hot Shellfish with Garlic and Lemon Juice* on p. 205.

CLAMS

Until recently it was virtually impossible to get any clams in Britain except the large, hard-shelled clam, which is only really useful for chowders. All the delightful little clams that you get in France, the *palourdes*, the *praires* and *vernis*, were unavailable. Now things are beginning to improve. The recipes for *Mussels in the Shell with Linguine, Garlic and Parsley* and *Grilled Mussels with Pesto* can be made with clams.

PERIWINKLES

I don't think I've ever seen periwinkles on sale in a fishmonger's shop in Britain. But they're very easy to pick on the seashore; turn over the seaweed on any rocky beach and you'll find them underneath. They come in various colors: yellow or a browny green but normally black or gray. They're all the same species and all edible. Wash them in cold water, bring them to a boil in well-salted water, then boil for just 2 minutes. Drain them and eat with some *Shallot Vinegar* (see page 53). Get yourself a pin or a periwinkle picker, dig them out, dunk them in the shallot vinegar. I think it tremendously civilized that even in the cheapest restaurants in Brittany, they offer you a little *amuse-geule* (appetizer) of a pile of periwinkles with maybe a little bowl of mayonnaise or shallot vinegar. You could even try making up some hot garlic butter to go with them. They are, after all, just sea snails.

MUSSELS

Thank goodness that mussels are becoming so easy to buy now. One of the main problems with writing a cookery book is that there are always some ingredients that are difficult to get hold of: take lovage or Japanese bread crumbs, called *panko*, for example. I included the recipes with these difficult ingredients because they are easily replaced, but the worry about whether people could get hold of mussels used to be a little depressing.

Most mussels available in fish markets and large supermarkets with fish counters are rope-grown.

That means the spats (that is the mussel seeds) are encouraged to attach their threads (called a byssus) to ropes suspended in the sea. You can tell whether the mussels you buy are rope-grown or not by the occasional strands of rope still attached to the mussel. A great advantage of rope-grown mussels is that they tend to be relatively clean and free of barnacles and weed. Those that are harvested from the rocks tend to be harder to clean. As to flavor, the rope-grown ones tend to be sweet and plump, the rock ones more seaweedy and ozony in flavor. But for the best flavor there is nothing to beat the small mussels that you can gather at very low tides on the beaches in the west and probably elsewhere in the country. The problem with these mussels is that they're a bit too small for mussel dishes, but we use them very effectively as accompanying shellfish in fish dishes.

Mussels can be picked anywhere around the British coastline but, because of the way we dump our sewage into the sea and seem to forget about it, there is always a risk of food poisoning from polluted water. For example, around Padstow we find that shellfish in the bays facing the open sea are pretty safe, but those in the estuary are not. Any pollution that goes into the open sea tends to be well diluted, whereas pollution in a partially enclosed estuary is far more concentrated. I am a bit of an optimist and I do feel that we are all now aware of the unacceptability of dumping sewage in the sea and that eventually, over the next ten or twenty years, we will see a revolution in the improvement of pollution levels in the sea around us.

But let's put things into perspective. Most of the time it is safe to pick, cook and eat shellfish from the beach—and there is nothing like it as far as I'm concerned. Leading what one might call a bit of a stressful life, I find there is nothing quite as relaxing as going down to the mouth of the estuary on a low spring tide looking for butterfish (a small type of clam), tellins (another type of clam), mussels, cockles and even the occasional razor-shell clam (razor clam) if the tide is exceptionally low.

OYSTERS

There are two types of oyster on sale in Britain, the Native oyster (*ostrea edulis*) and the Pacific oyster (*ostrea gigas*). The Native or European oyster usually costs about twice as much as the Pacific. The Pacific oyster is only called Pacific because that's where it originates from. It grows perfectly happily in British waters, though it doesn't reproduce here because the water is slightly too cold. Baby oysters are grown in oyster hatcheries and then sown into the water when they're about the size of your thumbnail. The Native oyster fetches a high price because it takes longer to grow. The Pacific oyster grows much faster and is therefore the variety favored by commercial growers.

The Native oysters from the west of England are called Helford oysters. They are still dredged from natural beds and are not farmed. The supply is restricted by a very sensible conservation method whereby oyster fishermen are only allowed to use sailpowered dredgers to fish for oysters, which slows them down considerably.

Since the Native oyster costs twice as much as the Pacific, it might be pertinent to make some observations as to the taste: does it taste twice as good as the Pacific? The answer is that it doesn't, any more than you can quantify the taste of a bottle of good white Burgundy as being twice as good as a bottle of Australian Chardonnay. However, after 20 years of running the restaurant, last autumn I managed to set up a comparative tasting which I consider to be exhaustive.

During the filming of the television series this book accompanies, we went down to the River Helford and the Duchy Oyster Farm where I buy Native oysters. About six dozen Native oysters were opened for us and three dozen Pacifics. We also had some wines to aid our tasting. We were aiming to establish what it was about the Native that set it above the Pacific. The Natives won hands down. While the Pacifics were fresh and sweet, the Natives had a sort of slightly bitter, slightly metallic finish to them that, in the end, proved subtle and exciting. Like a good wine, the complexities of the taste ended up being far more satisfying than the simple, straightforward flavors of the Pacific. As far as the wine was concerned, we found that Chablis was the best accompaniment.

SCALLOPS

The other day I was trying to decide what it is that makes me want to keep on cooking. After all it isn't the easiest way to make a living. But last night we'd just cooked for 90 (after about 60 I have this joke with the chefs where I say something to the effect that that was great fun now we'll go home, when we all know we've got another 30 to cook for), when a fisherman brought in a few scallops in a box with some red gurnards, weever fish, a few crab claws and a couple of small octopus. When I see a box like that of gleaming fish and the scallops tightly closed, damp with bits of seaweed and sand clinging to them, it doesn't matter how tired I am, I know it's all worth it. I see raw materials like those and I just want to do justice to them. I'd hate to have to work with frozen, soaked scallops. I have an almost possessive attachment to those beautiful fresh shells. Scallops are one of our most delicious shellfish—sweet and firm and relatively cheap. Only buy fresh scallops and steer clear of frozen ones, since they have often been soaked in water before freezing to increase their size and make the price seem more attractive. When they defrost, the water drains out of them along with a great deal of their flavor.

SQUID

Squid, like cuttlefish and octopus, belongs to the group known as cephalopods, which means "head footed," referring to the way the tentacles come out of the head. Cephalopods are in fact mollusks, like mussels and oysters, not fish. They are much underrated and seem to be one of the few species of marine life that have not yet been overfished. They all have a delicious flavor, more akin to lobster or crab than fish, and deserve to be much more popular. The general lack of familiarity with these excellent species reminds me of a Padstow boy who went to Spain for the first time, ordered a plate of deep-fried battered squid rings and remarked, totally astonished, to his friends, "Funny sort of onions they have over here."

Squid and cuttlefish can be cooked and eaten without any tenderizing (see p. 28 for preparing squid), but octopus does need something to help it. I think the easiest way to tenderize octopus is to simmer it gently in water (see p. 28).

There are various recipes for octopus stews in Mediterranean cookery books but I've never found them particularly satisfying. I think the best way of preparing octopus is in a salad as with the shark on p. 163-4, but you can just as successfully make the salad entirely with well-cooked, sliced octopus.

Hot Shellfish with Garlic and Lemon Juice

This Italian dish is a sort of hot fruits de mer. *The quantities of shellfish are merely a suggestion. You may like to make the dish out of fewer or more varieties, or include crab or lobster as well and make it into a main course. I have given cooking methods for all the shellfish but you may find that you can more easily buy it ready-cooked, in which case you will only need to warm it through.*

You will need to make a steamer to reheat the shellfish that has been previously cooked. Take your largest pan and pour a couple of inches of boiling water into it. Place some sort of trivet in it; the flower-petal steamer mentioned on page 35 would be ideal. Reheat the cooked seafood in the steam for about 4 minutes.

If raw, cook the conchs and periwinkles in well-salted, boiling water. Add the conchs, allow the water to return to a boil, then simmer for 4 minutes. The peri-winkles should be added to boiling salted water, returned to a boil and then drained at once. Keep them both warm.

Place the periwinkles and conchs (if already cooked) and the langoustines in a pan of well-salted, boiling water and warm them through.

Put the mussels in a large pan with a lid; splash in a little dry white wine. Place the pan over a fierce heat, cover and leave until they have opened. Remove with a per-forated spoon and keep warm. Do the same with the cockles, the clams, large and small, and finally, the oys-ters. These will take the longest and will not open fully; you will need to lever them open with a short, thick-bladed knife or oyster knife.

Strain the cooking liquor into a small pan through a fine sieve to remove any grit.

Arrange the shellfish on four large, warmed plates or on one very large serving dish. Add the olive oil, garlic, parsley, chili and lemon juice to the shellfish liquor, bring to a boil and pour over the shells. Serve with plenty of French bread.

Serves 4

4	cooked or raw conchs (whelks)
32	periwinkles
8	cooked langoustines (lobsterettes) or 8 cooked large shrimp
24	mussels
•	A little dry white wine
20	cockles
4	large clams
16	small clams
8	oysters
6	tablespoons extra-virgin olive oil
2	garlic cloves, finely chopped
1	small bunch fresh parsley, preferably flat-leaf, roughly chopped
1	red chili, seeded and finely chopped
•	Juice of 1/2 lemon

(LEFT) Mussel, Cockle and Clam Masala (*see page 210*), (BELOW LEFT) Grilled Mussels with Pesto (*see page 209*), and (BELOW) Mussels in the Shell with Linguine, Garlic and Parsley (*see page 208*)

Moules et Frites and Moules Marinières

Long have I tried to sell Moules et Frites *(mussels and chips with mayonnaise) at the restaurant, but without much success. It has long been one of my favorite dishes. I love chips and mayonnaise far too much, I'm afraid, and this combination is, to me, exquisite. The mussels are cooked very simply. You can, of course, serve the* moules marinières *without the chips and mayonnaise, maybe with some fresh baguettes and a bottle of Muscadet.*

Wash the mussels in plenty of cold water. Scrape away any barnacles with a short-bladed knife. Pull off all the beards and wash the mussels again. Discard any that are open and do not close when tapped sharply.

Take a large lidded pan that is big enough to hold all the mussels. Add the mussels, butter, onion, white wine and half the parsley and set over a fierce heat. Turn the mussels over every now and then as they start to open. Keep the lid on the pan when not turning them. When they are all open, remove from the heat and leave for 30 seconds or so to let all the grit settle to the bottom of the pan.

Serves 4

Scoop out the mussels with a big spoon and divide among four large, deep plates. Wide soup plates are ideal but you can use deep bowls as well. Pour all the juices from the pan over the mussels, holding back the last tablespoon or so, which will be full of grit. Sprinkle the rest of the parsley over the mussels and serve with the mayonnaise and chips.

3½	pounds mussels
¼	cup unsalted butter
1	medium onion, chopped
4	tablespoons dry white wine
1	tablespoon roughly chopped fresh parsley
1	quantity *Mustard Mayonnaise* (see p. 43)

Mussels in the Shell with Linguine, Garlic and Parsley

I used to think that spaghetti alle vongole *was a second-rate pasta dish using small tasteless clams in a much-reduced tomato, garlic and onion sauce, having ordered it more than once in restaurants who knew nothing about the importance of not overcooking shellfish. I'm afraid I'm an eternal optimist as far as food is concerned. My wife, Jill, often laughs at my soon-to-be-dashed enthusiasm in restaurants where she can see by the look of the place that we are going to be disappointed.*

But not so long ago we went to the coast of Italy below Rome and spent a week eating the real spaghetti alle vongole: *pasta with the sweetest of clams, the type we know as carpet shells. Sometimes the same dish was made with mussels, which I thought was possibly even better. We ate other seafood too, for a week we ate nothing else, but it was mussels and clams with pasta that really captivated us.*

The most important part of this dish is getting the pasta just right. The Italian interpretation of the words al dente *is much more severe than ours where pasta is concerned. You can get away with much more bite in pasta than you think and, in this dish, the slight hardness of the pasta against the soft shellfish is what makes it so special.* →

The pasta is part-boiled in salted water, then the cooking is finished with the liquor from the shellfish. The shells are not removed from the mussels because it is not a problem to eat the pasta with the shells—and the dish looks so much more exciting with them. You can use thinner pasta for this dish, but reduce the initial boiling time of the pasta to about 3 minutes.

Wash the mussels in plenty of changes of cold water. Scrape the mussels with a short, thick-bladed knife to remove any barnacles or seaweed and pull out the beards. Wash again and discard any that do not close when given a sharp tap.

Bring a large pan of well-salted water to a boil and cook the *linguine* for 5 minutes. Meanwhile, heat the olive oil in a small pan and soften the sliced garlic, then add the chili and parsley. Remove from the heat.

Drain the pasta through a colander and return the pan to high heat. Add the white wine, then the mussels and then the pasta. Cover the pan to trap the steam and speed up the cooking of the mussels, but occasionally stir the mussels and pasta to redistribute them.

Serves 4

When the mussels have all opened, remove the lid and add the oil, garlic, chili and parsley and let the juices reduce for about 2 minutes. The pasta should be just cooked, but if it is too hard for your liking, replace the lid and cook gently for a couple more minutes. Serve with plenty of bread.

Serve with a bottle of Vernaccia di San Gimignano or a Pinot Grigio.

2	pounds mussels
12	ounces *linguine*
4	tablespoons virgin olive oil
4	garlic cloves, thinly sliced
½	red chili, seeded and very finely chopped
3	tablespoons roughly chopped fresh flat-leaf parsley
2	tablespoons dry white wine

Grilled Mussels with Pesto

The mussels are opened and served in one shell, which is filled with a garlic, basil and pine nut pesto. For this recipe the pesto should be made quite dry and coarse, more like a stuffing than a sauce. You can make various other grilled mussel dishes in the same way using various flavored butters like Garlic Butter (see p. 49) or Cilantro and Roasted Hazelnut Butter (see p. 50). Also try the recipe on p. 45 for Charmoula as a filling and mix with some finely chopped almonds, or the Rouille on p. 45 mixed with bread crumbs.

Wash the mussels in plenty of changes of cold water, swirling them round until the water is clear. Scrape the mussels with a short, thick-bladed knife to remove any barnacles or seaweed and pull out the beards. Wash again and discard any that do not close when given a sharp tap.

Open the mussels by steaming them with a splash of dry white wine (or water) covered in a large pan over

fierce heat. Remove from the heat as soon as they have opened and discard one side of the shell. Strain the liquor through a colander and pour off into a small pan, holding back the last tablespoon or so of mussel liquor, which will contain a lot of grit.

Reduce the rest of the liquor to about 1 tablespoon by rapid boiling. (This will be added to the pesto ingredients.) →

Put all the pesto ingredients with the reduced mussel liquor in a mortar and pestle or food processor and pound or blend until roughly chopped.

Preheat the broiler. Arrange the mussels on a broiler pan. Spoon the pesto into all the mussel shells, then sprinkle over the bread crumbs and broil until the bread crumbs are beginning to brown.

Serve an Italian Chardonnay from the northeastern wine region of Trentino or a good Californian Chardonnay..

Serves 4

60	large mussels
•	A splash of dry white wine or water

For the Pesto

½	cup fresh basil leaves
2	large garlic cloves
¾	cup olive oil
2	tablespoons freshly grated Parmesan cheese
2	tablespoons pine nuts
2	slices white bread made into bread crumbs

Mussel, Cockle and Clam Masala

I have specified rather more masala paste than you may feel you need for this recipe as the chili already makes it very hot, but if you like your Indian food hot, then add it all.

You will need a large pan, preferably a wok, to cook this dish.

In a frying pan, dry-fry the cilantro seeds and cloves over medium heat for a few minutes, then add the cumin seeds, heating them for another 30 seconds. Grind in a clean coffee grinder or mortar, then put this mixture with the remainder of the masala ingredients into a food processor and blend to a paste. If the masala paste is too stiff, add a little vegetable oil to loosen it.

Fry the masala in the vegetable oil until the spices separate from the oil.

Wash the mussels, clams and cockles and toss them in the masala paste. Cover with a lid and, shaking from time to time, steam-cook until the shells open. If you feel the mussels haven't produced enough liquid, add a little water. The recipe contains no salt as mussels are salty, but taste to check the seasoning. Throw in a generous amount of chopped cilantro and serve in bowls.

Serves 4

2	tablespoons vegetable oil
3½	pounds mixed mussels, clams and cockles
6	tablespoons water

For the Masala

1	tablespoon coriander seeds
1	teaspoon whole cloves
2	tablespoons cumin seeds
12	ounces onions, finely chopped
8	large garlic cloves
2	ounces fresh ginger, peeled and chopped
•	Walnut-sized knob of dried tamarind pulp, seeded
1	teaspoon ground turmeric
3	fresh red chilies
2	tablespoons red wine vinegar
3	tablespoons coconut cream

For the Garnish

2	tablespoons fresh cilantro leaves, chopped

Oysters with Beurre Blanc and Spinach

The oysters in this dish are hardly cooked at all. This combined with the beurre blanc is fresh and pleasing.

Prepare a steamer to cook the oysters (see p. 205). Thoroughly wash the oysters and steam for about 4 minutes. Remove and open, keeping the liquor that comes out of them. Put the spinach leaves in the steamer and steam for 2 minutes.

Put the shallot or onion, vinegar, wine and water into a small pan. Add the juice from the oysters and simmer until only about 2 tablespoons of liquid are left. Cut the butter into small squares and whisk it in a little at a time, off the heat, building up a light emulsion.

Serves 4

Remove the oysters from their shells. Lay a folded leaf of spinach in the bottom of each shell. Place the shells on a flameproof serving dish and push briefly under the broiler to warm the spinach. Put the oysters on top and pour the *beurre blanc* over each. Place under the broiler again to warm through, then serve.

16	oysters
16	spinach leaves, stems removed
1/4	cup finely chopped shallot or onion
1	tablespoon white wine vinegar
1	tablespoon white wine
4	tablespoons water
2/3	cup unsalted butter

Oysters Charentais

This is a seemingly odd combination: freshly opened oysters with hot, spicy sausages. The idea is that you eat an oyster, take a bite of the sausage, then a good gulp of cold white wine like Muscadet. We use caul fat for the sausages—a membrane laced with fat that comes from around a pig's stomach lining. It should be reasonably easy to order half a pound or so from the butcher.

Put all the sausage ingredients into a food processor and blend until the mixture is coarse, that is, the bits in it are about the size of coarse sugar. Remove and portion the sausages into balls about the size of a golf ball and mold into rough sausage shapes. Wrap them in 4-inch squares of caul fat.

Twenty minutes before serving, open the oysters but keep them flat, taking care not to spill too much of the salty liquor. (Refer to the notes on p. 29 for instructions on opening oysters.) Divide the oysters among four plates.

Serves 4

Preheat the broiler and broil the sausages. Place three sausages beside each serving of oysters—don't forget the Muscadet.

20	Pacific oysters
	For the Sausages
12	ounces belly pork
1/2	teaspoon salt
1/2	teaspoon paprika
1/2	teaspoon black pepper
1/2	teaspoon dried thyme
1/2	teaspoon cayenne pepper
3	ounces *chorizo* sausages, skin removed
4	ounces caul fat, for wrapping the sausages

Steamed Scallops with Ginger, Soy, Sesame and Green Onions

This recipe came to me as a result of a visit to a restaurant in Gerrard Street, Soho.

It is fascinating to me how the Chinese restaurants in London's Soho have grown in everyone's estimation in the last 30-odd years. I can recall in the early days seeing dark red ducks hanging in every front window and wondering how anyone except the Chinese would dare to eat such frightening-looking food. The smell was enough to scare you rigid and the look of the stuff—wow!

Then about 25 years ago I went with a more adventurous friend to the Lido in Gerrard Street. He said I should try anything; it would all be good. So I ordered the most dreadful sounding dishes on the menu, Boiled Eel in Black Bean Sauce and, I think, Steamed Fish Heads. It was all totally wonderful and I've been back many times since.

My early reserve about foreign food is not something I feel very proud of, but I do use my own former reluctance to try things as a reminder that if I can become a convert, anyone can, including my youngest son, Charles, who won't touch much more than spaghetti hoops. Very vexing for a father who is a chef, but maybe he'll change.

This dish is a classic. It's incredibly easy to cook and a reminder to all cooks to keep it simple. Scallops are usually ill-treated by overcreative cooks because they seem to go well with almost anything; consequently, they are combined with almost anything. But if, as a result of such a combination, you can't really taste the scallop, why waste money? Why not use something like tofu instead?

Prepare a steamer following the suggestions on p. 205.

16	scallops in the shell
1	teaspoon finely chopped fresh ginger
1/2	cup Asian sesame oil
2	tablespoons soy sauce
1	tablespoon roughly chopped fresh cilantro
3	green onions, finely sliced

Sprinkle the scallops with the ginger. Place in the steamer and steam for about 4 minutes until only just set. While they are cooking, put the sesame oil and soy sauce in a small pan and warm through. Lay the scallops on four plates and pour over the sesame and soy sauce. Sprinkle on the cilantro and sliced green onions, then serve.

Serves 4

Scallops with Noisette Butter

This is the simplest of recipes but noisette butter needs to be made correctly to taste really good. It goes very well with grilled or fried fillets of any flat fish and any number of the cod family like whiting, hake or haddock. →

If you are making this as a starter, it would be more appropriate to use queens. Queens are a type of small scallop. The only difference between it and the larger bivalve is that it has two concave shells whereas the scallop has one concave and one flat shell.

Preheat the broiler.

Cut up the butter and place in a small pan. Set the pan over medium heat until the butter has melted and started to brown. This is the important bit of the recipe—the butter needs to go a delicate but not dark shade of brown. The word *noisette* means nutty and that is how you can tell when it is cooked enough— when it smells of warm nuts. Remove from the heat as soon as the butter has reached that stage and keep warm.

Brush the scallops with a little of the *noisette* butter and grill for 5 minutes. Remove and place on four warmed

plates. Squeeze over the lemon juice and season with salt and freshly ground black pepper. Pour the *noisette* butter over all the scallops. Garnish with the parsley.

Serve with plenty of fresh crusty bread to mop up the juices.

16	scallops (or 24 queens) in the shell
1	cup unsalted butter
•	Juice of 1/2 lemon
1	small bunch fresh parsley, finely chopped with a few whole sprigs reserved
•	Salt and freshly ground black pepper

} **Serves 4**

Sautéed Scallops with Basil, Saffron and Pasta

Scallop shells make excellent containers for seafood. You will need 20 scallop shells for this recipe. If it is at all possible, buy the scallops and shells together, though you will need to buy a few extra empty scallop shells as well.

Slice the scallops in half. Put the stock, the white wine and the saffron in a pan and boil rapidly to reduce by three-quarters. Add the cream and the butter and reduce further until the sauce coats the back of a spoon.

Boil the pasta in salted water until tender but firm to the bite (*al dente*). Toss it in a little butter with the sliced basil leaves.

Warm the 20 scallop shells under a broiler and arrange on 4 plates. Distribute the pasta among the

shells and bring the sauce to a boil. Add the scallops and cook for 2 minutes. Spoon the scallops and sauce into the 20 shells and serve.

12	good-sized scallops
2 1/2	cups *Fish Stock* (see p. 36)
4	tablespoons white wine
•	A good pinch of saffron
2/3	cup heavy cream
1/4	cup unsalted butter
4	ounces thin pasta such as vermicelli or *fedelini*
6	fresh basil leaves, sliced

} **Serves 4**

(TOP LEFT) Oysters Charentais (*see page 211*), (BELOW LEFT) Scallops with Noisette Butter (*see page 212*), and (BELOW) Sautéed Scallops with Basil, Saffron and Pasta (*see page 213*)

Sautéed Scallops with Lentils and Chardonnay

I use oaked Australian Chardonnay in large quantities for this dish, along with a pinch of spice normally associated with Indian cookery.

Serve with a heavily oaked Australian Chardonnay or similar wine. You only need about an eighth of a teaspoon of spice to go into the sauce, so I have had to specify the quantities as small pinches and large pinches.

To make the sauce, put the spices, 1 tablespoon butter, the onion and carrot in a pan and cook over gentle heat for about 4 minutes. Pour in the Chardonnay and stock and bring to a boil. Simmer until the volume has reduced by about two-thirds. Strain the stock, add the cream and simmer again until the volume has reduced by about two-thirds.

While the sauce is reducing, simmer the lentils with the fish stock, clove, bay leaf, onion and salt until tender. Drain.

Cut each scallop into three disks. Put a frying pan over high heat. When hot, rub a little of the butter over the pan, then put in half the scallops. Cook for 30 seconds only on one side to caramelize, then turn and cook for a further 30 seconds on the other.

Remove and keep warm. Pour any juices into the sauce. Heat the pan again, add a little more butter and fry the second batch of scallops.

Place a pile of lentils on each of four warmed plates and arrange the scallops on top. Whisk the rest of the cubes of butter into the warm sauce and pour round each plate.

Serves 4

12	scallops
	For the Sauce
•	A small pinch of ground allspice
•	A small pinch of ground cloves
•	A small pinch of ground nutmeg
•	A large pinch of curry powder
1	tablespoon unsalted butter
1/4	cup chopped onion
1/4	cup chopped carrot
1 1/4	cups oaked Chardonnay
2 1/2	cups *Fish Stock* (see p. 36)
4	tablespoons heavy cream
1/4	cup unsalted butter, cut into cubes
	For the Lentils
1/3	cup small green lentils, preferably Puy lentils
3/4	cup *Fish Stock* (see p. 36)
1	whole clove
1	fresh or dried bay leaf
2	slices onion
1/2	teaspoon salt

Grilled Squid with a Pepper Marinade

Squid marinated in olive oil with black pepper, Sichuan pepper and red chilies. The squid is best cooked on a charcoal grill but you can also get good results using a ribbed grill pan. I got the idea for this dish from the River Café in London.

This recipe can be equally well made with cuttlefish.

Grind the black and Sichuan peppercorns coarsely. Use a mortar and pestle or put the peppercorns on a chopping board, cover them with a clean tea towel and roll over them with a rolling pin. Put them in a bowl with the red chili, olive oil, lemon juice, salt, soy sauce and garlic.

Prepare the fire in the grill. Cut the bodies of the squid into 3-inch pieces then cut each tentacle in half. Put the squid into the marinade and leave for 30 minutes, turning over once or twice. Remove the squid from the marinade and grill for 1 minute. Turn and grill for another minute.

Arrange the arugula leaves on four plates. Place the squid on top and drizzle over the rest of the marinade. Serve with a wedge of lemon.

1/2	teaspoon black peppercorns
1/2	teaspoon Sichuan peppercorns
1	red chili, seeded and finely chopped
4	tablespoons virgin olive oil
•	Juice of 1/2 lemon
1/2	teaspoon salt
1	tablespoon soy sauce
1	garlic clove, finely chopped
12	ounces squid, cleaned (see p. 28)
3	ounces arugula leaves
•	Lemon wedges to serve

Serves 4

Sautéed Squid with Olive Oil, Garlic and Parsley

I am very enthusiastic about quick and simple recipes. This recipe was inspired by a dish in a charming little book called The International Squid Cook Book *by Isaac Cronin. I love the way Americans get bees in their bonnets about things. He's a complete fanatic about every aspect of squid, and he says this recipe is the easiest and, many people think, the best way to cook it. Serve with chips.*

Clean the squid (see p. 28) and cut the body section into rings.

Quickly fry the garlic in hot olive oil and add the squid just as the garlic is beginning to brown. Add the seasoning and a pinch of chili. Turn over and sauté for 2–3 minutes. Add the parsley and lemon juice. Serve with more lemon wedges and the chips.

1	pound squid
2	garlic cloves, finely chopped
2	tablespoons olive oil
•	A pinch of crushed dried chili
1	tablespoon roughly chopped fresh parsley
•	Juice of 1/4 lemon
•	Salt and freshly ground black pepper
•	Lemon wedges to serve

Serves 4

I think that in the not too distant future we will all be enjoying seafood in Britain with the same general enthusiasm as the Americans from Maine, the Portuguese, French and Spanish. I want to be able to go to a beach and find someone grilling fish over a driftwood fire to sell to me. In any country where seafood is valued, there is someone selling good things from the sea to eat right by the beach. In Britain you can buy ice cream, windbreakers and surf-boards, but I want grilled sardines with a simple salad or fresh spiny lobster just out of the sea, as I had once on a beach in Greece.

The last two recipes in this book encapsulate every-thing I love about seafood, cooked simply with no fuss straight from the sea.

Sardines Grilled Over Driftwood with a Tomato, Red Onion and Basil Salad

You will need some sort of grill rack on which to cook the sardines. Make a fireplace with beach pebbles, something you can rest the grill rack on. Build up a driftwood fire, then let it burn down to hot ash. Remove the guts from the sardines and scrape off the scales. Brush with oil and season well inside and out. Slash them three times on either side down to the bone. Grill them for about 4 minutes on each side. Meanwhile slice the tomatoes and thinly slice the onion. Chop the basil. Make a dressing with the olive oil, white wine vinegar, salt and black pepper and mix with the salad. Serve the fish straight from the grill.

Sit with a glass of Chardonnay and watch the sun set.

12	absolutely fresh sardines (pilchards)
•	Olive oil for brushing the fish
6	tomatoes
1	red onion
1	bunch fresh basil
4	tablespoons olive oil
1	tablespoon white wine vinegar
1/2	teaspoon salt
•	Freshly ground black pepper

Serves 4

THE CLAMBAKE

Every July we hold a large barbecue on one of the beaches near Padstow for all the staff. We end up with well over 100 people. We load the old charcoal barbe-cue (which we used to have in the restaurant) into the fish van, make lots of tandoori monkfish, teriyaki mullet fillets, shark steaks marinated in charmoula and a bucketful of Thai prawns. We then fill an old tin bath with ice and bottles of beer and off we go.

This year we're going to have a clambake, too. We'll dig a shallow pit in the beach, about 6 feet by 2 feet and about 18 inches deep, and line it with large smooth rocks. Then we'll build a large driftwood fire on it to heat up the rocks and leave it burning for 2 hours. When it's burned right down, we'll brush the hot ash off the stones, put a layer of seaweed on top of the baking hot rocks and pile on the clams, small lobsters, crabs, langoustines (lobsterettes), some plump mackerel, corn on the cob and some small new potatoes. We'll cover them with more seaweed and an old damp sack and leave everything to cook gently in the steam of the seaweed for about an hour. They'll taste so good with all that ozone-iodine flavor of the seaweed—a real seafood extravaganza!

LISTING OF AMERICAN, AUSTRALIAN AND NEW ZEALAND FISH

The following list gives local names, where necessary, or suggests a similar fish as an alternative.

British Isles	U.S.A.	Australia and N.Z.
Anchovies	Anchovies	Anchovies
Brill	Petrale sole, Brill sole	Sole, Flounder
Cod	Cod, Pacific cod	Blue cod
Coley	Haddock	Hoki
Conger eel	Conger eel	Blue grenadier
Dabs	Flounder	Flounder
Dover sole	English sole, Gray sole	Sole, Flounder
Eel	Eel	Eel
Flounder	Flounder	Flounder
Grey mullet	Mullet, Striped bass	Groper, Coral trout
Gurnard	Searobin	Gurnard, Coral trout
Haddock	Haddock	Blue cod, Hoki
Hake	Hake, Silver hake	Hake
Herring	Herring	Sardine
John Dory	John Dory, Oreo Dory	John Dory
Lemon sole	Lemon sole, English sole, Flounder	Sole, Flounder
Ling	Ling, Cusk, Cobia	Jewfish
Mackerel	Atlantic mackerel	Mackerel
Megrim sole	Flounder	Flounder
Monkfish	Monkfish, Anglerfish	Monkfish
Octopus	Octopus	Octopus
Parrot fish	Parrot fish	Parrot fish, Snapper
Pilchards	Sardines	Sardines
Pollack	Pollack	Rock cod
	Walleye pollack	Hoki
Pouting	Cod, Whiting	Hoki
Ray	Skate	Ray
Red bream	Red snapper	Snapper
Red mullet	Goatfish	Red mullet, Barbounia
Salmon	Salmon	Atlantic salmon
Sand eels	Sand launce, Smelt	Smelt
Sardines	Sardines	Sardines
Sea bass	Sea bass	Groper
Sea trout	Sea trout, Steelhead	Atlantic salmon
Shark	Shark	Shark
Skate	Skate	Skate
Snapper	Snapper	Snapper
Sprats	Smelt	Sprats
Squid	Squid, Calamari	Squid, Calamari
Swordfish	Swordfish	Swordfish
Tuna	Tuna	Tuna
Turbot	Turbot, Flounder	Sole, John Dory, Flounder
Whitebait	Whitebait, Smelt	Whitebait
Whiting	Whiting	Whiting
Witch	Flounder	Flounder, Sole

SHELLFISH

British Isles	U.S.A.	Australia and N.Z.
Blue crab	Blue crab	Blue crab
Brown crab	Dungeness crab	Blue swimming crab
Clams	Hardshell clams	Clams
	Littleneck clams	Littleneck clams, Pipi
	Cherrystone clams	Clams
Cockles	Cockles	Pipi, Cockles
Crayfish, Crawfish	Crayfish, Spiny lobster	Yabbies
Langoustine	Lobsterette, Norway lobster	Scampi
Lobster	Lobster	Rock lobster
Mussels	Mussels	Mussels
Oysters	Oysters	Oysters
Prawns	Shrimp	Prawn
Queens	Bay scallop	Queen scallop, Tipa
Razor-shell clam	Razor clams	None
Scallop	Sea scallop, Bay scallop	Scallop
Sea urchin	Sea urchin	Sea urchin
Shore crab	Green crab	Spanner crab
Shrimp	Shrimp	Shrimp
Soft-shell crab	Soft-shell crab	Soft-shell crab
Spider crab	Snow crab	Blue swimming crab
Spiny lobster	Spiny lobster, Crawfish	Crayfish, Spiny lobster
Swimming crab	Green crab, Blue crab	Blue swimming crab
Whelk	Conch, Whelk	Whelk
Winkles	Periwinkles	Winkles

ALTERNATIVE FISH

The following is a list of the fish and shellfish used in the book and alternatives available to most Americans if they can't find what is called for in a recipe. The alternatives are not necessarily the most similar fish biologically, but rather ones that work almost, if not equally, as well.

Eel: Mackerel
Conger Eel: Shark, Swordfish or tuna
Herrings: Mackerel or Sardines
Pollack: Haddock or larger Whiting
Whiting: Haddock or Cod
Mackerel: Herring
Salmon: large Sea Trout
Sea Trout: Salmon or Trout
Smelt: Sardines
Whitebait: Smelt
John Dory: Barbecued Dishes — Sea Bass;
       Others — Turbot
Goatfish: Any of the Bream family or Sea Bass
Sea Bass: Mullet or Goatfish
Red Bream: John Dory
Cod: Haddock
Gurnard: Sea Bass
Monkfish: Charbroiled Recipes — Swordfish;
       Others — Turbot or John Dory
Haddock: Cod or Hake
Hake: Haddock or Cod
Ling: Monkfish
Swordfish: Shark or Tuna
Shark: Tuna, Swordfish or Conger Eel

Tuna: Swordfish or Monkfish
Dover Sole: Petrale, Sand Sole
       Fillets of Dover Sole — Petrale Sole,
       Lemon Sole
Lemon Sole: Flounder
Brill: Turbot, large John Dory
Halibut: Turbot
Turbot: John Dory
Skate: Angel Shark, Porbeagle Shark
Squid: Cuttlefish
Octopus: Large Cuttlefish
Cuttlefish: Squid
Conch: Octopus
Scallops: Slices of Monkfish
Shrimp: Small Prawns
Langoustine: Large Shrimp
Razor Clams: Any other species of clam
Clams: Cockles or Mussels
Mussels: Clams or Cockles
Periwinkles: Small Mussels
Cockles: Mussels or small Clams
Oysters: Mussels or Clams
Lobster: Spiny Lobster
Sea Urchins: Scallop Roe

INDEX